How To Get Your Deer

BY John O. Cartier

Illustrated by Richard Amundsen

Published by Outdoor Life Books

Distributed to the trade by Stackpole Books

Published by

Outdoor Life Books
Times Mirror Magazines, Inc.
380 Madison Avenue
New York, NY 10017

Distributed to the trade by

Stackpole Books
Cameron & Kelker Sts.
Harrisburg, PA

Originally published in 1976 as *The Modern Deer Hunter.* This edition completely revised and updated.

Library of Congress Cataloging-in-Publication Data

Cartier, John O.
    How to get your deer.

    Rev. ed. of: The modern deer hunter. © 1976.
    Includes index.
    1. Deer hunting.   I. Cartier, John O.   Modern deer hunter.   II. Title.
SK301.C37   1986   799.2′773′57   85-19830
ISBN 0-943822-62-9

Manufactured in the United States of America

To my wife Bernice
who long ago encouraged me to write
about the hunting and fishing sports
I've loved for over fifty years

Contents

Preface

For almost twenty years I served as a full-time field editor for *Outdoor Life* magazine. It was my privilege to work with scores of deer hunters and deer biologists while gathering material for magazine articles. I filed the best of the deer-hunting tips because I figured that some day I'd have enough to fill a big book dedicated to helping deer hunters.

Some of the secrets of the old pros still work like charms. Some are a waste of time for the modern deer hunter. This book describes the techniques that will work best for you today. It is my conviction that *How to Get Your Deer* includes the best advice from old-timers as well as all the new knowledge needed to cope with today's conditions in the field.

And there *is* a great deal of new knowledge. New research findings have become a tremendous help to deer hunters. Much of this knowledge was undreamed of only a few short years ago. For example, there is an organization in Wisconsin called The Stump Sitters, Inc. It's a nationwide group of hundreds of deer hunters who spend thousands of hours hunting and observing deer. Members' data are collected and subjected to intensive study. One recently completed Stump Sitter project involved ten years and over 10,000 hours of field research on whitetail deer. Other intensive studies have been made by university wildlife departments and by state and federal wildlife biologists. Much of the accumulated information was unknown a decade ago, and much of it that relates to successful deer hunting is condensed in various chapters of this book.

Though some types of hunting have declined in recent years, deer hunters face a glowing future. A great deal of that future will result from scientific, modern game-management techniques that have much potential. Those techniques are also discussed in this book, and they point out why deer hunting could get even better than it is in many parts of our nation. Your future as a successful deer hunter has much more to do with your knowledge of how to hunt than it does with any apparent lack of deer.

John O. Cartier

How To Get Your Deer

DEER OF NORTH AMERICA

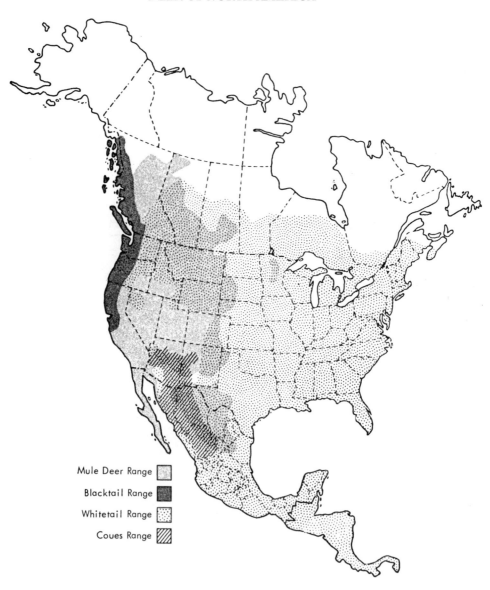

Mule Deer Range

Blacktail Range

Whitetail Range

Coues Range

Whitetail Deer

The normal life span for unhunted whitetails in the wild is ten to fourteen years. In captivity where excellent living conditions are provided these deer can live to the age of twenty. A legal buck will have his first set of antlers at 1½ years of age. This means that every buck in most woodlands will be dodging hunters each fall for his entire adult life. These facts should point out dramatically why a mature whitetail buck is a pretty clever character, especially when you consider his physical capabilities.

Senses

Much has been written about how well a whitetail can hear. But just how acute is a deer's hearing? In a test, a whitetail buck heard the clicking of a man's fingernails 75 yards downwind. I once had an experience that was even more enlightening.

I was on a stand when I spotted three deer approaching me. They were 100 yards upwind of my position and walking straight on at a steady pace. Suddenly they stopped, looked toward me, and cupped their ears. I was sure they couldn't see me and I hadn't made a sound since long before I'd spotted them. Still, they wheeled and trotted out of my view. Several minutes later I heard another hunter walking up behind me. It was obvious those deer had heard the man long before I did even though I was much closer to him.

To sum it up, a deer's hearing is so superior to yours that sneaking up on a whitetail in normal hunting terrain is extremely difficult. But forget the noise factor for a moment and concentrate on a whitetail's eyesight.

Regardless of what you may have read or heard, a deer sees exceptionally

When alarmed, whitetails normally show their flags—that is, raise their tails—exposing the white undersides. Note one of the lead bucks, though, fleeing with his tail down.

well, especially in semi-darkness. Dawn and dusk are the periods when most shooting opportunities are offered. During these periods their eyesight is far superior to yours. Even during midday deer can see astonishingly well. They sometimes don't notice motionless hunters, but they can spot movement from incredible distances.

I've often moved into a suitable position for glassing hunting terrain and then spotted deer which were far out of rifle range. In just about every instance those deer were staring at me. They'd seen me before I saw them, even though I was using a spotting scope or binocular. So don't ever base your whitetail hunting plans on the notion that deer don't see well. If you do you won't be successful.

Which gets us to the question of a whitetail's sense of smell. It's unbelievably sharp. It's so sharp that a buck relies more on discovering danger by scenting than by hearing or seeing. With a favorable wind or thermal current a deer can smell a man from far away. If you get upwind from even a distant buck there's no way you're going to fool him unless you use special techniques we'll discuss later.

For example, if we put a smart man in an uncharted wilderness, leave him without a compass and tell him to find his way back to his starting point, he will be confused and lack a sense of direction. On the other hand, you've probably heard stories of dogs or cats that were lost on family vacation trips far from home, yet which traveled long distances over unfamiliar country to return home. How did they do it? The answer has to be that they used an instinct unknown to man.

Man can learn to do many things well, but he does these things by thought processes or constant repetition of the act, not by instinct. What makes birds migrate unerringly from a specific summer area to a specific winter area thousands of miles apart? Much of it has to be instinct. Even the most experienced jet pilot couldn't make such a trip without benefit of dozens of scientific instruments, yet birds do it with no problems at all.

Years ago, whitetails had natural enemies such as wolves. Today, except in places such as northern Minnesota where some wolves still kill deer, the whitetail finds man and free-ranging dogs as his only predators. Is it any wonder that the whitetail's instinct on avoiding human hunters is being honed to an ever-finer edge as the years pass? This edge isn't as developed in mule deer because muleys have less contact with man than most whitetails; they are still killed by mountain lions in many areas; and they react more out of habit than does the whitetail, which has more capacity to adapt to the world of man. If you go along with the instinct concept you'll have to conclude that today's whitetail is more difficult to bag than were his ancestors.

Everything I've mentioned so far points out that the whitetail is much superior to man in physical endowments and instinct. With this knowledge the smart hunter recognizes that the only advantage he has over deer is his far greater ability to reason things out. The guy who consistently scores on whitetails is the guy who takes advantage of a deer's relatively small degree of reasoning power.

Speed

Okay, so if a buck does get wise to you through sound, sight, or scent, how fast can he escape by running? The answer isn't so surprising to veteran

Speed of escape is a whitetail hallmark. Whitetails can average 30 mph for several miles. Bucks have been clocked in 40 mph sprints. Broad jumps of 30 feet are common. Jumps over 8-foot fences, from a standstill; have been seen.

hunters who have seen deer blitz away from danger, but it's still interesting to know that whitetails can run at 30 miles per hour for several miles. Bucks have been clocked at 40 miles per hour during sprints. This still doesn't sound so impressive till we make a comparison.

Ruffed grouse are often found in whitetail country. The explosive, rocketing flight of these birds seems so fast that the average hunter would state flatly that a grouse can escape faster than a deer. Not necessarily so. Flight speeds of ruffed grouse have been clocked at 25 to 40 miles per hour. This means a deer can run as fast as a grouse can fly if he really wants to pour it on.

Another shocker is the whitetail's phenomenal jumping ability. There is a record of a deer jumping an eight-foot fence without even taking a preliminary step. Broad jumps of around 30 feet are common. A downhill jump of over 100 feet was observed by a naturalist.

Whitetails are great swimmers too, especially during hunting seasons when they wear their hollow-haired winter coats. Wisconsin researchers clocked deer many miles from land swimming at thirteen miles per hour.

So a buck won't hesitate to escape by swimming if he figures that's the best way out. And this brings up another interesting item regarding a whitetail's physical capabilities: in northern states, during late November deer seasons, the water is so cold that a man would perish in it in minutes, yet a deer can swim in the same frigid water for miles with no ill effects at all.

Survival Instinct

There's one thing about deer that I've never found discussed in print, but which I've heard promoted as an important point among a few veteran hunters. Let's call the subject "instinct for survival." From my experience this instinct is well-pronounced in deer, though all birds and animals have it to some degree.

Adult bucks in the northern states are in breeding condition from September to February, but does are receptive to these bucks only from October through December, during "heat" periods which last twenty-four to thirty-six hours and which recur every twenty-eight days until a given doe is bred.

This cycle is important because it shows why a buck will travel out of his normal home range during the rut. He doesn't collect a harem as does a bull elk, and if he can't find readily available does in his local terrain he'll go looking for them. If your deer-hunting season falls during the rut you may find bucks in areas where you never saw a sign of them during scouting trips before or after the breeding season.

Deer biologists tell us that a wild buck can service six to eight does without trouble. (A penned buck can service up to twenty does.) This generally means that some does will get bred despite heavy hunting pressure. Habitat is the all-important factor in determining survival of the species. On good range having few deaths from disease or winter loss, the whitetail herd nearly doubles between the pre-fawning and post-fawning periods. Even many doe fawns get into the act by getting pregnant at the age of six months. They have their own fawns at the age of twelve to thirteen months. Also, studies have shown that wild does seldom become too old to bear fawns. Females more than ten years old have been observed with their youngsters.

However, you should keep in mind that although all does get bred, the breeding may be accomplished by few bucks or many. In an area holding few bucks each male will service many does. So it doesn't follow that an area automatically harbors lots of bucks just because it may harbor lots of deer. An area that produced a tremendous buck harvest last year may not be so good this year because a lot of the bucks have been shot out.

This is why it's not always a good idea to hunt the same place year after year as tradition called for in the old days. Years ago, deer hunters didn't have the mobility they have today; now there is no reason to suffer through the ups and downs of buck populations in a given area. The secret is in pre-hunt scouting for the definite signs of bucks. I'll get into all the details of this technique in Chapter 4, "Why Stands Beat the Odds."

A magnificent whitetail buck during the rut (above). In the breeding season, bucks often travel outside their home range in search of does.

Whitetail does (right) can become pregnant at age six months, and they may continue to bear fawns after they are ten years old. The old doe shown here tends twins, the usual number of fawns to a doe on good range.

Hunters seldom find dropped antlers even though an area may contain many bucks. Dropped antlers quickly become bleached and softened by the elements. They are then gnawed by rodents for the calcium, phosphorous, and salts.

Research shows that male deer outnumber females about 110 to 100 at birth. Buck fawns are also usually stronger and heavier than their sisters, about seven pounds to five. They have the best odds for staying alive after birth, so hunting pressure often is the only reason buck populations may be low in a given area.

Yearling does usually produce one fawn. Thereafter, on good range, healthy does produce an average of two. Occasionally a doe will produce three fawns, rarely four. The gestation period is about 200 days.

In either-sex hunting areas, and in those areas where does may be harvested on special permits, it's common for some hunters to claim they killed dry does. They assume from this that such does did not produce fawns that year. The assumption is usually wrong because fawns nurse heavily for only about two months and are weaned at about twelve weeks. A doe can "dry up" about one month after nursing stops. So a doe that is dry in November could easily have had twin fawns in June.

Though even novice hunters are aware that bucks shed their antlers each year in winter, many beginners claim there are few bucks in a given area because they don't find dropped antlers in the woods. The real reason they don't find them is because the racks usually don't last long. They quickly become bleached and softened by the elements, then they're gnawed by rodents. Most dropped antlers are completely devoured. In northern states whitetail bucks shed their antlers in December and January. They begin growing new sets in April. Growth is finished by September, and polishing is usually complete by mid-October.

Habitat

When I discuss deer-hunting techniques later I'll point out that the normal home range of a whitetail buck living in ideal terrain may cover only a mile or two from place of birth. Unlike mule deer, whitetails are basically nonmigratory. But exceptions occur and the hunter should be aware of them. Today's deer biologists have facts about whitetail movements that the old-timers could only guess at.

In northern states, where yarding of these deer is common, movements may be greater than in southern areas where snow creates no problem for deer. Still, a Wisconsin study showed that most deer were bagged less than 3½ miles from their winter yards.

The rule of thumb is that where terrain conditions are best you'll find comparatively minor movement patterns. In less suitable areas, movements may be extensive. You should consider this fact if you hunt in marginal deer country, or if you hunt in an area where whitetails occupy various habitats on a seasonal basis. In agricultural states, for example, grainfields may provide good food from July well into the hunting season. But when the produce is gone, deer will pull back into the cover of stream courses or other permanent vegetation areas.

Where habitat is good only in widely scattered areas, deer may move

Unlike mule deer, which migrate many miles with seasonal change, whitetails tend to live their entire lives within a few-square-mile area. But they may migrate from marginal range.

long distances while seeking better homes. A good example of this is Nebraska, where tagging studies have shown movements which are considerably greater than normal. Recoveries of twenty-three whitetails which were tagged in the poor habitat of the Sand Hills showed an average movement of 38 miles. A yearling buck tagged southwest of Valentine, Nebraska, was killed the following year near Clearwater, 137 miles away. Another whitetail buck, tagged south of Valentine, traveled 125 miles before being killed the next year west of Lewellen. The implications are obvious: find the best whitetail habitat your area offers during deer season and concentrate your hunting efforts there.

Some of the better whitetail hunters I know kill their bucks close to towns and cities. One reason is that whitetails have learned to live near man and will prosper in good habitat no matter how close it may be to population centers, but another reason is far less recognized.

Practically all land near populated areas is privately owned. You can't hunt it unless you have permission. I learned long ago that landowners are much more likely to give permission prior to hunting season than later when they may be swamped with requests. This is one of the great benefits of pre-hunt scouting. Most landowners also allow only a limited number of hunters on their property, so if you're the first to ask you're more likely to

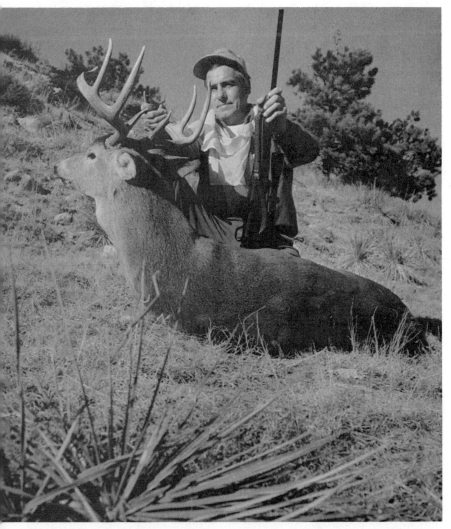

The author admires one of his better bucks, this one taken in Nebraska.

get an okay. What this boils down to is that some hunters get their bucks simply because they have hunting rights in good habitat that's unavailable to other hunters. The principle doesn't apply in public-hunting areas of the West, but it can make all the difference in the world in the East, Midwest, and South. Make friends with rural landowners and you'll up your odds on whitetail-hunting success significantly.

If you like to hunt on your own this principle takes on even more weight. Landowners will grant hunting permission to a loner much more readily than they will to a group. When a property owner grants permission to only one loner this guy can hunt a farm which, in effect, is a private hunting preserve. Not only that, but farmers watch their deer all year and can offer advice on the animals' habits and where they're most likely to be at any given time. The most meticulous hunters will tell farmers where they will park their cars and what type of clothes they'll be wearing so the landowner will be aware of trespassers.

Still another advantage is that some of the biggest bucks are found in farm country. This is true because the weather is usually milder than in the northern forests, food is more plentiful, and the same limestone fertilizer that grows crops also can promote exceptional body and antler growth. Further, the deer herds of farm country aren't so subject to the population cycles of forest deer. They're apt to increase more than decrease. A case in point is Michigan.

Michigan deer biologists say that back in the old days there were only a few hundred deer in the thirty-four southernmost counties. During the 1940s the herds had grown to several thousand whitetails. By 1963 the overall population of the area was estimated at 50,000 animals. Now those southern Michigan counties hold over 200,000 deer and provide some of the state's best whitetail hunting. But practically all of that hunting is on private land. I know of no better example pointing out how important it can be to get hunting permission long before the day of the hunt.

One of the reasons farm-country hunting can be so productive is that alien sights, sounds, and smells upset whitetails very easily. In forests, where deer are not used to people or human activities, the opening-day crowds of hunters make whitetails spooky in a hurry. Deer in farm country are used to human activity year-round. Thus, a farm-country buck seldom considers a hunter as an alien to his environment because he doesn't know the difference between a man with a gun and a man with a rake. This advantage is one of the few that whitetail hunters have over mule-deer hunters, and it's found only in farm country.

Proof that whitetails can accept man as part of their natural environment is the existence of many deer farms holding deer for tourist attractions. Most whitetails on these farms are completely tame.

Once a whitetail hunter has settled on a general area, the next step is selecting the best territory within that area. Whitetail hunting anywhere is only as good as the country hunted. Most of the best country contains the mixed cover of timber, grasslands, croplands, and lowland thickets which join together in all-important brushy terrain type referred to as "edge." Whitetails are often thought of by beginners as animals of the deep, unbroken forest. They're not; they far prefer lower, brushier vegetation. And they prefer this type of cover most of all when they find it bordering fields, clearings, swamps, lakes, timbered hills, and so forth. These fringes of thick cover are the "edge" areas that produce the best whitetail hunting.

Such cover is the precise reason why deer herds in agricultural states

Whitetails find little feed in mature forests except when mast crops such as acorns or beechnuts are available. They favor the combination of browse and protection afforded by country with mixed cover, such as woodlands, grasslands, thickets, and tangles.

have exploded in numbers. The "edge" in farm country affords ideal habitat for whitetails. It's also the reason why whitetail numbers boomed in the northern states after the mature timber was logged off in the early years of this century. As the tall trees were replaced with low brush (more browse) deer moved in and multiplied because habitat conditions became ideal.

Whitetails feed very little—except when mast crops are available—in heavily timbered areas because thick top foliage discourages the growth of browse. But these deer don't favor one type of food to the exclusion of any other. They prefer a varied diet, which is why edge in wilderness areas is as attractive to the animals as edge in farm country. In agricultural areas whitetails will utilize wheat, rye, corn, or other crop fields so long as the safety offered by brushy edge is nearby. Likewise, in wilderness areas, they'll move into forest areas to feed on beechnuts and acorns if they can escape quickly to edge when danger is present. You'll always find the most whitetails where there is a mixture of food types including much edge between the different types.

The main thing to keep in mind is that it's normally quite useless to look for whitetails in heavy timber. Right here, so I don't confuse the issue in the following chapter, I want to point out that there can be a difference in defining edge depending on whether you hunt in the East or West.

Edge in whitetail country usually means brush or low trees growing as tall as 20 feet. You'll seldom find these animals in brush so low that it won't cover their outlines when they're standing. It's a different story with mule deer. They'll often feed and bed in brushy areas so low it's necessary for them to bed down before they're out of sight.

But edge in the West, can also mean brush and small trees growing high above a man's head. Edge in whitetail country is always high enough to hide a standing deer; it may or may not be so in mule deer country.

Heavy hunting pressure has more effect on whitetails than mule deer. When the pressure gets heavy, whitetails become almost exclusively nocturnal in all their activities. About the only chance you have of seeing them then is very early and very late in the day when they're moving to and from feeding areas. This is another reason why hunting edge is very important. Deer will take a chance on moving in fringe cover as dawn or dusk comes on, but they'll seldom be caught in clearings, fields, or openings in heavy timber during hunting season.

Body Language

A whitetail's intentions are often revealed by its body language. Know these specific reactions and use them to be a more successful hunter.

When a deer wags its tail stiffly in a horizontal plane it often is an "all clear" signal, alerting other deer that danger has passed and they can come out of hiding.

A somewhat similar swishing of the tail indicates relaxation. In this case the tail is not stiff nor is it held in a horizontal position. When a deer wags its tail that way it means it is not alerted to potential danger. Also, deer that are routinely browsing, scratching and interacting with nearby herd members are not alerted.

A deer that stands stiffly erect with head high and ears cupped is very concerned with possible immediate danger. It may bound away immediately, but the longer it stands absolutely still the more likely it will soon relax. All deer have short attention spans. They always react quickly to what may be danger, but they'll soon calm down when no problems develop. Hunters often feel they should take a quick and poor shot at a buck as soon as they spot him standing in an alert position. Often they'll get a far better shot if they wait for him to resume unalarmed routine. If you spot a relaxed tail wag, a relaxing of cupped ears, or the dropping of an erect head, look for your buck to return soon to normal routine.

If, on the other hand, the first indication you have of a nearby whitetail is the all too familiar fully raised white tail flashing through thickets, you can be sure the deer has detected danger and is running for its life. Studies have shown that does are far more likely to show the white flag than bucks. The better trophy bucks tend to react to flight by holding their heads and tails low. If you jump several deer together, and note one is running with tail down, you're likely looking at a buck. If you have tracking in mind, that's the one deer to go after.

A whitetail that stamps and/or paws the ground with one front foot is signaling two facts. It is telling other nearby deer that potential danger is at hand, and it is trying to make that danger show itself. Such a deer has not yet identified you. If you can continue to remain unidentified the animal may revert to normal routine. But if you move or in some way establish your presence, the deer will bolt.

A feeding deer always twitches its tail before raising its head to look around for danger. Keep that in mind if you're stalking a buck in relatively open country.

A whitetail's tail can tell you many other things, too. Unalarmed deer normally carry their tails low, but usually raise them with the first sense of trouble. A deer that greatly suspects danger will raise its tail high and flare the white hairs. In most situations, a deer showing erect tail hairs is split seconds away from bolting. As panic takes over a deer's thoughts the animal will also flare its white rump hairs. This is signal enough to shoot, especially if such a deer also lays back its ears. A flared tail and laid back ears is a sure sign of immediate flight.

Mule deer inhabit open country where shooting opportunities are more numer-ous than in whitetail habitat. This deer is not as wary as the whitetail, and is generally considered easier to hunt.

Mule Deer

The first mule deer I ever saw astonished me because it was so strikingly different from a Michigan whitetail. A friend and I were driving into Wyoming on our first hunting trip in the West. It was shortly after noon on a mild, sunny day. We drove around a curve in ranch country and spotted several cattle grazing on a hillside clearing 100 yards to our right. Suddenly I noticed a deer among the Herefords.

"Look," I stammered to my companion. "There's a deer out there in the open. It's a buck. A six-pointer."

We pulled off onto the shoulder of the road and stopped to stare at the deer. He paid us no heed for several moments.

"Hard to believe," my partner said. "Back home in Michigan we'd never see a whitetail buck feeding in the open during broad daylight. Look at the enormous ears on that critter. No wonder they're called mule deer."

We got our next surprise when the buck finally decided we couldn't be up to any good. Away he went, bouncing into the air and coming down stiff-legged on all four feet in a kind of pogo-stick gait we'd never seen. He didn't seem to be in any hurry heading for cover. A Michigan whitetail would have flashed across that clearing on a dead run.

We were also surprised to note that the muley was much grayer than a whitetail, that his tail was far smaller. He didn't hold his tail high as he ran, and that his antlers appeared higher and much less inclined to curve than those on our deer back home. Then the buck pulled another stunt that left us shaking our heads.

He pulled up to the top of a knoll 200 yards away, stopped in his tracks, and turned to look at us. We couldn't believe it. A jumped whitetail usually runs till he's out of the immediate area and he never stops to look back. Broadside to us, the muley stared in our direction for a few moments, then calmly walked over the knoll and melted from view.

Eastern deer hunters making their first trips to mule-deer country often have similar experiences, which emphasize that the muley has a far different make-up than the whitetail. And to hunt him successfully, there are many other factors you should be aware of.

Mule deer are far less abundant than whitetails, and their range is much more restricted. Only eleven states offer good mule-deer hunting, and only six others offer even poor to fair hunting for this species. On the other hand, most mule-deer hunters enjoy a success ratio that's twice as high as that for whitetail hunters. In areas showing the best mule-deer hunting, the success ratio may be four times as high. This shows that mule deer are easier to hunt.

There are two general reasons for this. One, mule deer are usually hunted in much more open country than are whitetails. This means that shooting opportunities are easier to come by simply because you'll see more deer. Second, mule deer generally aren't as cautious or as clever as whitetails. This, again, means that shooting opportunities can come more often.

The above statement has been challenged in recent years by some veteran mule-deer hunters who claim the western deer is adopting the habits of the eastern whitetail by hiding in deep thickets, showing himself less in daylight and becoming far more clever. They say that many hunters are unsuccessful because they're taken in by the tradition claiming mule deer are easy to hunt. These veterans insist that modern hunters should go after muleys as if they were going after whitetails.

I agree—if we're talking about trophy bucks, those monarchs who have made it through a few hunting seasons and have lived long enough to learn the ways of hunters. I've had a few big mule-deer bucks make a fool of me when they used evasive tactics in thick cover which they refused to leave. These bucks are adopting the traits of whitetails for the same reason the whitetails have: ever-increasing hunting pressure.

But it's a different story with the younger bucks that most hunters bag. There are all kinds of facts to prove the point. The most obvious is hunter success-ratio statistics. The states with the top ten hunter-success ratios are all west of the Mississippi River, and they're all in mule-deer country. The top mule-deer states, in terms of deer-herd numbers—Wyoming, Colorado, New Mexico and Utah—harbor far fewer deer than the top whitetail states east of the Mississippi River. The conclusion is obvious: It's much easier to bag a deer in good mule-deer country than it is in good whitetail country.

Another fact that sheds a lot of light on the subject is the availability of deer-hunting licenses. In many of the eastern deer states licenses are unlimited to residents and nonresidents alike. Anybody can hunt deer in these states by paying the fee for a license. The reason this situation exists is that it's almost impossible to over-harvest bucks in the typical whitetail states of the East. These bucks are just too clever to be killed easily.

Not so in the West. The majority of the best mule-deer states limit the number of nonresident hunters; some of the "fair" hunting states limit the numbers of *resident* deer hunters. Lottery or drawing systems determine which applicants get a chance to hunt. The reason? Mule deer herds can be subjected to overharvest by too much hunting pressure. This again points out that it's generally far easier to score on mule deer than whitetails.

I've seen many examples of how easy it can be. One time I killed a fine buck in the mountains of Colorado during a late season when there was deep snow on the ground. My guide told me time and again before our actual hunt started that I shouldn't take the first buck I saw unless it was a trophy because there were plenty of big bruisers in the area. "These deer are migrating at this time of year," he told me. "The area we're going to hunt is a concentration area where the muleys gang up on their migration route before moving down to lower elevations. It's not really hunting up there, it's more a matter of picking the buck you want and nailing him."

Years ago, Ben Gregory, a local deer-hunting partner of mine, and I planned a Wyoming hunt with several other friends. Just before we left home for the drive to Wyoming, business matters forced Ben to postpone his trip. As it turned out, the business problems were solved sooner than Ben expected. He packed his gear in a hurry and made the drive to Wyoming to join us and utilize the two-deer license he had purchased by mail months before.

As Ben drove into the general area the rest of us were hunting, he spotted a herd of mule deer crossing a knoll behind some ranch buildings. He drove into the ranch, asked and received permission to hunt, loaded his rifle and took off on foot for the hills where he'd seen the deer. A half hour later he peeked over the top of a ridge and saw two fine bucks in a clearing 100 yards below him. He dropped them both with quick shots from the same spot.

Hunting mule deer with pickup trucks has been common procedure in the plains and foothills of the West. You simply drive cross-country in good deer areas till you jump deer. A few years ago the system got so out of hand in North Dakota that it's now illegal for hunters to drive off established roads and trails in that state. This is as it should be. Hunting from a vehicle is no sport and no challenge. Such things just don't happen in the East because no self-respecting whitetail buck will allow himself to be killed so easily.

I'll concur, however, that it's standard practice in the heavy brush country of South Texas to hunt whitetails by pickup truck. This is a special situation. Some of the ranches there are hunted so lightly the whitetails aren't overly cautious. But the main reason for using a vehicle in some areas is that the brush is so thick a man can't see a deer from ground level. So the pickups are specially rigged with platforms built about six feet above the beds of trucks. Hunters, while riding or standing on the platforms, can look down into the brush.

Regardless of these factors I certainly don't want to imply that hunting mule deer is always easy. On the contrary, most of my mule-deer hunting has been far tougher than my whitetail hunting, especially from a physical standpoint. A mule deer is much more of a wilderness animal than the whitetail. The latter has learned to cope with man's civilization and is often hunted on flat country along the edges of towns and cities. You'll seldom find mule deer in such places because they are fundamentally animals of the mountains, canyons, draws, and slopes. If you want a good buck you'd best figure on getting back into the wilderness away from the beaten track.

This does not contradict the notion that mule deer are easier to kill than whitetails. It simply points out that once you get into good mule-deer country—which often requires hard work in the form of backpacking, going on horseback, or hiking over rough country—your chances of downing a buck are better than if you were hunting whitetails. Beginners at mule-deer hunting are always encouraged by learning that their odds of taking a buck are high, but their enthusiasm often fades when they make their first hunt and find that the work involved in getting a mule deer can be a lot tougher an adventure than they anticipated.

Personality Traits

Mule deer have several personality traits that make them vulnerable once you get into a good hunting area. This deer is a far more placid animal than the whitetail. His personality is deliberate. He'll react more out of habit than the impulsive whitetail, which is nervous and jumpy and far more clever. I've already mentioned that jumped mule deer will often move a short distance, stop, and then look back at a hunter. They also frequently run across openings, they bed down in spots where they can be spotted easily, and they can be driven along predictable escape routes. Whitetails seldom exhibit these traits.

Mule deer are far less suspicious of man. Many times I've watched these animals, caught by surprise in the open, stare at me for a few moments then walk slowly away as if I presented no danger at all. Bedded muleys also have the unhealthy (for them) habit of jumping up and looking at a hunter before taking off. When you combine all these factors with the realization that mule deer are found in more open country than whitetails it's no wonder that a lot of them are shot at.

Mule deer are far more gregarious than whitetails, and this is another great advantage to the hunter. It's not unusual to see herds of ten or more muleys feeding on a single ridge or slope. And, except during the rut, bucks of this species are often found in groups. It's not uncommon to spot three or four bucks feeding together. This is one reason why proportionately more trophey muleys are taken than whitetails. When a hunter comes upon a group of these bucks he'll naturally try for the best head. The whitetail hunter normally sees only a single buck at a time. He'll usually take the first one he sees, and the odds are good the animal will be a younger, less-clever buck without much of a rack.

A characteristic habit of the mule deer is to bolt when danger threatens, but then stop and stare for a moment at the intruder.

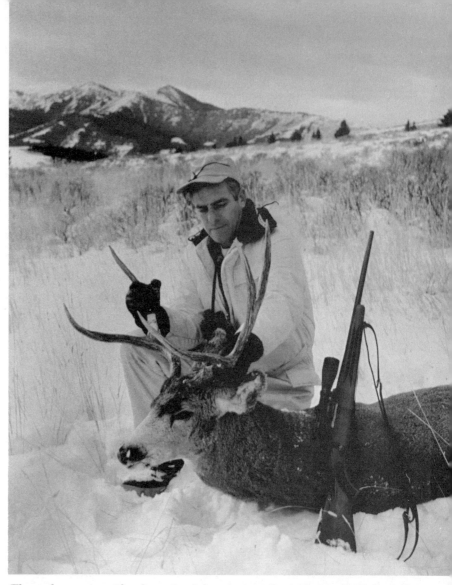

The author poses with a long-tined three-pointer he took in a foothills feeding area. Mule deer often feed in the foothills and bed on the slopes.

Successful hunting of the muley often involves knowledge of the animal's migration tendencies. Mountain deer will range high in summer and low in the dead of winter. During hot weather these animals range near timberline to avoid heat and insects. The really big bucks—in an attempt to escape hunters—will often stay high till snow becomes belly-deep. (Unlike elk, which graze off the ground, deer are browsing animals and can find food above deep snow.) If you want those big bruisers you'll have to go up there after them.

Still, as I touched on earlier when I told about one of my Colorado hunts, mountain mule deer tend to migrate down along general migration routes and they tend to concentrate in given areas. The experts who know the general boundaries of these routes and areas have little trouble killing fine bucks each year. Migration is another trait that's insignificant to whitetail hunters.

The top periods for hunting deer are dawn and dusk. This principle holds true for both mule deer and whitetails. All deer are basically nocturnal animals. By dawn they are moving from feeding to bedding areas. At dusk the reverse process begins. You're likely to see the most deer by being in hunting country during these two periods.

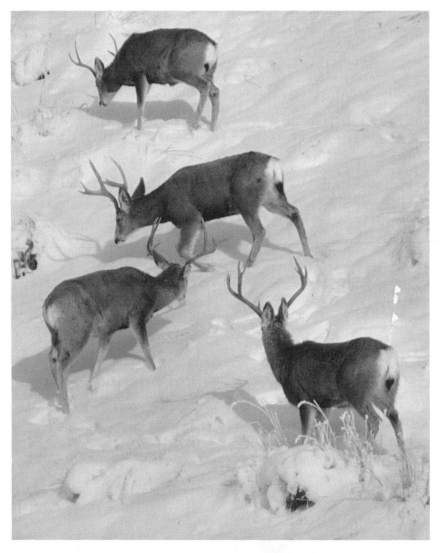

Mule deer bucks are more gregarious than whitetails. Though whitetail bucks are usually loners, it's not uncommon to see three or four muley bucks together.

However, you should be aware that some big mule deer bucks tend to be quite active—especially in oak brush and other thicket areas—during the period from about 10 A.M. to 1 P.M. I've never heard any reasonable explanation for this, but if you'll check a lot of kill records you'll discover that a considerable number of trophy muleys are downed during this midday period by experts at stillhunting. These fellows move quietly through the brush looking for the browsing bucks who seem to feel an urge to feed during midday. It's a tendency that whitetails don't have.

Another trait that distinguishes a muley buck from a whitetail buck is the former's desire to watch his back track. Though I've mentioned in several places in this book that I believe tracking is mostly a waste of time, here is another good place to point out one reason why I feel this way.

A hunter-wise mule deer watches his back track because he has learned it's one of the best ways to stay alive. Consider that a deer has far better eyesight, hearing, and sense of smell than you do. Consider further that a buck watching his back track is doing so from a stationary position behind at least some cover. Is it any wonder that a moving hunter is easily detected? You have practically no chance at all to get a shot at a mule-deer buck by following his track if he has the least suspicion you're after him. I shake my head every time I meet a hunter in the West who tells me he's tracking a big buck he jumped. The man is usually wasting his time.

The only time tracking may work—note that I say *may* and not *will*—is when there's enough snow on the ground so you can see your buck's tracks from a considerable distance. If you follow the tracks from 100 yards or more to the side it's possible you may surprise the animal before he's aware of your presence, especially if you move in from behind cover above the deer. Being on the uphill side of the trail accomplishes two purposes. First, deer seldom look up so you're less likely to be seen. Second, you'll be able to see a deer's tracks in snow a lot better and from a greater distance if you're above the trail, which means you can stay further away from the back track area your buck is watching.

It's been my experience that mule deer pick up movement a bit better than whitetails. This is probably because movement, rather than sound or scent, is a more common warning of danger in the open country of the West than in the thick forests of the East. This is why it's important for the mule-deer hunter in open and semi-open terrain to avoid getting into places where he can be seen easily. Never walk along the top of a ridge where you'll be skylighted. If you want to go high it's best to work along just below the top of ridges. Never go up or down an open slope if you can pick another route that offers some cover. When you're stillhunting or stalking it's best to stick to the heaviest cover available.

Being inconspicuous often has a good deal to do with your equipment. Don't use anything that will shine or glitter. In some areas it seems to be a fad today to have shiny instead of blued rifle bolts. This seems to me to be a mistake simply because a shiny bolt will glitter. So will other items such as the cheaper grades of Blaze-Orange shooting vests. Purchase the better quality, which is soft, pliable, and nonreflective.

Back in the late 1800s mule deer were almost wiped out across the West by settlers who hunted for meat and by market hunters who hunted for hides. Today this species is well-established in so many different types of terrain and in so many different climates that there's no such thing as typical mule deer country. I've hunted them along creek bottoms at low altitude and far up on the slopes of mountains. The one generality I have made is that muleys like rougher and more open country than do whitetails. We can narrow this down a bit by adding that the mule deer tends to inhabit brushy coulees and draws while the whitetail prefers taller cover.

Hunting Techniques

One of the greatest attractions of mule-deer hunting is the possibility of coming up with a real trophy rack. This species grows the largest and handsomest antlers of all North American deer. Even a young mule-deer buck will boast antlers far larger than young whitetail bucks. The difference is even greater as each species matures.

To make the record book in the North American Big Game Awards Program, you'll have to take a typical whitetail scoring a minimum of 170 points. But to make the book with a typical mule deer you'll have to take a rack scoring 195 points. If you study the latest record book (published about every six years) you'll find there are well over 300 mule deer listed scoring 195 or better, but very few whitetails score above 195. I'll discuss the record book in Chapter 21.

The rack of a typical mule deer is dichotomous, which means that it is evenly branched. The antlers are basically "Y" formed, and the upper ends form into two smaller "Ys." The points of a whitetail buck all come off one main beam, much as the points on a garden rake. A branched rack can, of course, be much more massive. Mule-deer antlers also curve inward less than whitetail racks, which means their size can be more impressive because they tend to be higher and wider. These facts are probably the basis for the somewhat confusing terminology on how many antler points a buck actually has. Hunters in eastern whitetail country count all points on both the left and right antlers. Thus, a buck with four points on each side would be an eight-pointer. In mule-deer country this same buck would be a four-pointer because western hunters count only the points on one antler. A whitetail buck with antlers measuring 20 inches across the outside spread could very well be a candidate for the record book, but veteran mule-deer hunters don't consider a muley a top trophy unless the buck boasts an outside spread in the 30-inch bracket.

Though mule deer in general are easier to harvest than whitetails, these big bucks with the enormous racks can be very difficult to fool. The antlers of a mule deer reach their greatest size when the animal is at least five years old. A five-year-old has seen plenty of hunting pressure. The only reason he's still alive is that he learned how to be clever.

These bucks seek terrain that is not overrun by hunters. When hunting season comes on they normally bed in areas hunters find almost impossible

This young mule-deer buck is still in velvet. Note the two "Y" branches on each beam that characterize the "typical" rack for trophy scoring purposes.

to reach without being heard or seen. Choice areas are just under rimrocks. That's why these crafty old bucks are often called "rimrockers." They'll also bed at the upper ends of canyons or draws offering a screen of brush or weeds.

Such sites are ideal for safety because the hunter who tries approaching from below is readily seen. Sometimes trophy bucks consider the wind direction when picking these bedding spots. They like to have the wind at their backs so they can smell or hear an intruder approaching from behind.

One way to outsmart these bucks is to cash in on the mule deer's trait of seldom allowing a hunter to approach closer than 100 yards. Where a whitetail may lie in hiding while a hunter passes within a few steps, the muley will jump and move out when he figures you're getting too close. The hunter who moseys along about 100 yards or so below rimrocks or to tops of canyons and draws often lulls a buck into thinking he isn't seen. The ones that decide they're not in trouble till it's too late get shot at. The principle to remember is to take your time, move slowly in zigzagging directions and never walk straight toward a spot a buck may lie up in. If he thinks he has been seen while you're still several hundred yards away he'll slip out behind cover or go over the top.

If you have a partner you can try ambushing a buck if you already have

The antlers of this aging monarch show many long, abnormal points in addition to the two basic "Ys" on each antler. For trophy scoring of this head in the "typical" category, the total length of abnormal points would penalize the score. In the "nontypical" category, the abnormal points would improve the score. Scoring aside, this is a very impressive head.

spotted him. One partner sneaks in behind the animal and takes a stand along the route the buck will likely use when escaping the downhill man. In this case the lower hunter simply moves uphill toward the buck in a straight-on approach designed to make him scared enough to try escaping. When he moves out he may get waylaid by the hunter in hiding.

Another trick is to hunt from above if you have the wind in your face or at least quartering into you. This technique takes advantage of the knowledge that deer seldom look up. Also, they expect danger from below and consequently they'll bed in a spot harboring some cover that screens them from below. Often this cover affords little or no camouflage from above. A buck picking such a spot will be in plain view of the hunter above. In addition, the hunter who works high while looking down can see anything that moves over a considerable area.

This last trick is almost sure death to a buck if you discover his hiding spot while you're still so far away you don't worry him. This is the reason why spotting scopes and good binoculars are of far more value when hunting mule deer than whitetails. Experienced hunters know the types of areas where mule-deer bucks are likely to lie up and they glass these areas thoroughly. When they spot a buck they then decide which of the tricks I've mentioned should work best.

Because of the vast terrain and distances where mule deer are hunted they usually are not driven with the same techniques used so successfully with whitetails. However, a partner can help in much the same way when you're hunting small canyons or draws. The accepted procedure is for one hunter to circle around in advance and post himself on a stand at the head of a canyon or draw where deer are likely to emerge when jumped. The other man then zigzags up through the cover as he tries to jump deer. Another good system is for each man to work opposite sides of the depression, moving slowly and on the same elevation. Deer jumped by one man will often run across the depression with the idea of escaping out through the other side. Therefore, any game moving out is likely to be seen by one or the other of the hunters.

A good trick for a single hunter working these depressions is to select a spot at the top where he has a fine view of the terrain below him. Then he pitches or rolls rocks down into the cover where deer may be. The noises so produced are very irritating to mule deer. They'll take only so much of it, then out they go. This trick again takes advantage of the fact that muleys just won't take a chance on hiding with the tenacity of whitetails.

Though the watering habits of mule deer are no different than those of whitetails, it's good to keep in mind that watering holes are fewer and farther between in the West than in the East. This means that taking a stand by a known watering area in mule-deer country can be quite productive simply because a lot of deer are likely to be using the spot.

I have a rancher friend in Wyoming who kills his buck every year near the overflow puddle produced by one of his windmills. He takes a stand 100 yards from the puddle and waits for deer to come down out of the hills at dusk. It's an easy way to kill a deer, and it's very effective. Smart western hunters keep their eyes open for watering areas used heavily by deer.

As a general rule mule deer will water—and feed—at lower elevations, then move high to bed down as dawn comes on. It follows that a good hunting technique is to climb above feeding and watering areas under the cover of darkness and take a stand along the edge of game trails leading up through canyons, draws or gullies.

Good binoculars are almost a must for this type of hunting. From an outcropping of rock or other high vantage point a man can glass a lot of country. He may see deer moving directly toward him, but it's more likely he'll spot animals bedding down somewhere below. In this case he can switch to one of the hunting methods I described earlier. In any event, if you get above the animals before they start moving up you'll be in a far better position to spot them than if you hunt the low country.

If your favorite technique is stillhunting, don't expect to hear alerted mule deer snort as whitetails often do. And, as I pointed out in the beginning of this chapter, muleys don't run with their tails erect, which is standard whitetail procedure. But they do move out in various gaits, and these gaits can offer clues as to what the deer intends to do.

If your buck takes off with the peculiar pogo-stick gait I described earlier, it usually means he is alarmed but not quite sure of what to do next. Chances are he will cover a short distance, then stop and offer a standing shot. If a buck starts off this way it's often best to hold off shooting and wait for the best opportunity.

If the buck really wants to blow out of there he'll move with astonishing speed and power in a dead run. But even then he may not go far. He may flee wildly for 100 yards or so, then stop on top of a knoll or ridge to stare back at you. Though I've never tried the trick, I've heard many veterans tell how they stopped a running mule deer simply by yelling or whistling at him. The unusual noise apparently makes the deer curious enough to stop and wonder what's going on.

If you jump a buck in thick cover and he takes off running, you'll probably have no chance to score unless you try a quick shot. But if the terrain is relatively open, chances are your buck—especially if he's a young one—will stop before he goes far. Even if he doesn't, it's very possible you can get another opportunity to shoot. Once a mule deer runs over a ridge or knoll, he's likely to stop when he has the hunter out of sight. These deer seem to have an out-of-sight, out-of-mind attitude.

Once in Wyoming I jumped a herd containing two bucks. The six animals ran over a knoll and disappeared. It was a small knoll, which I circled in several moments. When I came around to the other side the herd was standing dead-still in wide-open prairie watching their back tracks. I lined my rifle on the larger buck and dumped him. Such incidents are common in the West, but they're almost unheard of in whitetail country. Once a whitetail buck starts running, he's long-gone.

Another dramatic example of the differences between the two species is shown in their requirements for bedding spots. A whitetail buck will always select a dense thicket or other heavy cover while a muley buck may bed in cover so scant the average hunter would never believe a deer could be there. I've seen them bedded near a single bush in otherwise open terrain. I've already pointed out that muleys like to bed high—primarily because a high spot offers the best view of potential danger—but once they're high, they'll often bed with scant thought of cover. This, again, is why good binoculars can be such an important hunting tool in the West. The careful glassing of any slope or ridge during midday hours may turn up a bedded buck. And don't overlook the vast rocky areas that course these types of terrain. They may seem incapable of hiding deer when viewed from below, but once you climb up you'll find endless crannies in which the muleys find ideal bedding sites. The best mule-deer hunters spend far more time glassing than do the best whitetail hunters.

And many of these same mule-deer hunters make a point of knowing what the deer feed on in the areas they hunt. The chief forage of deer can vary drastically from region to region. Concentrating your hunting efforts in an area of top food supply can often be the major factor contributing to a successful hunt. If you don't know what the favorite plant species are and what they look like, you can get the information from local game wardens or veteran hunters. Keep in mind, however, that mule deer are migratory in states with mountainous terrain. A forage area heavily used by deer in December may not harbor a single animal in October. Be sure you're hunting the right area at the right time. A big muley buck needs over seven pounds of food per day, he isn't going to use an area unless the range supports the best menu he can find.

One theory that has carried over from the old days is that a mounted man can get closer to game than one on foot because game isn't alerted by four-footed critters. Don't put much stock in this theory today. Too many mule deer have been shot at over too many years by hunters who stepped off horses and blazed away. Modern bucks have been bred with the instinct to be wary of anything that isn't a normal part of their habitat. It's best to accept the principle that a horse only helps get you up to where the game is. From there on, you'll usually be more successful if you hunt on foot and employ the techniques I've discussed.

When to go hunting during deer seasons isn't nearly as important for mule deer hunters as it is for whitetail hunters. In whitetail country most of the deer harvest is cropped off the first few days of each season. Many whitetail bucks, especially the young ones that haven't yet learned the ways of hunters, are caught by surprise on opening day when nimrods flood the woods. It may take the survivors a couple of days to find hiding places, but when they do, they become exceedingly difficult to hunt.

Hunting pressure in mule-deer country isn't usually as heavy; consequently, the deer aren't as spooky. Also, as I have mentioned several times, mule deer in some areas are migratory. A whitetail buck, not being migratory, is in danger all season in the same small and usually quite accessible

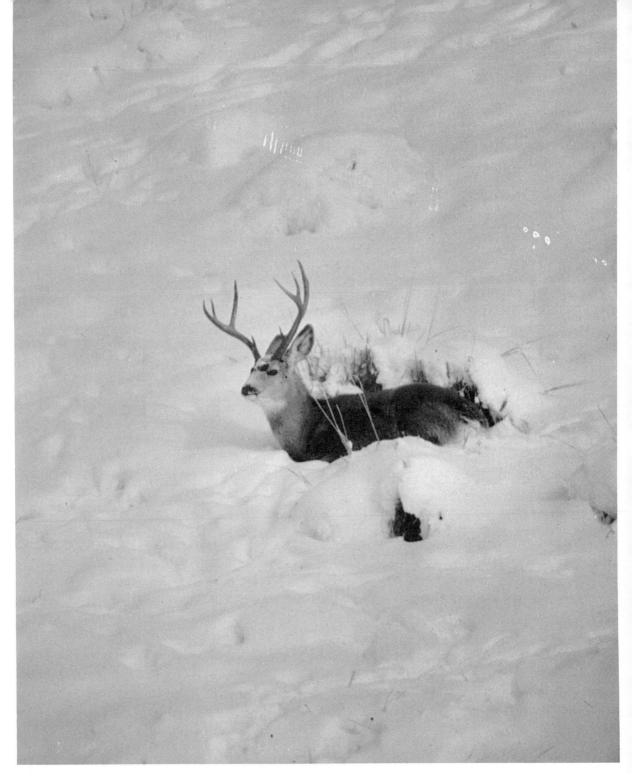

Mule deer will often bed down in areas that offer little concealment. Contrasting snow thus makes them easy to spot.

To avoid hunters, mountain mule deer often stay high up until the snow becomes belly deep, making food scarce. Clever bucks are the last to migrate down, yet most travel along established routes, just as the bucks in this photo are doing.

area he calls home. But a muley often moves out of a given range and into another. When he does this he loses some caution because of his tendency to think he has moved away from trouble. This is one reason a good share of big muley bucks are taken late in the season.

So your chances of success with mule deer are just about as good the last day of the season as the first. They may be a whale of a lot better if you hunt late when there is snow on the ground, especially in the deer-concentration areas utilized during migration, or if you use the glassing technique. A deer bedded in snow is far easier to spot than one bedded on bare ground.

Furthermore, early-season hunting in the West can be tough because deer seasons get underway much sooner than in the East. September hunting can be hot, which restricts your physical activity. The rut has not

In relatively open country, mule deer favor bushy coulees and draws that afford food and cover.

started, which means the big bucks are off by themselves and are cagier than they are when the rut begins. It's a fact that mule-deer hunting may be at its worse when the sun is shining, the temperature is hot, the ground is free of snow, and the most hunters are out.

A last big distinction between eastern whitetail hunting and mule-deer hunting is the readily available guided hunt in the West. The guided mule deer hunt is tailor-made for the man who is too busy to learn hunting techniques, and who has little time to spend on the adventure itself. Guides and outfitters are few in whitetail country, but numerous in the West. The busy hunter, for a price, can probably get his mule-deer buck with little more preparation than sighting in his rifle. This type of deer hunting has become so prevalent today that I'll devote much more emphasis to the subject in a later chapter.

CHAPTER
3

You Can't Shoot
What You Don't See

Warren Holmes and I were pass-shooting ducks on a knoll in North Dakota. Scattered clumps of brush varying from house-size to several acres dotted the prairie around us. During a lull in the shooting my companion pointed to a small patch of thickets 300 yards away.

"Big buck," he said.

I stared at those thickets till my eyes watered. I couldn't see anything that even resembled a deer. I shook my head and said, "Warren, I think you're seeing things."

"Well, darn it," he answered, "he's standing right there next to the north edge. There, he's moving out. Surely you can spot him now."

I finally did see the deer, but not until his body began taking shape as a silhouette against the golden prairie. Even then it was difficult to spot his antlers till he turned his head to look at us.

Warren has worn glasses since childhood. At that time I'd never worn them and we were both in our late forties. My eyes are better than his, but he has made me feel like a fool on several occasions when he had to point out game to me.

One time in Wyoming we were hunting mule deer. Our host was a rancher who had hunted deer in the West for many years. His idea of hunting is to drive back-country trails in a pickup while looking for game. He is used to the system and used to the terrain, but Warren often spotted deer before he did. I recall one time we were driving slowly down through a gully.

"Hold it," Warren grunted. "Back up about 15 feet. I think I saw the top of a buck's head in those rocks 100 yards to our right."

35

Ken backed up and stopped. Warren had been correct. He pointed toward a precise spot and told us a small three-pointer was lying flat out while trying to hide. Neither Ken nor I saw the animal till it decided to jump up and bolt.

"I'll be darned," our host said, "how'd you ever spot that little buck?"

Later in the day Warren decided he'd have a better vantage point if he rode in the truck's bed instead of its cab. Several times Ken and I were surprised by his sudden pounding on the roof. It was Warren's signal that he'd spotted more deer.

That evening Ken told Warren that he was astonished with his game-seeing abilities, particularly because Warren had little experience hunting in the West. He asked what the secret was.

"Well, I guess a deer is a deer," my partner began. "Even though I don't have much knowledge of mule deer I've hunted whitetails all my life. I seem to have a natural knack for recognizing cover where deer may be. I search that cover with my eyes, and I look for colors or shapes that could be parts of a deer."

Larry Price, a guide with whom I've hunted in Colorado, also has a great facility to see deer. He explained his ability in another way.

"Most hunters fail to see deer in heavy cover unless the animals are moving," he told me. "Movement is easy to see so I don't worry about missing it. I concentrate on looking for unnatural objects that aren't moving. When you think about it you'll realize that most objects in the woods are vertical. Sure there are blowdowns, logs, and rocks that are horizontal, but everything that's growing is vertical. Deer bodies are not. So I pay special attention to horizontal objects, and I really scrutinize anything that approaches a deer's size or color."

Wayne Fitzwater, a Montana game warden, once told me that experience is the most important factor in seeing game. We sat on the edge of a mountain ledge one evening and watched mule deer by the dozens come out of forests surrounding a logged-off area across a canyon. He claimed it isn't much of a problem to see game if you've had enough hunting experience to hunt where game is likely to be.

I'll have more to say about his theory shortly. But first I want to mention that Wayne's system had to be more complicated because he was pointing out bucks that were several hundred yards away. Not only that, he was seeing the animals as they were just beginning to walk out of the timber. Often I couldn't tell deer from stumps until they were well into the clearing.

That night in camp we discussed the art of seeing game, and Wayne mentioned something that I'd never thought about before. He just passed it off as matter-of-fact, but I believe it's an important principle most hunters are unaware of.

"Many hunters miss seeing detail because they take a wide-angle view of everything," he began. "That's because a panoramic view is naturally most

You might hastily conclude that the photo on the left has no deer in it. But a careful study of the photo on the right will help you locate a buck in both pictures. Successful hunters study suspicious areas and forms.

interesting. The trick is to spend only half your time with the wide-angle view, the other half should be spent looking for detail. You were having trouble telling deer from stumps because you were trying to see everything at once. After you concentrated on a particular deer it suddenly didn't look like a stump at all. That's because you narrowed down your field of view. You saw a lot of stumps that looked like deer, but after you focused your attention you didn't see a deer that looked like a stump. It's just a matter of training your eyes to see detail."

How important is the art of seeing game? It's all-important for deer

When scanning for bedded bucks, hunters expect to see a prominently displayed head, as shown in the top photo. But the savvy hunter will be alert to the tip of an ear or part of an antler. Had the buck below been a doe, it probably would have gone unnoticed.

hunters because today's deer depend far less upon running to safety than did the bucks of yesteryear. *Today's bucks know their odds of staying alive are much better if they hide instead of run.* Deer still panic and run, but they are apt to run for shorter distances, then hide sooner and longer.

When I started hunting mule deer years ago in the western states I was astonished to see so many deer in pastures, in fields along roads, and in plain sight in woodland clearings. That fact was brought home to me during a 1973 hunt with Ray Lyons, an outfitter in Collbran, Colorado.

We drove down out of the mountains one evening when a blizzard was brewing. In fields along the valley road we saw quite a few deer, often several of them feeding in groups. I mentioned to Ray that I'd spotted no deer along the same route during the several previous days we'd been driving it.

"They're feeding early because a storm's coming," he said. "There are plenty of deer down in these valleys but they normally don't come out of hiding till dark. Years ago you used to see deer all over the place, even during hunting season. They're much more secretive now and they're wizards at hiding. You have to look a lot harder to see deer today."

That statement comes from a man who has been a full-time guide and outfitter for nearly forty years. It's some of the best advice a modern deer hunter can get.

As for seeing whitetails, I believe Warren Holmes' convictions are about as solid as any. His score for the past eighteen years is eighteen bucks. He took all of them in a heavily hunted area of Michigan, a state where the deer-hunter success ratio is only about 11 percent. How can he score so consistently when nearly 90 percent of the hunters around him fail to go home with venison? Well, he hunts hard and he hunts only from stands, but it's likely that much of his success stems from his knack for seeing deer. One time he said to me, "The best shot in the world isn't going to eat deer liver unless he can see a deer to shoot at."

One of Warren's favorite topics is deer size. He points out that almost all hunters delude themselves into expecting the average whitetail to be much larger and taller than it really is. Tell a hunter that a big buck seldom stands taller than 40 inches at his shoulder and you'll have a doubting hunter, but you'll be telling the truth.

As I point out in other parts of this book, I think the odds are pretty well stacked against many deer hunters who go after their whitetail bucks by using the stillhunting technique. But I know one guy, now an old man, who used to be fairly successful with the system before his area became crowded with hunters. Years ago when I began to get serious about deer hunting I'd often visit with this fellow and ask him about the tricks of the trade. I've never forgotten one comment he made, and it's better advice now than it was then.

"I'd tell any hunter to use his eyes more than his feet," he began. "Most hunters are in too much of a hurry to see what's over the next hill. The plain fact is that once you're in good deer country your buck is just as likely

There are seven whitetails in this photo. The casual hunter would probably spot only the doe at left. The key to success is in looking for parts of deer. The illustration on the opposite page will help you locate all seven deer.

to be in the thicket next to you as he is to be in one three miles away. You won't get a shot at him unless you see him before he sees you. You have to focus all your attention on the most suspicious things you see. That's the way to spot deer. Successful stillhunting is about 90 percent looking."

My ability to see deer is far better than it was twenty years ago. Last fall I downed a mule deer buck that was almost invisible. He was standing motionless in a stand of timber so thick you could barely see the snow background behind the trees. When I first spotted him, all I noticed was a patch of gray that was out of place against the white snow and pale-green aspen trunks. Seconds later I picked out part of a rack of antlers, then I noted another patch of gray that was part of the buck's shoulder. I'm positive I'd never have seen that deer unless I'd known what to look for.

Everything I've mentioned so far points out that much of the skill used in seeing deer is a skill that can be learned. I believe that most successful deer hunters develop much of this skill without being aware of it. In acquiring an extensive outdoor background a man automatically learns to interpret what he sees. As warden Wayne Fitzwater told me, an experienced hunter learns to recognize good deer country which, in turn, presents the possibility of seeing more deer. He learns to analyze where deer travel, feed, and bed; he literally thinks like a deer. In short, a man with lots of hunting experience knows where to look. The most successful veteran hunters also know *how* to look.

Is the deer in the top photo a doe or a buck? Patience reveals that it's a buck—for a good shot.

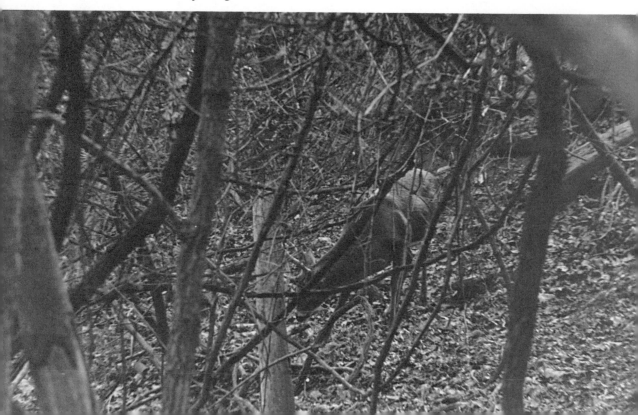

Glassing for Deer

The most obvious way to get a better view of what you're looking at is to inspect a questionable object with binoculars or your rifle scope. Glassing for deer is especially important in western states where you're likely to see animals at greater distances than in the heavily forested East, Midwest, and South. Several guides have told me that average deer hunters have great difficulty putting their glasses or scopes on partially hidden deer even after they have located them with the unaided eye. That's because most hunters seldom use their binoculars or scopes except during the few days each year when they are actually hunting. They aren't familiar enough with their equipment to use it efficiently. This is one fault I don't have because I'm a nut on using binoculars year-round.

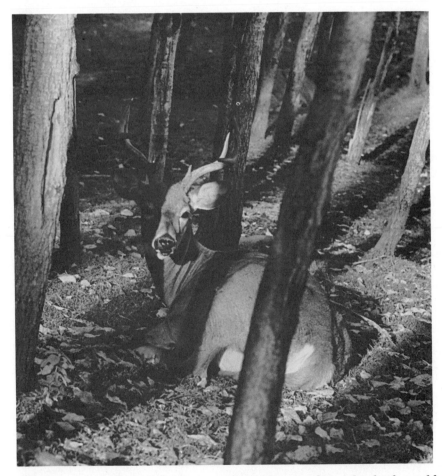

Bedded where light and shadow provide good camouflage, this buck would probably go unnoticed from a distance unless the hunter studied the scene with binoculars or a riflescope. Optics can be as important as the rifle.

Whitetails often bed where deadfalls or rocks conceal most of their outline. A flicked ear or a head movement may be your only tip-off unless you've drawn a sharp focus on the right spot.

My office windows face out on a large inland lake. I delight in studying migrating ducks in fall and spring, fishermen in summer and winter, and birds and squirrels and other interesting objects just about anytime. Scarcely a day goes by in which I don't use my binoculars several times. I'm as familiar with using those glasses as I am with touching a match to my pipe.

This familiarity often has enabled me to see game that would have gone unnoticed. I go along with the guides who claim that the average hunter would do himself a big favor by learning to use optics efficiently. A deer antler that appears to be a branch in the distance can be identified for just what it is with the use of glasses. I could list many such examples.

Deer hunters of years ago didn't bother much with scopes or binoculars because they were relatively bulky and inefficient. Modern optics are far superior, and they represent one of the most important advances ever made in deer-hunting equipment. For today's deer hunter a good binocular can be just about as important as his rifle.

Mistakes Hunters Make

A problem among Eastern hunters who go after mule deer in the West for the first time is that they don't look for deer in the right places. Most whitetails seen from stands or during drives are likely to be spotted 50 to 75 yards away. In the more open country where mule deer are hunted, it's common to see potential targets several hundred yards away. Also, whitetails are much more likely to hide than muleys. A whitetail may not bolt until you're practically on top of him, a mule deer will seldom let you approach closer than 100 yards.

Hunters with whitetail backgrounds often go on their first mule deer hunt and continue to use the short-range vision they used back home. They

If you can hunt upwind, try to move eastward in the early morning and westward in late afternoon. This will help silhouette deer against the brightest area in the sky.

miss seeing deer that may be in plain view across a canyon, down in a draw, or up on a ridge. The cure is to get local advice on where to look when hunting a new area for the first time.

A couple of years ago one of my Michigan friends joined five other fellows and drove to the Colorado Rockies for a mule-deer hunt. They had never hunted the area, they had no experience with mule deer, they had no guide, and they didn't bother to ask for local advice. They camped for six days, saw few deer, and scored on only one small buck.

In contrast, I booked a hunt in approximately the same area with a reputable outfitter. There were four hunters in my group, and we nailed four big bucks in only 2½ days of hunting. The difference was that our outfitter put us in the right spots and told us where to look for deer.

One of the main reasons hunters don't see deer is that the animals see or hear them first. Mule deer, more so than whitetails, are likely to spook and run when confronted by man. It's common sense to expect to see deer farther ahead if you're walking on crusted snow or very dry ground than if you're walking on wet or soft ground. You'll also make less noise if you eliminate noisemakers like keys or change in your pockets, canteens or binoculars banging against rifle stocks, or crinkly clothing and rain gear. The human voice is especially startling to deer. When hunting with companions it's best to save talkfests until after the day's hunting is finished.

The time of day can be a very important factor in seeing deer. One time in the prairie portion of Wyoming, I wondered why my guide started the day by stillhunting directly toward the brightening sky in the east. My unasked question was answered in a hurry when a three-point buck got up from his bed near the top of a rise 250 yards ahead of us. I'll never forget the coal-black silhouette the animal made against the dawn sky. Even his antlers were outlined in perfect detail. One of my companions shot the buck. When we reached the kill site I commented that the deer must have been stupid to let a hunter in plain sight shoot him.

"No, we weren't in plain sight," the guide answered. "Look back down to where we were when he stood up. It's still in shadows down there. He couldn't see us nearly so well as we could see him. If a man can hunt upwind he should go east in early morning and west in late evening. He'll see a lot more deer that way. On clear days, with the sun up, it's best to hunt with the sun behind you because it will shine on the deer. That's when the flick of an ear or flash of an antler really shows up."

The smart hunter knows where to look for the animals in various kinds of weather. On warm days, deer seek shade. On cold days, bucks often bed on slopes or ridges facing southern exposures where sunshine filters through the cover. Deer don't like windy places. When a strong wind is blowing it's best to look for them on the lee side of hills and ridges or in lowland pockets of cover.

The most dramatic experiences that have shown me how weather affects deer happened within a few miles of where I'm writing these lines. Deer live all around my place in mixed woodlands of hardwoods, birch, brush, and conifers. These forests are fairly thick, except where they give way to huge areas of sand dunes along the Lake Michigan shoreline. The dunes are mostly rolling hills of sand with low areas harboring scattered pockets of pine.

You could roam those dunes for days during spring, summer, and early fall and you'd be lucky to see a deer track, let alone a deer. But as fall wears on, the herds begin moving into the dunes. When heavy snowfall hits, they converge on the area. Take a trip through there in winter on a snowmobile and you'll see deer all over the place.

It's likely that deer movements in your area are affected to some degree by weather, too. I can't tell you how your local deer react to changing weather conditions because even the same species react differently in various parts of the country. But if you'll take the time to study your local situation and talk to local experts, you'll probably gain additional knowledge that will enable you to see more deer.

I believe it's possible for a man to train himself year-round to see game better. For example, I get a kick out of watching squirrels in the clearings and trees around my bird feeders. Sometimes they approach with caution, hiding against a tree trunk, flattening out on a limb, or jumping into a bush and freezing motionless for minutes. You learn something about the motions and movements of game by watching any wild animal or bird. I'm not saying you could train yourself to see deer by watching birds and squirrels in a big-city park, but I do believe that the more movements of wildlife you watch, the more you'll train your game eye to see those movements. Also, you'll be training yourself to understand what you see, and the benefits of that type of education can add up fast.

The average hunter has been led astray by the photos in outdoor magazines and deer hunting books. Almost without exception these photos show big bucks in areas harboring little cover. No editor is going to use a photo of a buck that's hard to see; he wants a dramatic photo that says "big buck" at first glance. That's fine, but it's misleading because when a hunter sees a deer under normal hunting conditions, the scene won't resemble any of the photos in magazines and books.

The first mistake is expecting to see deer that look as huge as they look in photos. As I mentioned earlier, the average whitetail seldom stands taller than 40 inches at his shoulder. Trophy mule deer bucks are larger, but even these animals can be mostly hidden in weeds that stand only three feet tall. When a hunter realizes that he should "think small" he'll see more deer.

The next most important mistake that most hunters make is expecting to see a whole deer, like those they see in photos. Under most hunting conditions, you'll see only parts of a motionless animal, unless of course the deer is moving. Even then you'll likely get flashes of movement—a pair of legs or parts of antlers. When I'm hunting in woods I don't expect to see a whole deer until after something alerts me that I'm probably seeing parts of one. I really stare at anything that moves, and I thoroughly scrutinize anything that approaches a deer's size or color.

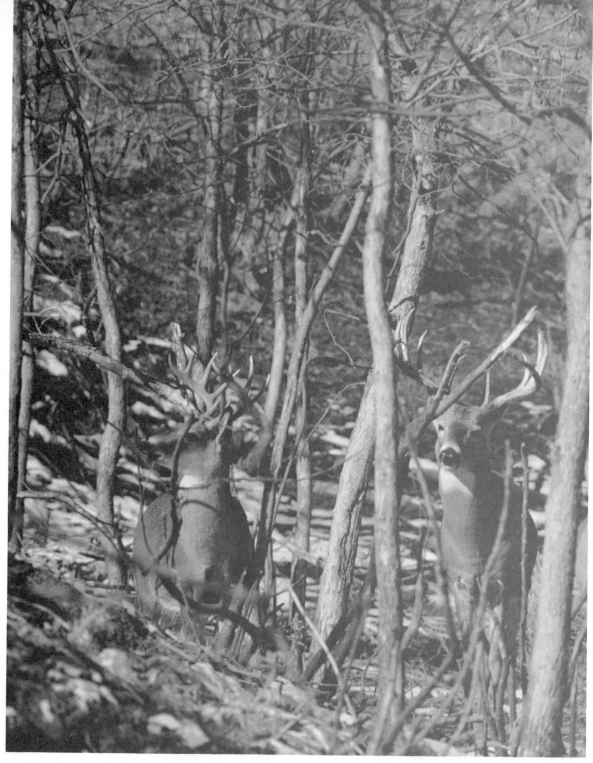

Many hunters fail to consider the weather's effects on game movement. In this photo, bucks have retreated into a hollow to escape heavy winds.

When you do that you eliminate the wide-angle view. Let's say we're watching the Indianapolis 500 auto race. From our seats in the stands we're watching a bunch of racers come around a turn. With our normal wide-angle view we see a great deal of action, much of the track and parts of the infield and stands. Suddenly one of the cars spins out of control. Immediately our view is narrowed down and centered on the car in trouble because it naturally becomes the focus point of our attention. The smart deer hunter does the same thing when he suddenly sees something that may be a part or parts of a deer. It's a matter of training your eyes to see detail.

You have to concentrate. You have to expect to see a deer at any moment. Pay particular attention to the thickest cover near runways. *Don't waste time looking at such terrain as clearings, bare sidehills and open ridge tops.* Deer know they are easily seen in such places, so they avoid them. With experience, you'll develop a talent for recognizing cover where deer are most likely to be. This is why veteran hunters see far more deer than beginners.

When you do see a deer it's very important to interpret the animal's actions. If it's walking slowly, or feeding, it's likely unalerted. If it appears edgy and often looks toward its backtrack, there are probably more deer coming. This situation is particularly important if the deer you see is a doe and you have a buck-only license.

In such a case the average hunter can't resist watching the deer he spots because it's naturally the most interesting thing to do, but it's a big mistake. Forget the doe that you can't shoot anyway. Really scrutinize her backtrack area in an attempt to spot the buck that may be following.

Seeing Deer from a Stand

Most of what I've mentioned so far emphasizes that the skill used in seeing deer is a skill that can be learned. The ability to see unalarmed deer is even more important, and this objective can be planned.

Let's say you're on a stand and you suddenly spot a deer. The animal is standing dead still and staring straight at you. You'll be lucky to get a shot because your presence has already been discovered. Now let's change the scene and say the deer you suddenly see is walking slowly, maybe browsing, but in no way suspicious of trouble. Now you have the ideal situation. Instead of spotting a deer that is ready to bolt and frighten other deer that may be following, you're looking at a potential target that may be the first of several other potential targets about to walk into view.

The key to viewing such scenes is to hunt from a stand that arouses no suspicions in passing deer. Today's wary bucks won't approach a hunter they can see even if the man is motionless. Down through the years old stumps, fallen logs, or outcroppings of rocks often made fine stands; but they don't anymore, unless they at least partially conceal you.

I feel that permanent blinds are the best answer. I build mine with weathered boards cut long enough to conceal my body to eye level while in sitting positions. I build them in the spring for two reasons. Spring terrain (before the leaves develop) resembles November hunting terrain in my area. In spring I can study the lay of the land and determine the best stand sites from a vantage standpoint. I can't do this if I wait until after the leaves are out.

More important is the fact that a blind built in spring—no matter how conspicuous it is—eventually becomes a normal part of the landscape, as far as deer are concerned. By summer the animals will have passed it so many times that they cease to pay it any special heed. Such a blind makes the best possible stand.

The last factor is comfort. The more comfortable you are the longer you can sit still, and the longer you can sit still the better the odds that deer won't see you. Dress correctly for sitting. You'll need far warmer clothes than you would for walking. Warm boots are important, but a warm hat is even more important. More body heat escapes through the head than anywhere else. Hand-warmers are fine, and a Thermos bottle of some hot drink is almost a necessity. Nuts, dried fruit, or other snacks—as well as sandwiches—help maintain body heat.

A "hot-seat" or foam pad makes long periods of sitting more comfortable. So does a built-in backrest in your blind. Mittens are far warmer than gloves. Don't pay any attention to hunting buddies who say that true hunting is toughing it out in the elements. The techniques of hunting from stands have been around a long time, but many deer hunters don't appreciate how effectve they are when adapted to today's hunting picture.

CHAPTER
4

Why Stands
Beat the Odds

Hunting from a stand is the most productive technique in areas where many hunters are in the woods. They are bound to move deer, and the more they move, the better the odds for the hunter on a stand.

The trail-watching hunter is the only one who can beat a deer at his own game. Any moving hunter is matching his ears and eyes against an animal whose senses are far superior. Not only is the hunter on a stand silent, but he can control his scent and he can limit his vision to the area where action is most likely to occur. Also, he is most likely to get standing shots because he is hidden and quiet.

Scouting

Being a successful stand hunter calls for careful reconnaissance. Deer often change location from season to season as browse and weather conditions change. Reconnaissance work done in summer may lead to an area loaded with deer, but they may not be there during the fall hunting season. Deer that fed in crop fields have to find a new dinner table when the crops are harvested. A field that was fallow during summer may offer a food bonanza when its winter wheat begins sprouting in fall. Summer runways that led through leafy bushes may be abandoned when the leaves drop in fall because the concealment is gone. A woodland that attracted deer last year because of an outstanding mast crop may not produce nuts this year. If the food is absent you'll find no deer.

The point is that you should do your scouting for stand locations as close to the opening of deer season as possible, or during the season. Deer react differently when they're being hunted. I'll explain in a moment.

One of the best—and most enjoyable—ways of scouting is to combine it with other activities. When I hunt grouse and woodcock in my local area of Michigan each October I'm always looking for deer sign. I have a friend who took up squirrel hunting in farm woodlots mostly because he was in those woodlots anyway looking for signs of corn-fed bucks. Another guy I know killed a big buck last fall in a swamp near a river. There were so many deer in there that he took two friends back to the area and they killed bucks, too. He found his hotspot runway while walking the river's bank when he was fishing for steelhead. Still another friend jumped a herd of whitetails while he was out picking fall mushrooms. He scouted the area, picked a spot for a stand, and then went home with venison when deer season opened.

There is one all-important tip to keep in mind when scouting for runways: it's best to do your scouting a day or two after a heavy rain. If you do

In heavily hunted country, you can depend upon other hunters to unwittingly keep deer moving for you. The key is to take up a stand along an established runway, making sure the wind won't carry your scent to approaching deer.

this you'll know that all the deer tracks you find will be fresh. There's no sense picking a stand site along a runway that isn't being used.

The best sites are near feeding areas, bedding areas, scrape areas, watering areas, the trails connecting these areas, and the trails used as escape routes. Locating a stand anyplace else probably will be a waste of time.

Some veterans claim the first thing to look for is a feeding area. This is sometimes true in mule deer country where the animals often feed in herds on ranchlands in early morning and late evening, but whitetails often feed in cover. There are important reasons why looking for well-used runways is the best bet in whitetail woods.

Whitetails don't roam as far between feeding and bedding areas as mule deer do. Mule deer roam the open country as a matter of habit. They'll often feed in low-lying valleys and bed down in high buttes or rimrock, and they may take different routes to their destinations from day to day.

Deer may feel secure enough in the "edge" along farmlands until the first day of hunting season. When hunters suddenly decend on the area, the deer often head for heavier cover. With this knowledge, you can choose a stand offering likely shooting each opening day.

Deer use trails in all types of weather and terrain. Thus, your odds improve if you can locate these trails and hunt near them by means of trail watching, stalking, stillhunting, or driving.

Whitetails don't have these habits. They often bed down just over a hill from a feeding area. Their runways are used more consistently and are well-worn and easier to find. Whitetails always have a movement pattern that you can discover by studying runways.

From my experience, it's a lot easier to find a whitetail's runway than it is to find his feeding area. The key point here is that once you find his runway you can find his feeding, watering, and bedding locations simply by backtracking on his trails. That's a relatively simple job because a whitetail's home area seldom covers more than one square mile, which is the key to deciding where to hunt.

The one thing a runway can't tell you is whether the deer using it are bucks or does. There's no sense selecting a stand site in an area not used by bucks. The best way to discover that some of the tracks on a trail belong to bucks is to get a good look at the animals. This is best accomplished by scouting just before deer season opens.

Another good trick is to look for rub marks in the brush along runways. Rub marks are made when bucks clean and polish their antlers on sturdy saplings. A rub mark looks as if someone had cut a foot or two of bark off a tree with a dull knife. Most are made about two feet above the ground on saplings of an inch or less in diameter. The important point is that fresh rub marks are positive evidence that one or more bucks are using the area.

Fresh scrapes offer similar evidence, but you'll find them only during the rutting season. A scrape is a calling card a buck leaves for does in heat. A buck makes a scrape by pawing out a fan-shaped spot in the ground. It measures from a foot to several feet across, and it will be completely cleared of leaves, twigs, grass, and other debris. The buck's calling card is actually his scent, which he leaves by urinating in his scrape.

A stand site by a scrape is effective because bucks usually return to their scrapes at least once a day to see if they have attracted ready-to-breed does. If your deer season is open during the rut you'll be smart to be constantly on the alert for buck scrapes.

Locating a Stand

If your choice of a stand site is to be near either a feeding or bedding area there are several factors to consider.

Whitetails leave their beds and move toward a feeding site sometime during the last hour before night. They travel slowly, scheduling their arrival to coincide with dusk. All during this time shooting light worsens. On the other hand, they'll leave feeding areas on a schedule enabling them to reach bedding locations shortly after dawn. During this trip, shooting light improves. You also should realize that stormy weather, often encountered during deer-hunting seasons, prolongs daylight movement of whitetails. In short, a stand near a bedding area offers more shooting light potential than does a stand near a feeding area.

Always remember that a deer's most basic instinct is to travel upwind.

Antler rubs along a deer trail are proof the trail is being used by one or more bucks. Rubbing is done primarily before and during the rut, and it involves both antler cleaning and mock battles. This buck is fighting a tree in rutting season. Tree and saplings (see opposite page) show clear evidence of buck rubs.

The clever buck depends on his nose to tell him of danger ahead. For this reason whitetails have alternate runways leading to feeding and bedding areas. Your stand must always be downwind of any well-used trail, but be sure your site is near a trail the deer will be using during the time you are hunting.

It's my contention that locating a stand on potential escape routes is one of today's best bets for bagging deer. A lot of gunners kill deer because the

One of the best sites for a stand is near a watering area which is connected by a trail with a bedding area.

animals happen to blunder upon them after being jumped by other hunters. The guy who kills his buck in this fashion seldom analyzes why the deer happened to be where he was at that specific time. If the hunter did figure it out, he would come to the correct conclusion that the buck was running an escape route. I could mention dozens of examples of what I'm talking about, but a few particular incidents that stand out in my memory will illustrate my point.

In my local area whitetails are normally scattered all over a terrain of hardwoods; pine and cedar pockets; and mixtures of brush, clearings, and farm fields. But when rifles begin roaring on the opening morning of deer season, many of the animals begin moving to what might be termed safety zones.

Within a few miles of where I'm typing these lines there is an area consisting of a few thousand acres of very thick jackpine clumps intermingled with grassy clearings. The area is not used by deer during the summer, but they flock to the place when they become harassed by hunters. Not too many locals know this, but it is known by the hunters who have done enough of their scouting *during* previous deer seasons to discover the movement patterns of those whitetails.

These hunters locate on stands along the low-lying escape routes the deer use when moving from their normal fall range into the range they use when rifles begin booming. Such stands have nothing to do with feeding, watering, or bedding areas. Their sites are selected with a simple principle in mind: "If I were a deer, which route would offer me the most cover for getting from where I am to where I want to go." Stand hunters who utilize this theory are among today's most successful hunters.

I have a friend who gets at least one shot at a buck almost every opening day. His stand is near the bottom of a ravine where a power-line opening crosses the beginning of a huge cedar swamp. The cedar swamp is within a mile of the end of a large area of farm fields and small clumps of brush. Whitetails wax fat in that area before hunting season. They feed in the farm fields and bed in the small pockets of brush. But as soon as hunting season opens, those small clumps of brush offer less hiding security than some deer want. Then the deer head down the ravine leading into the cedar swamp, and they walk right in front of my friend's stand.

Several times during deer-hunting trips in the West I've heard a rancher, guide, or outfitter say something like this: "The deer in this area usually bed down in the thickets at the bottom of that canyon to our right. I'll hike down there and jump them. Chances are they'll run up the canyon and top out over there by those two tall pines. I'll give you an hour to walk over there and get settled on a stand, then I'll go downhill and see what I can kick out."

My most dramatic experience with this sort of deer behavior took place in Saskatchewan. In the southeastern part of the province whitetails are hunted with a technique locally termed "pushing the bush." Most of the cover in that area consists of small pockets of brush ranging from the size of a city block to several hundred acres. Stand hunters are positioned near one end of a brush patch, then drivers work through the cover from the opposite end in an attempt to drive deer to the standers.

During my hunts in the province I was impressed with the fact that my guides always told me to stand in precise areas. One time Glen Holloway, a local guide from Wapella, said to me, "Stand right here behind these trees."

Then he pointed across 100 yards of plowed field toward the end of a large patch of brush. "If there's any deer in there they'll come out right next to those two big rocks when I push the bush from the other side. They'll run the field and cross into that cover on your left.

"A deer knows the best route to safety," Glen explained. "Unless he's unusually alarmed he'll run the same route every time he's jumped as long as he doesn't have to run downwind. I'm so familiar with this area I know those routes almost as well as the deer. A guy who does a lot of scouting gets that kind of knowledge."

All of these examples point out the importance of knowing where deer are likely to be and where they're likely to go when they get into trouble. A stillhunter or a stalker would have practically no chance for a shot at these traveling animals. But the man on a stand has the odds in his favor.

Concealment—Ground Blinds

Although a hunter on a stand usually won't spook a deer by creating sound, he still has the animal's nose and eyes to contend with. As I've already mentioned, no wild deer will approach a person he can smell, and, though naturally curious, no deer will approach something he sees that looks suspicious.

The subject of concealment of a hunter on a stand can promote plenty of arguments. Down through the years many deer hunters have thought of a stand as no more than an old stump, a fallen log, or an outcropping of rock. You may find such objects on perfect stand sites, but they won't be perfect stands because you're underestimating a deer's eyesight. Few clever bucks will approach a hunter they can see even if the man is motionless.

Another factor is comfort. I've heard hundreds of hunters discount hunting from a stand because they "just don't have the patience to sit on a hard stump all day." This is nonsense. A deer certainly doesn't know or care if you're sitting on a hard stump or a soft lawn chair if he can't see you, and he won't see you if you are properly concealed. It follows that if you're properly concealed you might as well have some of the comforts of home. It also follows that if you have a few comforts you'll be able to stay on your stand longer, and that's all-important because it's the guy who stays put who shoots a deer.

Some years ago my son Jack and I built a deer blind that a lot of veterans would laugh at. We put four corner posts in the ground, connected the posts with wire, and tied clear cedar and oak branches to the framework. We used cedar and oak because the foliage from these two species doesn't

Stands take many forms, but essentially they are places where you wait and watch. This hunter may be able to see the trail, but deer would be likely to see him before he could take a good shot.

fall when it dies. If we'd built the blind with branches from maple and hemlock it would have been a skeleton by deer season. It was quite an elaborate affair, big as a duck blind. Our stand didn't blend in well with the surroundings because it had a boxlike appearance, but it worked perfectly for several reasons.

First, it was located on a knoll above two crossing runways. A stand located on such a spot doubles your chances of seeing deer. Second, we built the blind long before deer season. The whitetails using those runways no doubt were suspicious of the structure for weeks after it was built, but as time passed and it produced no trouble the deer accepted it as harmless. Third, it offered perfect concealment because it was constructed of thick cover.

The opening morning of the deer season produced rain mixed with snow. But we were quite comfortable, sitting on soft lawn chairs. We were able to move around because we were concealed. We watched deer move past us long after many other hunters probably had become wet, chilled, hungry, and disgusted. Similar experiences through the years have cemented my belief that hunting from a stand doesn't have to be a dull and lonely experience. Anyone can sit longer if he is warm, comfortable and concealed well enough so he doesn't have to sit like a statue.

Years ago I used to hunt from deer blinds that were more conspicuous than the one I just mentioned. The area we hunted covered several square miles of sand dunes intermixed with pine forests. The deer in that region fed on dune grass and bedded in the thick conifers. They were vulnerable to rifles only when they traveled from one clump of forest to another, and the only vantage points from which they could be viewed clearly were the tops of bare dunes.

The problem, of course, was that if a hunter stood in the open on top of a sand dune he would be spotted by deer before they left the fringes of cover. So we built blinds on the dunes long before deer seasons opened.

We did our best to camouflage those blinds. First—and it's a good trick to consider wherever you can use it—we dug in. We dug foxholes in the sand to conceal the lower halves of our bodies. We lined the foxholes with upright weathered boards cut long enough to conceal the rest of our bodies to eye level while in sitting positions. Then we lined the rims of the blinds with pine branches.

The blinds were built high enough to break the wind, and big enough so a man could move around while showing a minimum of movement. They were built in wide-open places, were constructed mostly of unnatural materials, and were of unnatural contours. Did they work?

The first day I hunted from one of those blinds I saw twenty-eight deer, three of them bucks. The first buck was behind me. I didn't spot him till I stood up to stretch. We saw each other at the same time. He bolted back into cover before I could get my scope on him. The second buck offered a fair shot but I missed him. The third offered a good shot. I piled him up with one .243 slug. None of those twenty-eight deer were wary of that blind because they had passed it so many times without trouble before deer season that they didn't associate it with danger. Again, that's one of the most important points a stand hunter should remember.

Hunting from specific locations can boost your odds in another way, too. You can mark a trail to your stand which can be followed by flashlight. This means you can eliminate the mistake many hunters make by arriving at their site too late and leaving too early. Deer begin traveling at the first hint of dawn. If you wait till it's light enough to walk to your stand without a flashlight you'll miss seeing a lot of deer. You should be on your stand long before dawn, and you shouldn't leave in the evening until all shooting light is gone.

I don't mean to imply that you should be on your stand all day. Most hunters just don't have the patience for that, and it isn't the best technique, anyway. Many expert stand hunters agree that six hours of waiting per day is about right. The sitting periods should consist of the first two hours of daybreak, the last two hours before darkness at night, and two hours at midday. The off-hours should be spent scouting for new or better stand sites. I've already mentioned why it is so important to scout when the hunting season is open.

Though deer normally are bedded at midday, these hours are producing ever more venison as the hunting army continues to increase in numbers. Most hunters take a break in late morning to return to cars or camps for lunch, and they return to hunting areas in early afternoon. This means there is much activity in the woods during midday hours, and this activity moves deer.

Another factor contributing to the success of midday standers is the growing use of gang-type drives. Going hunting early in the morning serves no useful purpose for drivers, so they normally don't get organized until after deer have bedded down. Since the purpose of a drive is to move bedded deer, the drivers also aren't active late in the day. This means that the man on a stand who hunts only during early and late daylight hours is missing a chance at deer moved by drivers. If you hunt where driving is popular you can up your chances by hunting from a stand when drivers are in action. I'll cover gang drives in the next chapter.

Having more than one stand has definite advantages. Most hunters who think about hunting from a stand have the idea of building one blind. However, it's a good idea to have several stands in the area you hunt. Then you can go to an ideal site regardless of wind direction, time of day, thermal currents, driving activity, or time you have available to hunt. An obvious example is a wind shift. Suppose you're in a spot downwind of a runway when the wind reverses itself. If you have a stand on the other side of the trail, you can move to the new site in moments.

Standers who don't have the inclination to build good blinds underestimate the value of concealment. A buck will usually materialize out of

This hunter has pulled pine boughs around a foxhole on a ridge from which he has a good view all around. Whenever you plan to make stands that will alter the natural environment, be sure you check with landowners or managers for permission and then restore the area before you leave.

nearby thickets and be in plain sight before you suspect he's anywhere near you. At this point it's too late to think about concealment. He'll bolt and be gone before you get your rifle half way to your shoulder if you're not hidden. It's a shame to do everything else correctly, then miss getting your buck because you didn't take a few moments to properly conceal yourself.

If you don't build a blind in advance, the first thing to consider is light density. Locate in a shadowed area low to the ground so any movements you must make are less noticeable. Then take advantage of natural concealment such as windfalls, ground-hugging limbs, stumps, or clumps of brush. If there isn't any natural material where you want it, perhaps you can put some there. Dead branches will help to break up your outline. A good trick in areas where there are conifers is to cut off a few twigs and jab them into the ground.

The important point to remember about temporary concealment is that it must be as natural as possible. If you upset the landscape appreciably, a deer is sure to notice it. Any deer knows his home-territory objects as well as you know the furniture arrangement in your house. If you come home and see a chair out of place it stands out like a sore thumb. A deer will notice something out of place just as readily. It then becomes a potential source of danger.

One reason this principle is so important is that bucks normally follow does on runways. Your concealment must be so natural that all deer will freely use the trail without the slightest suspicion of your presence. Does and fawns must move along as if there isn't a hunter within 10 miles. If they don't, and they act wary, you'll never see the buck that may be following them.

This lesson—among several others—was driven home to me one time on a hunt in northern Wisconsin. My job was to take a stand ahead of the rest of my group while they organized a drive. I was told to locate near a creek.

When I got on location I found several choices for stands. One was in a thick clump of blueberry bushes near the creek, but I passed it up because the ground was mucky in there. Instead, I picked a spot on a small knoll. The cover was meager but the vantage point offered an excellent view toward the woods my companions were to drive. At the appointed time they showed up. I hadn't seen a deer. After I told them that they hadn't moved any whitetails I got a real surprise.

"C'mon," said Lyle Laurvick, my host. "I want to show you something. Those woods were full of deer. We had 'em moving straight toward you."

We walked 100 yards along the edge of the woods, then cut in to where the drivers had come through. In moments Lyle pointed out a runway which was loaded with fresh deer tracks. We walked down the trail a few yards, then Lyle gestured toward a place where the deer had left the runway and headed into some hills.

"Right here is where they spotted you," he said. "You can't expect whitetails to walk by a man if they can see him. I'll bet the first mistake you made was that you were standing up. Never do that on a stand. Always sit down. Get as close to the ground as possible. That cuts your silhouette in half and it restricts your area of movement.

"Your second mistake was picking a stand site on that knoll. Not enough cover there for one thing, but you also made the common error of trying to see too much territory. The object isn't to see a lot of deer, it's to see one deer that doesn't see you. That's the only way you'll get a good shot. If you'd been in the thickets near the creek that herd would likely have walked right past you. You wouldn't have seen them till they got close, but they probably wouldn't have spotted you either. You've got to pick a stand on the hard-nosed basis that deer won't see you."

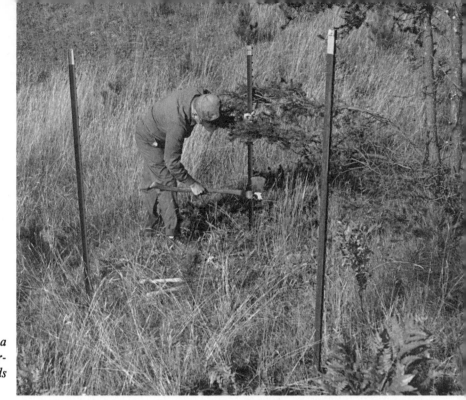

1. *If possible, Holmes uses a standing tree or two as corner posts. If not, he pounds in green steel fenceposts.*

In this sequence of photos, veteran deer hunter Warren Holmes demonstrates how he builds a blind. He sites the blinds near runways or deer crossings, and he builds them long before the season opens so deer get used to seeing them.

2. *Then he wires four branches to the uprights at eye level when he's standing, and four more at eye level when he's sitting on a crate.*

3. *When the horizontal branches are wired to the uprights, Holmes is ready to weave in pine boughs.*

4. *Here Holmes is wiring green pine boughs to the cross members; he also works in some horizontal boughs.*

5. *Standing, Holmes can peer over top of blind, but usually he watches for deer through shooting slit, keeping his head back and in shadow. Slit runs all round blind. Final step is to mark blind with fluorescent tape to warn other hunters.*

Few deer would notice the hunter in the photo above. But the overhead view (below) reveals the reason why the birds are announcing an intruder.

That lesson was emphasized later in the day when another member of our group nailed an eight-pointer ahead of a drive. He showed me his stand site. It was behind an old pine stump on a hillside.

"It's a good idea to get behind something when you're on a temporary stand," Don Johnson said. "Stumps, blowdowns, thick tree trunks, or rock piles all make natural hides. I also like to locate above a runway because deer don't expect danger from above. They seldom look up. Anyway, two does walked down the runway minutes before the buck showed. Those does had no idea I was behind the stump, so there was no way they could alert the buck."

Don touched on an all-important point when he mentioned that deer seldom look up. In states where tree stands are legal, they're the best bet by far. Earl Hoyt of St. Louis, Missouri, has some thoughts on why this principle is so valid. Earl is a nationally known manufacturer of quality archery equipment and is a veteran bowhunter.

"The first suggestion I'd make to the novice bow hunter is to hunt from a tree stand," said Hoyt. "I'd guess that 65-75 percent of bow-killed deer are taken from trees. They offer a lot of advantages. Deer are not bothered much by movements in trees. It's because they are used to seeing wind-blown branches moving and they just don't expect danger from above. Also, deer do not scent hunters in trees as well as hunters on the ground. Further, I've found that sound from tree blinds doesn't seem to have as much effect as sound from ground stands.

"Even so, I don't think the novice hunter is careful enough with his movements. He tends to look around while turning his head and body rapidly. He should make slow turns or rely on eye movements. This works well in a tree because a hunter can see through brush much easier if he's above it than on the same level with it."

Earl emphasized another factor that I've already mentioned, but it's important enough to be highlighted again.

"Another big mistake I see among archers is trying to hunt the whole state," he said. "One place this weekend, another place the next. Hunters should become totally familiar with their hunting location and know the habits of the area's deer. You can't select a good stand without knowing when and why deer are likely to move past it."

Tree Stands

Tree stands range from a crotch between limbs to deluxe, weatherproof and heated miniature cabins placed on top of A-frame piers. The latter are used in Texas, the former can be utilized anywhere tree stands are legal. The most common tree stand is a platform, mostly because a platform offers far more comfort and freedom of movement than does a crotch between limbs.

Tree stands that consist of only a crotch are all right for short waits but are usually too uncomfortable for long trail-watching sessions. They can lead to shaky offhand shooting that may result in hazardous loss of balance.

The burlap screen around this tree stand breaks the wind and helps mask the hunter's silhouette.

Permanent and comfortable platform stands are often erected in the Texas brush country.

The first thing to consider when building a tree stand is that the tree belongs to somebody. Defacing a tree without the landowner's permission is unpardonable. So is digging foxholes for blinds.

Once you have permission there are a few things to consider. Weathered boards will show up less than fresh-cut boards. Remember that lumber construction in a tree will creak as the tree sways. You can eliminate much of this creaking by building the platform as small as possible. It should be no larger than what you need for a comfortable seat. Creaks are also produced by hunter movement. You can deaden these sounds somewhat by placing an old piece of carpet on the platform.

An important consideration in tree stands—or all stands for that matter—is freedom of movement to shoot. After a stand is completed you should dry-fire your firearm through any expected shooting area. If it knocks against branches they should be cut away. A deer will bolt when he hears an unexpected noise whether or not he's looking up.

The same thought includes proper housekeeping. Never position your rifle where it can fall. Place thermos bottles and other gear in locations where they won't be knocked over. Clear away dead leaves or twigs from your sitting area. It takes only seconds to do these things, but they help insure against making unnatural noises.

The Scent Problem

Even if your stand site is perfectly located, you can ruin your chances of getting a deer by not controlling your own scent. If a hunter crosses a deer runway shortly before the animals begin using it, the runway usually will be abandoned for that day. Few whitetails will continue down a runway beyond a place where it has recently been crossed by a human.

Before I head for a stand I always consider two scent factors that I have no direct control over, wind direction and thermal currents. Most deer hunters know that their stands must be downwind of runways, but few are aware that thermal currents (vertical air drifts) carry scent in the same way as the prevailing wind except they carry it up or down instead of horizontally.

At dawn, as temperatures normally begin to rise, the thermal currents flow upward. As evening approaches and the day becomes cooler, the thermal currents begin falling. A dawn stand should be above an area where you expect to see deer because you want your scent to be rising skyward, not downhill. However, a hillside stand should be avoided in the evening because your scent will be going downhill.

You can lick these wind-direction problems the same way a smart buck does. He depends on his nose to tell him of danger ahead, so he has alternate runways leading to his bedding area. On any given day he'll use the route that allows him to keep the prevailing wind in his face. The smart hunter has alternate stands. On any given day, or at different times during the same day, he'll utilize stands where wind direction and thermal currents flow in his favor.

In spite of everything I've written so far, even the smart hunter can't es-

THERMALS

In the absence of an apparent prevailing wind, it's good to remember that thermal (heat) currents travel uphill in the early morning and downhill in the late afternoon. This will help you locate your stand so that your scent isn't carried to the runways you want to watch.

cape the fact that humans smell. Because a whitetail's sense of smell is so acute, the less smell you bring to the woods the less chance a buck has of picking up your scent.

Begin each deer hunting day with a bath or shower. Use a scent-free soap or Phisoderm. It's a cleaner that is not a soap. It's sold in squirt containers, it leaves no scent and can be found in drug stores. After bathing use a quality deodorant that does not have an added scent. Some deodorants, such as roll-on "Ban," have neutral scents.

Dress in clean clothes, from underwear out to outerwear. It doesn't help much to clean your body, dress and then slip into a hunting coat that hasn't been cleaned in years. Hunting clothes should be cleaned and aired before each new season begins. I know some veteran deer hunters who have their hunting clothes cleaned after the season closes, then they store them in air-tight plastic bags containing freshly cut cedar twigs. I don't go that far; I store my clean clothes in a closet that's constructed of cedar boards.

Some fanatics on the use of scents for deer hunting go to the extreme of washing their boots, air drying them, then applying masking scents to the outsides. Is this silly? Can the use of scents be way overdone?

Tink Nathan is one of the leaders in the $37 million annual deer scent manufacturing industry. His company, Safariland Hunting Corporation, P.O. Box NN, Department OL, McLean, VA 22101, has been selling deer scents for decades. Does Nathan believe that going deer hunting without using scents is a big mistake?

"The average hunter's ignorance of the effects of human smell can easily be his greatest handicap, but there's a limit to what can be accomplished," says Nathan. "Food-based masking scents are not strong enough to mask human odor, they're a waste of time and money. Some hunters like to rub a masking scent such as apple or acorn on exposed hands and face. This doesn't do much good as far as masking human smell is concerned, and it lulls the hunter into a false sense of security.

"We sell what people want, but we try to sell the stuff we recommend," Tink went on. "You should definitely use scents, but you should use those that work, and you must use them in the right way. Using something like pine oil to kill human smell won't work. Good skunk scent or red fox urine are the best bets, but skunk is the best of the two. Fox scent, while strong, isn't as strong as many hunters believe. The hunter who puts either on his boots will go a long way toward masking his smell."

But don't use more than a few drops each day. Masking scents come in highly concentrated form. You've used enough when you can barely detect the odor on your boots. A deer's sense of smell is so far superior to yours that too much of this stuff does more harm than good. A buck that begins picking up far more skunk or red fox smell than is natural becomes suspicious.

Common sense dictates other things you can do to mask human smell. Bathing won't help much if you follow up with after-shave lotion or hair tonic. Avoiding foods that contribute to body odor is important. The worst offenders are onions, garlic, and highly spiced foods. Eat bland foods before going hunting, and take non-spiced sandwiches for eating on your stand. A good trick is to chew gum such as Clorets. Breath-cleansing gums help eliminate mouth odors that develop after eating.

Smoking is almost a sure way to eliminate your chances of getting a deer. My father-in-law was a farmer living in excellent deer country, and he was a deer hunting nut. He was also a dedicated pipe smoker, and he had a theory on how farm-country deer react to smoke.

"Whitetails living near normal farming activity don't pay much attention to smoke because they're used to it," he said. "Cars and trucks are always going down roads that deer cross. Many times I've watched deer pay no attention to smoke from brush fires I've built. Smoke-belching tractors don't alert deer, so why should smoke from my pipe?"

Paul always felt that he was born to be an unlucky deer hunter because he seldom got shooting. It used to make him mad because he claimed he knew more about deer than any ten city hunters put together. I'm convinced that if he had left his pipes at home when he went to his stands his luck would have vastly improved. Anyway, if you smoke while on stand you must use skunk scent to overcome the odors.

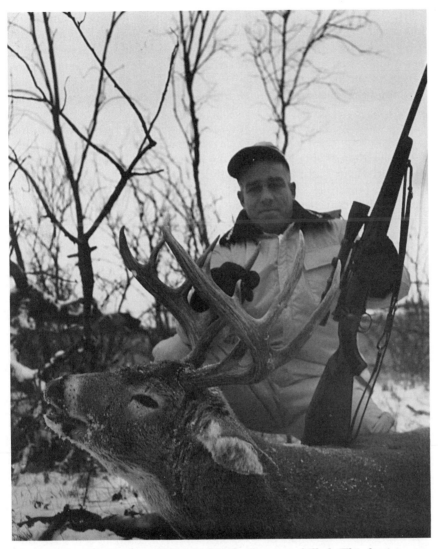

The author with the best whitetail deer he has ever killed. This bruiser was downed from a stand in Saskatchewan.

A better trick is to substitute chewing for smoking if you must have tobacco. Spit in a can and take the can and contents with you when you finish the day's hunt. Not dumping the contents near your stand is just as important as not urinating on the ground in or near your stand. Urinate in a small plastic bottle with a screw-cap lid. Dispose of the contents later when far removed from your stand.

Tink Nathan brings up another important subject.

"Every deer hunter is faced with the necessity of bowel movements, and when he makes his movement he is creating an enormous amount of human smell," Tink began. "Obviously he should walk at least a few hundred yards downwind before doing his job, but he should know that toilet paper alone won't clean the body area enough to eliminate the fresh smell. I recommend the use of Tucks or Wet Ones, premoistened disposable pads with mild skin cleaners. Both are sold in packs that can be carried in your pocket."

There are two hunting techniques that have a great deal to do with controlling human smell. One is knowing the route your buck will most likely use while approaching your stand, the second is understanding why hunting in drizzle or rain can be so deadly.

Serious bowhunters often devote a lot of time to trying to kill one particular big buck that they have seen in a given area. Through a lot of scouting and hunting effort they determine where the animal feeds and beds, and what routes he uses for his travels. They get to know so much about the buck that they can almost predict where he is going to be at any given time. I often hear an expert bowhunter say something like, "I've been after that same big buck for five years, and I finally got him. I knew he'd come by my stand sooner or later. This morning he made his last mistake."

Dedicated scouting effort can tell you a lot about normal travel habits of deer in your area, and dedicated hunting effort always leads to knowledge of change in travel habits after the shooting begins. All experienced deer hunters have heard stories about some fellow who shoots a buck every year from the same stand. Sure, he has a hotspot, but he has it only because his stand is in the right place and he knows from which direction his buck is most likely to approach. That knowledge enables him to select a stand site (or sites) where prevailing winds blow in his favor. All of this scouting and hunting effort takes a lot of time, but it's the reason why some fellows get a buck every year while most hunters may get lucky once in every four or five years.

Rain or drizzle dramatically reduces human smell. It drives a hunter's scent into the ground. So your odds add up. When hunting from a stand near an active bedding area on rainy days you're apt to see less wary deer, you'll probably see them in good shooting light, and if you have used proper human smell control you should be scentless at almost point-blank range. You can't get a better combination.

CHAPTER
5

The Gang Drive

Years ago the old-fashioned gang drive was one of the best techniques for producing venison anywhere in whitetail country. It worked well in those days because when deer were jumped they ran for their lives. They ran straight away from the drivers and into the rifle sights of standers who were posted ahead of the drivers. In those times of less hunting pressure than we have today, deer were startled at the mere presence of a hunter. The naive critters bolted as soon as they realized men were in their area.

It's all a new ball game today. Modern bucks who flee for safety without thinking about the consequences wind up in freezers. Those that make it through their first hunting season have learned that the way to stay alive is not to run but to hide or sneak. That's precisely why the old-time gang drive—a line of hunters moving aimlessly through good deer woods—is seldom productive today. The keys to success of the modern drive are organization and leaving nothing to chance.

How determined to hide are today's bucks? Let me relate some incidents to illustrate the cleverness of modern deer. Here's a story from a local friend, Jim Sutton.

"It was during pheasant season," Jim began. "My dad and I watched about 15 shotgunners work out a valley of underbrush no more than 150 yards wide. They were only a few yards apart as they walked down through the thickets. When they moved on over a ridge a rooster flew in and landed behind them. Dad and I walked down and zig-zagged all over the area trying to flush that bird. Finally Dad came close to stepping on a big eight-point buck that bolted from almost under his feet. Some of those pheasant hunters must have passed within 20 feet of that deer. The thing that got me was that this took place over a month before deer season opened, yet that buck was so determined not to move that he didn't blow out of there till his last hope of not being seen was gone."

I have a personal story that's comparable. Last fall while grouse hunting I tumbled a bird I couldn't find. I put my cap on a bush at the spot where I thought the bird had gone down, then I searched in ever-widening circles around the cap. After I'd worked around that small area for about ten minutes a buck jumped up and roared out of there. I must have been within a few yards of him several times before he decided enough was enough.

Again, this incident happened long before deer season. How cagey do clever bucks get when rifles begin roaring? Here's another story, told to me by a retired newspaper writer:

"I had twelve deer that came to my orchard every day," he began. "I fed them apples. I knew those deer so well I had names for them. I knew their exact habits, especially in the evening when they came in for food. The night deer season opened they didn't show. I didn't see any of those whitetails again until about a week after the season closed. One night seven came back, the next night ten, the following night eleven. Only a fawn was missing, yet the surrounding woods had been full of hunters. Those deer simply hid out when the gunning began, and they didn't revert to normal movement patterns till the shooting was over."

Two years ago an archer friend of mine discovered a large herd of whitetails feeding on acorns along an oak ridge. He bowhunted those deer for weeks. During that time he identified seven different bucks. When gun season opened he and six other riflemen stillhunted the same area. They never saw a single buck.

A Montana hunter told me that his uncle had hunted a specific snow-covered small area for four days. Finally he climbed a lightning-killed deadfall for a better view of his surroundings. He happened to glance into the thick brush immediately below him. He couldn't believe his eyes when he spotted a buck lying motionless in the thickets. He slowly inched his rifle to his shoulder and killed the animal in his bed. The astonishing thing about this story is that there wasn't a single deer track leading in or out through the six inches of two-day old snow on the ground around that small thicket. The buck hadn't moved for at least two days.

If these stories aren't enough to convince you that many modern deer won't run blindly in front of drivers, let me pass on some information from a man I consider a real expert on driving deer. I've mentioned Lyle Laurvick several places in this book, simply because he has had as much deer-hunting experience as anyone I know. How much experience? Well, I'll let him tell you about his hunting years and his driving techniques. Driving and hunting from stands ahead of drivers are the only systems he uses.

"Since I got out of the service after World War II, I've missed only a few days of our total Wisconsin deer seasons," he began. "You've hunted with my group, so I don't have to tell you we hunt from daylight to dark every day of the season or until each member of our group kills a deer. As soon as

Hunters on stands are often surprised by a nearly silent blur of motion as driven deer flee past. At other times frightened deer may make a noisy, brush-breaking approach. They may sneak away from the drivers toward the standers; or they may double back through the ranks of the drivers.

a man downs his buck he's automatically a gunless driver for the rest of the season.

"Working as a driver is hard labor if it's done right. That's why a lot of so-called drivers give up too soon. Some will work a drive for a couple of hours in the morning, then go from tavern to tavern. By the time they reach the sixth gin mill they're convinced there isn't a buck in the whole county, and they've got proof from all the would-be hunters in the last five bars they visited.

"Then there are the guys who do most of their driving in cars, not on foot. They cover 200 or more miles in good deer territory in a car, but only two or three miles in boots. They can't understand how they can cover all those miles and never see a deer. A good driver doesn't spend his daylight hours anyplace except back in the boonies where the deer are. But there's a lot more to it than hard work because modern deer are far more clever than their forebears.

"Years ago a given area could be driven and the deer of this place always went to that place, via this or that trail. That's why the driving technique used to be so successful, even when used by drivers with little skill. But no more. The hunter who lives in the past and refuses to change his driving tactics is bound to be lost in the shuffle because he can't break the new codes of our modern bucks.

"Many of the places we used to drive years ago still harbor good deer herds, and they still can be moved. The big difference is in the way they move and when they move. The buck of yesteryear used to break out across wide openings such as clearings, apple orchards or railroad rights-of-way in a headlong dash to escape drivers as soon as he was alerted to their presence. Today's buck won't jump unless he thinks he has to, and when he does he stays away from openings of any type. I've looked at thousands of fresh deer tracks that prove these points without question.

"Take a power-line opening in thick brush as an example. A running buck could clear such an opening in two leaps. Years ago, 90 percent of jumped bucks would take the gamble; today that figure is more like 10 percent. I couldn't begin to tell you the number of times I've followed the tracks of a jumped buck to an opening, then discovered that the cautious critter changed his route to parallel the opening instead of crossing it. This thinking is all-important when you consider the sites where you should put standers ahead of drivers. The standers who locate on the edge of openings—as was standard procedure years ago—seldom go home with venison today. It's best to locate near escape routes in thickets.

"There's another factor most drivers overlook. Many guys figure there are fewer bucks today than years ago because they don't see as many. In the old days 90 percent of the bucks ran as soon as they realized a man was headed toward them. Today 90 percent will lie still and hope the hunter will walk by. How do you lick this problem? The answer is several drivers working closely together while covering the driven area slowly and thoroughly. They've got to work out every thicket. The more men a buck has to cope with, the closer they are together, the slower they move, and the more thoroughly they work the cover, the more nervous the deer will get. The more nervous a buck gets, the more likely he is to move out."

Lyle is quick to temper that statement with another of his principles. He claims that a clever buck doesn't worry much about coping with a known danger, it's the unknown that makes him edgy. For instance, a buck won't worry much about one or two men invading his territory, particularly if the men are moving rapidly and making considerable travel noise. A clever deer knows he can avoid trouble by remaining hidden or sneaking around a man. However, when a group puts on a drive and the men move slowly and carefully, even a clever buck doesn't know what he's up against. He doesn't know how many hunters there are, what they're doing, where they're going, or whether they have already spotted him. That's when he's likely to jump, and it's the main reason well-organized gang drives can be successful.

Here are some more of Lyle's thoughts about how deer react to the known versus the unknown:

"Did you ever wonder why the whitetail harvest in most states is highest the first two days of each new season? I'm convinced that when the hordes of hunters first move into the woods and the rifles start roaring, many of the deer panic. They're caught by surprise. The ones that make mistakes get shot. The ones that survive figure out what's going on and they adapt by hiding or moving into remote areas.

"The principle is that if you can hunt a buck when he doesn't know what's going on you have him at a disadvantage, and that's when drivers can move him. This happens early in the season, but it also happens when the woods are damp or covered with a few inches of fluffy snow. If a buck can hear men moving he has little fear. His extremely sharp sense of hearing enables him to place himself where he'll be out of trouble. This is why so many modern deer sneak back through drives without ever being seen.

"But if you get conditions where men can walk quietly, especially if it's windy, deer often go wild because they realize danger can be upon them at any moment. It's the unknown that makes them commit errors and move out ahead of a drive. Our kill always goes up dramatically when new snow is on the ground. This is the best time to make a drive. Not only because the sounds of the drivers are reduced, but also because deer can be seen more easily against a snow background. In short, if a buck can't be sure where the drivers are and he can't be sure whether or not he'll be seen, he's much more likely to get on the move."

Planning Pays Off

Every successful driver I've talked with claims that good planning is the key to the successful modern drive. Haphazard driving of any ill-selected woodland won't work today for the reasons I've mentioned. The two most important considerations revolve around what areas to drive and how to drive them.

Throughout this chapter I've been talking principally about whitetails. These deer inhabit terrain most suitable for driving techniques and they're more apt to hide and sneak than mule deer. However, the tactics work with all deer found in woodlands regardless of species. Today's mule deer are developing the cleverness of whitetails as hunting pressure continues to increase. Muleys, more and more, are tending to seek safety in forests and to utilize the cunning of whitetails. Wherever you find mule deer in woodlands you'll find that they can be driven effectively.

The question of what areas to drive applies to all species of deer. Don't drive big woodlands where deer have too many escape options. You could put a couple of dozen drivers in a few square miles of forest and never see a deer, let alone get a shot at one. In big woodlands deer will keep doubling back and forth, always staying out of sight of drivers and seldom moving past standers. The trick is to drive toward areas deer are likely to use as escape routes.

An example is a wooded ravine bordered on both sides with open ridges. Since clever bucks won't want to top out in the open, they'll probably move up or down the ravine in a direction away from the drivers. When they reach the end of the depression they'll sneak out through the best cover available.

Consider in the above example how organization fits in. If the driving group is very familiar with the ravine, all the members have valuable knowledge of where the deer are likely to be hiding and where they're likely to go when jumped. All men in the group know where the standers will be and precisely how long it will take to make the drive. Everything is executed with military precision.

Drivers and standers can't execute such an operation without intimate knowledge of terrain, and this is why driving unfamiliar country is usually a waste of time today. You have to have all the advantages in your favor simply because modern bucks won't move unless they have to. And when they do move you have to have some indication of where they'll go and why they'll go there. There's no way you can have this knowledge when hunting unfamiliar terrain.

That's why—in every group of successful drivers I've hunted with—I always hear statements such as: "Tomorrow morning we'll make our first drive in Miller's Hollow if the wind holds north. After that we'll work Munson's Forty, then Blueberry Ridge." Such hunters have intimate knowledge of their hunting lands. They know exactly how to hunt those lands and, from past experience, they know that deer are likely to be there.

The first consideration is to select hunting country that can be driven efficiently. I just mentioned a ravine bordered with open ridges, but let's go to a simpler example.

Say we have forty acres of oak trees loaded with acorns and dotted with thickets of brush large enough for bedding areas. The oaks are surrounded on all sides by dense cedar swamps. Though the oaks and the thickets may harbor plenty of deer, there isn't a chance in the world of driving them efficiently because they can sneak out to safety in any direction.

When driven up a wooded ravine bordered by open ridges, clever bucks will usually hold to the ravine cover and head for an established escape route near the top. The stander should set up where the wind won't betray him.

WIND

83

Now let's assume we have an identical forty acres surrounded on two adjacent sides by wide-open fields. The other two adjacent sides border dense cedar swamps. In this case, because modern bucks seldom cross openings, we've cut down the whitetail's escape routes by 50 percent. A drive here would have a chance of success, but it would be slight because the deer still have too many options for getting away without being seen.

Now let's take another identical forty acres surrounded on three sides by open fields. The fourth side is bounded by scattered cedars, except for a narrow draw running downhill from the oaks into dense cedars. The draw is lined with relatively thick brush. Here we have an ideal situation. If the forty acres are driven from the side opposite the draw, any deer that are moved have only a single logical choice for escape. Their best route by far is through the thickets in the draw. Consequently, the best sites for standers are along the edge of the draw.

This example is somewhat simplified, but it illustrates the type of thinking that should go into the selection of driving areas. The key to success is to consider any areas used by deer, but to select only those areas bounded on at least two sides by openings which cautious deer won't cross. Such openings could be fields, highways, power lines, rivers, lakes, mucky marshes or any type of clearing. Barriers such as cliffs or steep hillsides serve the same purpose. Deer, when driven *slowly,* will almost always move ahead along the path of least resistance so long as it offers adequate cover.

The next thing is not to select too big a tract of woodland. The key consideration here is how many drivers will be in action. Ten drivers could adequately cover a woodland twice the size of one adequately covered by five men. (Laws of your state may affect the options you have on numbers of drivers. Several states limit the number of hunters who can operate as a group.) The type of woodland makes a big difference, too. A woodlot 200 yards wide and consisting of scattered ground cover might be driven efficiently by three men. The same three men could not efficiently drive a thick cedar swamp 200 yards wide. A clever buck probably wouldn't jump in thick cedars even if the drivers were only 25 yards apart because he knows his odds on staying alive in thick cover are best if he hides or sneaks around the drivers.

We also have wind-direction problems. Let's go back to the forty acres of oaks surrounded by openings except for the thicket-lined draw. If the wind happens to be blowing from the draw to the oaks there's no sense in making a drive because deer would scent standers along the draw. They'd turn back and take their chances with sneaking through the line of drivers.

At this point it's easy to understand why anything less than the best planning won't work with a drive. Today's successful drivers know exactly how they're going to drive an area and when they'll go into action. Again, this type of knowledge comes only from experience.

When I talk about experience with terrain I don't mean just the physical characteristics of woodland. I also mean experience with hunting success. For example, you could hunt two areas of the same size and physical characteristics and discover that one often harbored deer while the other seldom produced any animals. Why? There could be many reasons, but experience gained through hunting two areas soon tells the hunters that it's a waste of time driving the nonproductive area.

There are problems with weather, too. Some areas may hold deer early in the season but not late in the season. In northern states, whitetails often change locations when the woods become covered with snow. In all areas deer are prone to change locations in direct proportion to how much hunting pressure they're subjected to. That's why knowledgeable drivers don't waste their time driving some specific areas until the hunting season is well along. They know that deer don't move into those given areas till they're forced into them by gun pressure. Such areas are almost always sections of the thickest cover available.

So, knowing where to put on a drive all boils down to experience. If you can't join an experienced group of drivers you'll have to form your own group, and you'll wear out a lot of boot leather gaining the experience of knowing where and where not to put on drives. Choosing potentially good driving areas and then driving them is the only way you'll gain the experience of knowing which areas hold deer and which escape routes the deer are likely to use.

Sharing the Work

If you form your own group there are some thoughts to keep in mind. Deer hunting does not have the same objectives for all men. The guy who likes to hunt from a stand will not make a good driver because he's basically a loner. He wants a serious and quiet hunt by himself. Other men can't stand to sit on stands; they thrive on the get-togetherness and good times of groups. They're the kind you want if—and it's a big if—they're the types who take their hunting seriously. You can't put on efficient drives unless all members can be counted on to participate in each scheduled hunt. The fellows with little desire don't make good drivers.

However, one advantage to forming a driving group is that the members may include some novices and men of various ages or physical abilities. The novice can be told what to do and where to go by experienced members, and in that way he gains his own knowledge of deer hunting. He'll learn the tricks of the trade a lot faster by hunting as a member of a group than he will by stillhunting or trail-watching on his own. Driving also gives the out-of-shape or older members a chance to hunt efficiently. Since standers are always required ahead of the drivers, there's always a place for the weaker members. Many good stands are often reached by walking short distances from roads.

On the other hand, the drivers themselves may have to engage in very hard work. Some drivers—especially the end members on a sweep drive (which we'll discuss shortly)—may have to travel fast to keep up. Driving through swamps and tangles can be especially rugged. So it's good to have young members in your group, guys with the stamina to plow through the tough stuff and enjoy every minute of it.

In spite of such considerations it's best to be fair in sharing the work load. If all members of a driving group are in reasonably equal physical condition, the rule of thumb is that all members spend half their time driving and half standing.

Drive Savvy

All drives should use the contour of the land to the best advantage. Just as the flow of water is narrowed as it goes through a funnel, so should the escape options of deer be narrowed as the drive progresses. A pie-shaped piece of woodland should be driven from the wide end toward the narrow end. A ravine or canyon, which is normally narrower at its top than bottom, should be driven uphill.

But such considerations should take into account the direction of the wind. As I mentioned earlier, don't drive upwind toward standers because deer will never approach a man they can smell. At first thought it would seem that drivers should move with the wind because deer will scent them and move ahead. But I question this accepted procedure. We've discussed why deer are more apt to get edgy and move when faced with the unknown rather than the known danger. With a crosswind, the animals won't be able to smell either the drivers or the standers. Hence we introduce an unknown factor when deer can hear drivers but can't smell them.

Again, this is the type of reasoning that goes into an organized drive. Experienced leaders of successful drives take such things into consideration before they decide where each day's drives will take place. An east wind may be perfect for driving a given area, while a south wind in the same area may make a drive totally inefficient.

Another key to an organized drive is timing. Many things are involved here. Standers must be on their sites before the drive begins or all effort may be wasted. The obvious example is when deer are moved past stand sites before the watchers reach them. Without complete knowledge of the terrain to be driven, the drivers can't know where the standers will be or how long it will take them to get there. One factor in this chain of events happens when the drive is finished. If a driver doesn't know where the standers are—the point at which the drive ends—he may filter through

Since deer generally seek an escape route with cover, this tree stand was built with a good view of the busy draw. The "X" in the drawing shows an alternate stand site for use if the wind were blowing from the tree stand toward the woodlot. Sometimes a drive through a woodlot known to contain deer will fail because the deer sneak unnoticed through the line of drivers. If this occurs, a second drive can be staged from the same starting line, with one or more drivers dropping behind the others to watch.

WIND

them and proceed beyond the group. This can lead to great delay in beginning the next drive. It's just another example of why efficient drives require systematic organization.

This is as good a place as any to point out that there is no optimum number of drivers or distance between drivers. However, too large a group gets unwieldy and promotes the chances of mistakes in timing. I think ten or twelve hunters (where legal) is maximum for good control. As to distance between drivers, it all depends on terrain. In dense cover 20 yards is not too close, in open woods 200 yards could be about right. Spacing should be decided on the basis of how close drivers should be to each other to prevent deer from sneaking back through their line unseen.

Timing becomes most important when the drivers begin their part of the operation. The hurried and noisy drives of years ago won't work today for two important reasons. The noisy driver—the fool who shouts, blows horns, or beats on pans—is giving deer the exact information they want. Noise pinpoints a man's location and progress, which is all the information a whitetail needs to sneak away or hide. A hurried driver gives the animals the same options. Also, in a slow-moving drive, deer are apt to be little frightened. They'll tend to move ahead at a slow pace. This gives standers the best shooting opportunities.

Most novices assume that a line of drivers should be just that: a straight line of men moving forward. But today's experts feel that the line of men should more closely represent a U or V. The forward parts, or ends, of such formations tend to intercept deer which try sneaking around the ends of drives. Incidentally, some veterans shape their stander lines in inverted U's or V's. This produces a military-type "pincer" effect as the drivers move toward the standers. It helps prevent deer from sneaking around either drivers or standers, an option they have continuously if drivers and standers are formed in straight lines. Also, deer detest being surrounded. When they're confronted with this situation they'll keep moving while trying to find an outlet.

In order for the drivers to maintain a U formation, each driver must maintain the same rate of travel. Unless each man can see his right and left companions, and this is often impossible in thick brush, the formation is in danger of falling apart. Some experts time their drives based on past experience. They know that it should take, say, forty minutes to reach standers from the time the drive begins. If a man knows his terrain he knows his landmarks, and consequently he knows where he should be at any time during the forty minutes. In such drives the watch is an all-important tool.

Keying driver positions to natural sounds is another stunt used by drivers who can't see each other. Natural sounds in the woods include calls of birds. Some drivers keep in proper position by whistling bird calls to their companions.

One time I was on a stand in an area that I didn't realize was being driven. I eventually became aware of the occasional caws of crows. Imagine my surprise when I heard a crow caw right in front of me, then saw a man step out of the brush where I assumed the crow was. Until I saw the man I had no idea there was another human within miles of me. Such a sight is startling. I imagine the same discovery would be startling to a buck, and it would probably get him moving, which is the object of any drive.

Drivers should move ahead with the speed of a leisurely walk. Deer will use their normal escape routes if they know they don't have to hurry. Push them too fast and their reactions become unpredictable. Push them slowly and they'll likely come out in the natural places where your standers are located.

I've had many experiences proving my statement that deer will mosey along in normal fashion if they aren't pushed hard. One time several does moved slowly past my stand. They browsed and acted unconcerned in every way, except they'd look back over their back tracks occasionally. Eventually they moved out of sight.

A short time later two hunters came into view, following the deer tracks. They appeared to be ready to shoot at any instant. They obviously believed they were just behind the deer and that they would spot them soon. Those deer knew exactly where the hunters were, and they assumed they were safe as long as they traveled just fast enough to stay far enough ahead of the men to stay out of sight.

Though this chapter has nothing to do with stillhunting, I want to mention here that such experiences have convinced me that tracking deer, whether in snow or not, has little merit today. Most modern deer are simply too clever and cautious to get waylaid by the tracking hunter, unless he's an expert.

Another variation of the old-time straight-line drive, modified to fit modern conditions, is known in some areas as the "sweep" drive. A sweep drive sweeps around a pivot man (stander), who locates in cover on a point of land or on a hill where he has a good view. The drivers closest to the pivot man have to move very slowly because they don't cover much distance as the drive sweeps around, but the men on the far side of the line have to leg it fairly fast to keep up. Those are the positions for your young and sturdy fellows. The sweep drive is the only one requiring any drivers to walk rapidly.

The reasoning behind a sweep drive is twofold. In some areas deer have become so used to the old-time straight-line drives that it has become second nature for them to sneak around the end man. In a sweep drive, the pivot man never moves and he has a top vantage point. He'll see most deer that try sneaking around his end of the line. And, since the far men on the driving line are moving a definite arcing route, they tend to confuse deer. The animals don't know which direction is straight away from the line of drivers, so they tend to stay ahead of the men instead of trying to sneak back through the line.

However, as the years pass, more and more bucks are discovering that

WIND

These hunters are crossing a field and entering a large woodlot to begin a drive. Since deer generally shun open fields, their escape route will probably be in another direction.

In the sweep drive, the pivot man is also the stander. Drivers closer to him move slowly. Those on the far end usually have to step out swiftly to keep their end from bowing back and letting deer slip around them.

the best way to outwit drivers is to sneak back through their ranks. Once they accomplish this feat, and once their initial fear is gone, they'll revert to traveling established game trails to get to where they want to go.

Knowing this, many expert drivers check the beginning sections of their driven area after the drive is over. When they find fresh tracks of deer that had sneaked through the drive they note the routes the animals used to escape. Then, the next time the area is driven, the "dropout" technique is used. As the drive progresses a couple of men will drop out along the escape trails and take up stands as the other drivers continue forward. Many of today's bigger bucks, who assumed they had long ago figured out how to outwit any drive, wind up as deerburger when this modern stunt is pulled on them.

Years ago I wanted no part of drives because I figured they were dangerous. It seemed logical to assume that as a line of drivers moved toward a line of standers there could be bullets coming both ways. But as the years passed, and I hunted with driving groups who knew what they were doing, I found that they never had accidents. Why?

Organization again is the key word. When drivers know exactly where standers are going to be there's practically no chance a stander will be shot accidentally. More important, most deer killed during a modern drive are downed by the standers, not the drivers. No deer on the move is going to let a driver get too close to him. That means that by the time a buck goes by a stander he'll be far out ahead of drivers, particularly in more open country. In thick woods he'll still be far enough ahead of the drivers to insure a wall of trees behind him.

Even so, I wouldn't go deer hunting at all today unless I was wearing plenty of Blaze-Orange outer clothing. So many studies have shown that fluorescent blaze orange cuts down hunting accidents that it's stupid not to wear it. In short, a well-organized drive conducted by hunters wearing some Blaze-Orange clothing is a pretty safe way to hunt.

Maps

Good topographic (topo) maps are key tools for driving groups. They should always be used to orient group members as to location of stand sites, driving routes and meeting spots. But much of their value comes before members gain a lot of experience with a hunting area.

A topo map gives a good indication of the shape of the land and what's on that land. As such it can be used as a planning board. It will show you which patches of woodland are of good size for driving operations. You can select a few such areas, then check the map further to determine which of those areas are bounded by the most openings or natural barriers which deer don't like to cross.

An example would be a section of woodland bounded on one side by a river and on the other by steep slopes or high hills. Perhaps you can find an area on the map where a sharp bend in the river comes within 100 yards or

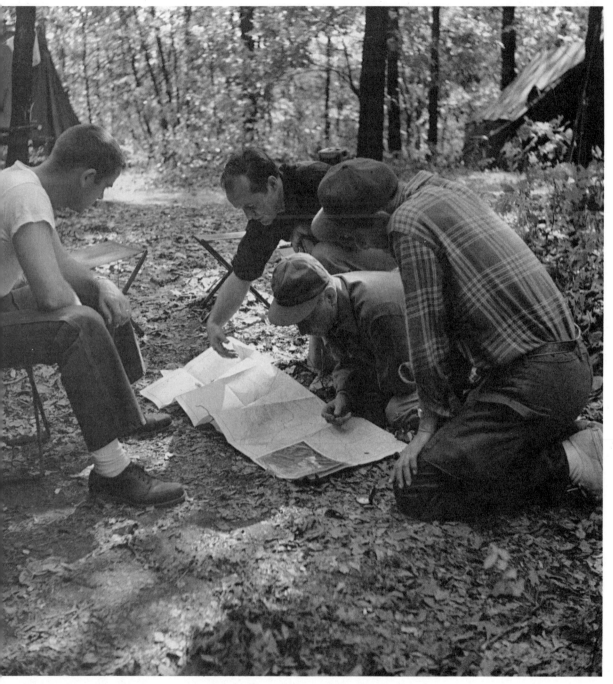

Some hunters mark "Xs" on their maps where standers have seen bucks. If a buck is killed, they draw a circle around the "X." As deer seasons pass, the hunters have a graphic record of the most productive stands in the area.

so of a point of high hills. Such a "narrows" is a natural for stand sites. Once good stand sites are chosen it's easy to determine where the drive should begin and what routes the drivers should travel. It's largely a matter of deciding how long you want the drive to last and how much area you want to cover.

As a new area is hunted over a period of years, you no longer need the map to acquaint you with the physical aspects of the terrain, but it can still provide you with great information if you use it to coordinate additional details.

For instance, it's a good idea to mark X's on the map where standers saw bucks. If a buck is killed, draw a small circle around the X. As the deer seasons pass you'll have graphic information showing which stand sites were most productive. Analysis of the terrain features at those sites often offers clues as to why they're good. Such information can be helpful in selecting stand sites in new driving areas.

There are many other advantages inherent in the use of maps. I'll discuss them all in Chapter 14, "Maps for Deer Hunting." In that chapter I'll tell you which maps are best, where you can get them, and more about how you should use them.

The Two-man Drive

There are several important reasons the two-man drive can be one of today's best bets for collecting venison. First, the odds per hunter always favor the small drive over the gang-type drive. Large drives seldom pay off in more than one or two bucks, for up to ten or twelve hunters. One buck per ten men is only a 10 percent success ratio. One buck for two men is a 50 percent ratio. The comparison becomes more meaningful when you consider that gang drives take much more time than small drives.

Deer also react differently when faced with one driver than when faced with a team of up to a dozen men. Whether a buck is a mule deer or a whitetail his reaction is to sneak or hide when confronted with a gang. But when faced with a single man he sometimes feels that safety is easy to come by with a simple dash for freedom. Sometimes a modern buck will be curious about what the man is doing and what he's going to do.

Because of this trait a buck will often circle a lone hunter, get downwind from him, and then follow him by scent. Today's bucks often pull this trick. They know that when they keep track of a single hunter's location they're in no danger. This trait can turn the tables on bucks when hunters employ a two-man drive. I'll explain the tactics later in this chapter, but I want to emphasize here that the system won't work for gang drivers. The principle is that deer always want nothing to do with gangs, but they're often curious about the goings-on of lone hunters.

Another advantage of the two-man drive is that the planning of the military-type tactics and organization necessary for a successful gang drive are not required. A small drive is easy to put into operation with a minimum of planning, and it's ideal for those hunters who dislike trail watching or mingling with large groups.

Best Terrain

Perhaps the top advantage of the two-man drive is that it often works best in areas never hunted by gangs. I'll mention a couple of examples that should serve to illustrate.

One time Bob Wolff and I were ruffed grouse hunting on 120 acres of second-growth woodlands. We were working along the edge of the woods which bordered an open field. Two grouse bombed out in front of Bob. He nailed one, the other flew out over the field and landed in a patch of brush no larger than an average house. The brush patch appeared as an island out in the wheat stubble.

"Well now," said Bob. "That bird made a hell of a mistake. We'll just walk out there and flush him again."

We walked the 70 yards to the brush, then separated to pull a circling maneuver. All of a sudden I heard a crashing of branches from Bob's direction, then a big eight-point buck bolted past me, not 10 yards away. He crossed the open field and ran into the main woodlands. If it had been deer season I would have had a fine shooting opportunity.

I've experienced similar incidents and I've been told about many others. They prove that some of today's cleverest bucks often bed in the smaller pieces of cover relatively close to much larger woodlands. Why?

Because those little hideaways are overlooked by most deer hunters. Deer get used to outwitting hunters in cover that looks like deer country. Country that looks as if it should harbor deer gets hunted. Habitat that appears to be the last choice a buck would accept for bedding security never gets hunted. Clever bucks learn this lesson. These are the bucks that are setups for the two-man drive.

The trick is never to overlook the little islands of trees or thickets close to the larger woodlands that are known to harbor deer. A buck doesn't live in these little patches of cover, he just beds there. He feeds and travels with other deer in normal range, but when the others bed down in natural areas he returns to his own little hideaway. This is why the hotspots are close to normal deer woods. Our buck doesn't want to get too far away from established feeding areas, but most of all he wants the security of bigger woods should a hunter accidentally stumble upon him. He wants to be able to bolt to the bigger woodland in seconds. Keep this principle in mind: The little pieces of cover 50 to 100 yards from big woods have potential; if they're over 100 yards from the safety of big woods it's not likely that clever bucks will use them.

Other small areas that are great for two-man drives are those places that are difficult for gang drivers to hunt, and that's precisely why they hold deer. A river boasting small islands of thickets is a top example. Gang drivers may work both sides of a river many times during deer season, but they'll never work the islands if they can't wade to them. Such a situation is ideal for a couple of men in a boat. They simply travel from island to island and put on their two-man drives. The system is deadly. Another good bet is a narrow draw leading to a big woodland.

The two-man drive can be effective when other techniques won't work.

Once many years ago I was walking the bank of a small creek while jump-shooting wood ducks. The section I worked meandered from a bridge over a dirt road down through farm fields to a big woodland bordering a large lake. Near the bridge the thickets along the banks of the creek consisted of scattered willows. Downstream about 100 yards from the woodland the creekside cover broadened into a circular island of cover about 50 yards in diameter. This patch of thickets contained willows, birch and cedars.

When I moved into the island of cover three wood ducks flushed off the creek ahead of me. After my first shot roared I heard a sudden commotion. My initial thought was that my gunfire had put more ducks into flight;

then it registered that the new noises came from a patch of solid ground to my left. I glanced that way and saw a fine buck streaking for the big woodland near the lake.

I jumped that buck from the same spot two more times while duck hunting. I figured I had him dead to rights when deer season opened, but when I went in there with a rifle he was gone. It's likely he had had enough interruption with my duck hunting and had found a new bedding area. In any event, my experiences with that little chunk of cover illustrates a couple of principles.

First, that general area—a band of woodlands bordered on one side by the lake and on the other side by farm fields—offered a natural area for a gang drive. But no gang of drivers would even consider working the cover along the creek because, except for the small island of thickets, the brush is only a few yards wide. So that buck bedded where he did because he figured he could stay out of trouble there.

Second, his cover was so ideal that he hated to give it up. He did so only after I had jumped him three times. That's a good indication of how appealing to bucks these tiny pockets of thickets near big woodlands can be.

Now we get to the all-important point of why a two-man drive can be so effective. Though I jumped that buck three times I never did get more than a fleeting glimpse of him. Not once did he offer a good shooting opportunity. But each time he dashed away he took the same route: straight toward the closest edge of the big woodland bordering the lake.

Take the same situation, assuming that deer season is open and I have a partner with me. My partner locates on a stand between the small-cover area and the big woodland. Then I walk into the small patch of cover and jump the buck. Unless something very unusual occurs, that buck is going to just about run over my partner as he makes his break for freedom. It isn't quite that simple, as we shall see, but the example serves to show how effective the two-man drive can be.

The small drive certainly isn't limited to hunting tiny pockets of cover. Let's go back to the curiosity trait I mentioned at the beginning of this chapter, the trait that often compels a buck to circle a lone hunter, or a hunter that he thinks is alone. Of course a buck won't do this in a small-cover area. He'll make his dash. But in big woods, he'll prefer not to run far. Let's use another example to show what can happen.

The Circle Drive

Say one hunter sneaks slowly and quietly 100 yards into a big woodland bordering a field, then takes a stand. When he's in position his partner starts from the edge of the field and walks a 200-yard-wide circle around the man on stand. If the walking hunter jumps a buck the chances are he won't get more than a fleeting glimpse of it. But, if the buck decides to circle the walking hunter to get his scent, he may move right past the man on stand. This trick can be worked anywhere in whitetail or mule deer woods.

The two-man circle drive may move a deer past the stander. But since the stander may not know where the driver is, the stander should try to set up in an elevated location to ensure that his bullets don't hit the driver.

Great care should be taken not to make noise when you're executing the circle drive because the drive takes place in a limited area. When two hunters arrive at a woodland they shouldn't converse, slam car doors, or make any other racket that a buck within hearing range can pick up. When a clever buck gets any indication he's dealing with more than one hunter he'll decide to hide or to sneak into another area. In either event the circle drive won't work.

Most hunters using the circle-drive technique alternate between walking and standing. They may make one drive in a small area, or walk many adjacent circles in a large woodland.

The Straggler Drive

Another system that takes advantage of bucks that circle behind a lone hunter might be termed the "straggler drive." In this instance, the lead man moves slowly, and with considerable commotion, into the wind. The straggler man follows quietly behind him. The distance between the two men will vary according to the denseness of the terrain, but 75 to 100 yards is about average.

Deer jumped by the front man are likely to move off to his side, then swing and circle behind him to pick up his scent. If all goes well, this maneuver may give the following man an excellent shooting opportunity. Keep in mind that both hunters must move into the prevailing wind. If they were hunting downwind, a circling buck would pick up the scent of the following man before presenting a shooting opportunity. Once again, as soon as a clever buck learns he's dealing with more than one hunter all bets are off.

Farmland Drives

The type of two-man drive I'm most partial to is the type I use in the farm country around my home. In this case the hunt isn't limited to two men; there could be three or four although two men can pull it off handily.

The key to success is farmer contact. They're the guys who live and work in farm-buck country year around. They see dear, they know where they feed and where they roam. The thing they don't know, unless they're deer hunters themselves, is the precise routes the deer use while moving between feeding, watering and bedding areas. It takes scouting to determine these runway locations.

The man who takes the time to develop friendships with farmers can gain a wealth of information. He'll hear such things as: "Last year there was only one buck on my place. This year there's at least two, and one's a real bruiser. Mostly I see them around my south forty. I think they're working the acorns in there."

What does such a tidbit of information offer? First it tells you there are two bucks in a relatively small area, and it tells you where the area is. It

WIND

The staggered drive exploits the wind and a buck's trick of sneaking behind a hunter to catch his scent and keep an eye on him. If both hunters move into the wind, the second hunter often gets good opportunities.

also gives you a clue as to where the deer are feeding and bedding. A man could scout big woods for days to determine the same facts a farmer can give you in minutes. That's one of the great advantages of hunting farm country, whether or not you elect to hunt with driving methods.

Anyway, with such information you can walk down to the south forty and do some scouting work. It shouldn't take long to finish as deer don't have too many runway options in farm country. I look first for well-used trails leading across roads. Deer almost always have to cross roads in agricultural areas simply because there are so many of them. Runways leading to road crossings will take advantage of best natural cover. Brushy fence-lines, valleys, unplowed swampland, fingers of thickets, and edges of woods that dead-end at roads are typical good bets. The trick is to find runways utilizing such cover, then backtrack on them to find feeding or bedding areas.

When you find a bedding area you'll know where your deer are likely to be during daylight driving times. Now you have all the dope you need to put on a drive. You select the runway the deer are most likely to use when pushed from the bedding area, put a stander on it or near it, then drive the woods. Pick the farm-country woodlots that are small enough for one man to drive effectively while working a zigzag course. Those are the ones that are ideally suited for the two-man drive.

I'll mention some of the typical hotspots in my area. They may give you clues as to what to look for.

Close to where I'm writing these lines there are four square miles of typical northern Michigan farm country consisting of grain fields, potholes, small tracts of timber, brushy fencelines, wooded hills, and brushy ravines. The entire area harbors deer. Where they feed and where they bed each year depends on crop production and whether the mast-producing trees produce bumper amounts of nuts. In any event, the deer are in the four-square-mile area every year but they'll use different runways, depending on annual conditions.

Last year one farmer put in eighty acres of winter wheat. The wheat field edged gravel roads on the south and north sides. The east side was bounded with a paved road. The west side was bordered with a 100-yard-wide strip of timber and thick underbrush. The timber thinned close to the north side road, but a narrow ravine of brush ran to the road, then led into a larger patch of timber across the road. This woodland ended at a lake.

A friend of mine got word from the farmer that deer were using his winter wheat. My buddy analyzed the situation. He guessed that the whitetails were bedding in the strip of timber on the west side of the field because it offered good security close to the food supply. He concluded that when those deer wanted water they would head north through the ravine leading into the timber that ended at the lake. He drove down to where that ravine was cut by the gravel road on the north, parked his car, and looked for fresh tracks. He smiled to himself when he noted the well-used runways coming up out of the ravine on both sides of the road.

"Okay," he told me later, "I figured that if those deer were pushed from the south they'd have to run north along the ravine runway toward the woods bordering the lake. That's just what happened. When daylight came on I had my partner Gordy work into the bedding area from the south end. The first deer that came out was a spike buck. He trotted right in front of me. I'm no trophy hunter; I nailed him in his tracks."

Right here I'd like to point out a principle involved in this incident. My friend would have had little chance if he'd tried stillhunting that buck in his bedding area. He might have jumped him, but at best he wouldn't have had a good shot because of thick cover. As it turned out, his partner who jumped the buck didn't even know he jumped him. He wasn't aware that he had moved a deer until he heard my friend's rifle roar. That's how effective the two-man drive can be in farm country. One man jumps the target, the second takes a stand along the route the target is most likely to use

WIND

Knowing the runways and likely bedding areas in small farm woodlots is essential in anticipating deer movement.

as an escape runway. These runways are limited in farm country, and that's the reason why they're relatively easy to find.

Not far from where my friend killed that spike buck there are two pie-shaped areas of bottomland too boggy to plow. Each area contains about 20 acres of weeds and thick alders. Their narrow ends are joined by 20 yards of trees, mostly small birch and maples. Deer use the bottomlands as bedding areas. Depending on wind direction, one can be driven toward the other. When jumped, deer normally route through the 20-yard width of small trees joining the two areas. The escape route can easily be covered by one stander, and each bottomland can easily be driven by one driver working a zigzag pattern.

A somewhat similar area contains a long, narrow swampland that dead-ends at a point of hardwoods. The point of timber is about 50 feet wide at the head of the swamp, but it rapidly broadens as the trees continue uphill to merge with about 80 acres of woodland. On all sides of the woodland are crop fields. Deer moving from the swamp into the woodland—or vice versa—have established a runway leading through the point of woods. This runway resembles a cattle trail leading to a barn. Even the most inexperienced of deer hunters would have little trouble locating such a well-used runway.

All of these terrain situations I've mentioned have one point in common: each contains a fairly large area (for farm country) of cover which deer require for bedding, and each is reached or left by a narrow escape route. They're naturals for the two-man drive because the cover areas are small enough to be driven by one man, and the escape areas are narrow enough to be covered by one stander. Find such farm-country areas, try to determine which routes deer should logically use for moving from one cover area to another, and then scout these routes until you find well-used runways. Hunters who do this and then employ the two-man drive are likely to stock their freezers with venison. Driving the farm country is deadly because deer have so few escape options.

A cardinal rule of any driving operation is that the most successful drives are those on which the hunters can best predict what the deer will do when pressed by drivers. In big woods deer have the options of running, hiding, or sneaking. In farm woodlots, which usually are quite small, deer will usually run when driven. Perfect the two-man drive technique in farm country and you'll be on to one of today's best bets for frying deer liver.

Not only is the system an excellent way to hunt, but it also has other things going for it. One feature that appeals to me is that the two-man drive in rural areas is not time-consuming. Your car will take you exceptionally close to your hunting locale, and you can often complete a drive in an hour or less. Some of my deer-hunting friends put on drives before going to church on Sunday mornings.

Mule-Deer Drives

Mule-deer country, especially the areas showing sparsely wooded canyons and draws of small to medium size, are excellent bets for the two-man drive. I once learned a neat system in Wyoming from a rancher who frequently had nobody to hunt with except his son.

"In this area we have a lot of draws that top out on level rims," he told me. "Many of these draws are in series, and they might be only 50 to 100 yards apart. We begin our hunting by having one man take a stand at the top of a draw. The second man works up from the bottom. If the drive is unsuccessful we'll walk half the distance along the rim to the next draw. Then one man walks downhill to the bottom, crosses over to the bottom of the draw and takes a stand. The man on top walks over to the top of the draw and drives it to its bottom.

"With this technique we hunt lots of draws and share the climbing work. The guy doing the driving almost never gets a shot because the deer sneak out ahead of him. It's the two-man effort that produces meat."

Although I've talked mostly about drives involving two men, I want to mention again that three or four men can pull the same stunts. All I'm emphasizing is that the systems can't be worked by a lone man. In cover areas larger than those I've described, it's often necessary to have two or three drivers. But I wouldn't consider tackling woodlands or outlets to such woodlands requiring more than three drivers and one stander. Give a deer too many escape options and you can't control his movement directions. Except for use of the circle and straggler drive techniques, it's best to tackle big woods with gang drives.

One last point should be considered when employing the two-man drive: the driver should never follow a straight line. Deer in small cover areas don't like to jump and dash unless they feel they have to. I've mentioned that single drivers should walk zigzag courses, but they should do so with definite intent. The idea is to penetrate the thickets, walk out the edges, and explore each area where a deer is likely to be. A driver using such tactics makes a deer nervous because he doesn't know what the man is up to. As soon as a small-cover-area deer decides the jig is up, he'll make his dash for safety. It's the brush-beating driver who moves deer on the small drive.

CHAPTER
7

The Art of
Stillhunting

Stillhunting is probably the least understood of all the deer-hunting techniques. To begin with, the term is a misnomer. It would seem to imply that a man hunts by remaining still. In some states in the Southeast this definition is still in vogue. If a man in that area tells you he got his buck while stillhunting he probably means he shot the animal while sitting still on a stand.

The basic concept of stillhunting is moving slowly and as quietly as possible while looking for deer you suspect to be in the area. In contrast, stalking means moving slowly and quietly as possible while trying to sneak within shooting range of a buck you have already spotted. Stillhunting can change into stalking on a second's notice when you suddenly spot a buck that's unaware of your presence, but stalking never changes to stillhunting unless the stalker blows his chance and has to resort to finding another buck.

Stillhunting won't work in heavily hunted country. You need solitude. In an area where there are many hunters there just isn't the room to practice sneaking tactics because there's too much human interference with normal movement patterns of deer. Stillhunting also doesn't work well in most of the heavily forested sections of the country east of the Mississippi.

In dense woodlands it's too difficult to move quietly and almost impossible to see very far ahead. If you hunt under such conditions it's almost always better to take a stand. The more open country of the West and Southwest is where stillhunting works best. And you can get results in isolated areas of the East where cutover lands mix with clearings that are lightly hunted. Some areas of the Great Lakes have sand dunes and jack-

pine clumps boasting soft floors of pine needles. That's stillhunting country, too—if it's back in the boonies and lightly hunted. I mention this to
point out that if you don't hunt in terrain that's suited to stillhunting
there's no sense in trying it. On the other hand, if stillhunting possibilities
are open to you, here are some further tips that should make your ventures
more successful.

The intriguing thing about stillhunting is that the action often is explosive. Of all the deer I've killed, some of the bucks I remember best hit the
ground while I was stillhunting. I recall these incidents so well because the
action erupted suddenly. Such activity puts a strain on a guy's nervous system.

You always remember the first deer you kill because it's such a highlight
in your life, but in my case I remember the situation more than the killing
shot. I didn't know much about deer hunting during those boyhood times.
On the day in question I was pussyfooting around my local Michigan
woodlands trying to imagine I was making like an Indian.

I walked across some oak-lined hills and then dropped down into a ravine that had a creek coursing its bottom. To my right, 20 yards downstream, a small clump of cedars fanned out on both sides of the creek. The
clump looked like a good place for deer to hide, so I turned toward it. As I
made my move those cedars seemed to explode with bounding and running
deer. There must have been a dozen whitetails bursting out of there. One
small forkhorn buck made the mistake of running right at me. The range
was almost point-blank when I pulled the trigger, and I guess that's why I
didn't miss. My first buck hit the ground dead and skidded into some blueberry bushes only yards away.

I believe most of those whitetails had been watching me from the time I
began walking down into the ravine. When I made a sudden change in direction and turned toward their hiding spot they decided it was time to
leave. The buck I shot must have become confused. He ran the wrong way
when the rest of the herd erupted.

I've walked into many similar situations in the years since. The stillhunter must sneak in among deer, and this calls for all the skill, stealth, and
caution a man can muster. The very nature of the game implies that you'll
occasionally come upon deer that are unaware of you until you get very
close. More often you'll come upon deer that are very much aware of your
presence, but these animals choose to try hiding till they no longer can
stand the tension of a nearby human. In any event, the shocking thrill of
deer exploding from cover at close range is almost always an adventure re-
served for the stillhunter.

It sometimes happens to stalkers, less often to drivers, and still less frequently to standers. A stalker may pussyfoot onto a deer while sneaking up
on another. A driver seldom experiences the explosive dashing of deer because he doesn't travel silently enough to get close without alerting them. A
stander is stationary except for the travel required to get to his stand, so his
opportunities for jumping deer are greatly diminished.

Move Slowly

To stillhunt properly in thick cover, you take a half-dozen slow steps and then stop to look and listen. During the stops you should look to your right and scan on a distant plane in an arc to your left. Then drop your line of view a few yards and scan on the same plane from left to right. Drop the sight plane again and continue inspecting the terrain ahead back and forth. The idea is to check out every piece of cover from the horizon to a few yards in front of you. What you're trying to do is see deer before they see you, or to see them before they become nervous enough to jump and move out. Seeing these animals takes the special skills I covered in Chapter 1.

If you travel more than a mile an hour you're not stillhunting properly; you're going for a walk. Some experts say you can't stillhunt at more than half a mile per hour and expect to see the details your eyes must interpret to spot motionless deer. They also claim that if you move at a faster pace you're bound to make too much noise to sneak in on a target. Which brings up another aspect of the misnomer of stillhunting.

The word "still" means remaining in one place or free from sound. Since a stillhunter is moving, however so slowly, he's bound to make some sounds. You should take it for granted that deer usually hear you because their keen ears pick up every approaching sound. There is no such thing as a completely noiseless approach. And herein lies one of the most important secrets of stillhunting.

The key is that game itself isn't noiseless. A deer moving down a runway makes sounds, but they're natural sounds if another deer hears them because he expects to hear them on game trails. The same deer would not expect to hear off-trail sounds, especially if they were loud and persistent. So the sounds of movement can be natural or unnatural, and deer positively know the difference.

The significance of this is that a stillhunter should work upwind on natural deer runways, and he should travel slowly. A deer moving along a runway stops frequently to look and listen, to browse a bit and to attend to natural functions. This is one reason why it's so important for the stillhunter to move slowly, it's the only way the few sounds he can't avoid making will come off as natural sounds.

It's best not to head directly across country without any regard for game trails. As soon as you do this the sounds you create become unnatural and have no counterpart in the wilds. On-trail noise is in order; off-trail noise is not. Your job is to duplicate in your movements both the sound and the pace of a deer; that's the best way to get in close.

The second reason for moving slowly is that you must have the time to carefully scan the terrain ahead, as I've discussed. The general rule is to take only enough slow steps to give yourself a new perspective of your surroundings, then stop and study them again in detail. It's usually impossible to discover a partially hidden deer unless you take the time to inspect every suspicious item as it comes into view. Don't forget that a deer hears better than you do and is probably aware of the sounds you can't avoid making long before he sees you.

But deer also expect to *see* movement on runways. The slight swaying of a bush or limb is not alarming to them. If you're hidden enough so that a deer can't tell you from another deer he'll pay little attention to the movements and sounds you make. Your advantage is that you're concentrating on seeing part of a deer, but your unalerted buck is not expecting to see part of a man. So stay hidden as much as possible. The only way to do this is to move slowly behind thickets or other types of natural terrain. Do your looking from behind a particularly thick bush or tree. The faster you move the more your body comes into view from any specific point where a deer may be. By moving slowly and studying every part of the land ahead, you have the best odds on seeing a buck before he sees you. And even if he does see you first, he normally won't move out till he sees enough to be sure you're an enemy. By moving slowly and sticking to cover I have several times made out deer standing and watching me. If I had been walking normally they would have run long before, but because of my very slow approach they were not at all sure of what I was.

In the West, where the country is more open than in the East, it's a tremendous help to do most of your studying of the terrain with binoculars. Good optics will show a piece of an antler or a section of deer body in brush far quicker than the naked eye. In this part of the country it's almost impossible to spot game before it sees you unless you glass more than you move. The almost constant use of binoculars will tire your eyes, but it's worth the effort. Adopt the policy of moving as quietly as you can for 10 yards or so, then stop and glass every detail of the land ahead. This sounds tedious, but when you master the technique you'll be amazed at the number of deer you'll pick up in your optics.

Another advantage of stopping so often is that you get a chance to use your ears. If you're dead still you have the opportunity of hearing deer that would otherwise sneak away without disclosing their presence.

There's no sense in stillhunting an area that doesn't harbor the animals. A good bet is to scout for recently used bedding areas. When you hunt a bedding area you should try to determine which trail deer would use in reaching it. For example, no unalarmed deer will travel downwind. If you approach a bedding area along a downwind trail, a buck will immediately become alerted to the unnatural sounds and movements that wouldn't concern him if you were traveling a trail in an upwind direction. The basic rule is always to stillhunt with the wind in your face or partially in your face.

Consider the weather, too. On windy days deer will lie upon the lee or most protected side of a bedding area. If a day is very cold but sunny you can expect to find the animals on southern exposure ridges or slopes. If the weather is hot they'll prefer thickets offering shade. Just remember that a wise buck can come into a bedding area from almost any direction. Try to determine what might have attracted him to take a specific route, then stick to the same trail. This is the type of thinking that takes the success of your hunt out of the "luck category" because you're depending on good basic hunting knowledge. Thinking out strategy always makes a hunt more interesting from start to finish.

The main advantage the stillhunter has is that he often has an element of surprise. Today's deer, much more so than their ancestors of years ago, are likely to try a sneak getaway when they're caught unawares. Here again is why those long and frequent stops of the knowledgeable stillhunter can be so productive. If you spend most of your time looking you're much more likely to catch one of these sneaking bucks in the middle of his act. It's also good to keep in mind that a deer can materialize out of the brush 50 feet away and be in plain sight before you know he's anywhere around. If you happen to be moving rather than looking at the time, he can be gone just as fast as he appeared and you may never know he was there.

Here, the first man stillhunts along the valley floor ahead of his partner, who moves through cover near the ridgetop. Thermals carry the first hunter's scent to a buck bedded on the slopes and rouse him to move opposite the route of the first hunter—and into view of the second hunter.

THERMALS

One time during a hunt in South Dakota's Black Hills I was stillhunting along the edge of a creek when I decided to cross to its other side via a fallen log. The operation didn't take more than about 1½ minutes, but during that time a fine buck got up just in front of me and sneaked away unseen. How do I know? Because some guy was on a stand 150 yards away and he watched the whole sequence. It shook him up so badly he rushed over and blurted, "Why didn't you shoot that buck?"

When I told him I hadn't seen the deer he took me to the spot where the whitetail had jumped up. Then he pointed out the fresh tracks leading away. So much for the importance of restricting your movements. Spend 90 percent of your time looking and only 10 percent pussyfooting along trails.

Stillhunting in Pairs

Many deer hunters have the mistaken idea that stillhunting must be practiced only by lone hunters. This thought is based on the principle that one man will make only half the noise of two men. Well, this principle isn't necessarily true. I came across some enlightening and conflicting information a few years ago when I was working with Linn Thomason of Tulsa, Oklahoma, on a magazine story.

THERMALS

"Two men can actually make less noise than one," Thomason told me. "The first trick is to use hand signals to eliminate all talking or whispering. The main thing is for one man to move ahead about 100 feet, concentrating entirely on traveling silently. His attention is riveted on not stepping on sticks or dry leaves or brushing against branches. The stationary man watches for game while his partner travels. Then the lead man watches while his partner moves up. The system is time-consuming, but it combines the twin advantages of practically noiseless travel with having one set of eyes and ears that are always alert for game. With this technique two men can hunt more efficiently than one.

"Another trick my partner and I use is to stillhunt about 150 yards apart," Linn continued. "One man walks in a valley while the other travels parallel on a ridge. The high man stays about 150 yards behind his partner. The principle is that air rises as a new day warms, and thermal currents carry the scent of the low man up the ridges. Deer like to bed below ridge tops. They'll pick up the scent of the low man while generally failing to detect his partner. It's typical of big game to determine the direction of travel of the lower hunter and then sneak back along the ridge in the opposite direction. The hope is that the animal will be seen by the high hunter who is stillhunting along at the same pace as his partner. The high man must keep concealed as much as possible, and above all he must not expose his outline to the open sky. The clever buck, especially when he's sneaking away, will be constantly on the lookout for danger ahead."

Somebody once told me that he wouldn't think of stillhunting without first covering his rifle with flat paint of camouflage colors. This guy claimed the glint of light from polished barrels and stocks has spooked many a deer from stillhunters who did everything else correctly. If you do a lot of stillhunting this tip sounds like a good one.

Cross-Country Hunting

Although I've emphasized the importance of hunting along established game trails, there are times when you almost have to stillhunt cross country. Such times include working from where you park your vehicle to where you want to go in a prime hunting area, hunting for feeding or traveling deer, and scouting out new areas. During such times you should be especially alert when approaching open areas, meadows, and the tops of ridges and hills. Make sure there's no game in sight before you show yourself at the edge of any opening. Stop just short of the crests of ridges and hills and peer over them so you don't sky-line yourself. A good trick is to sneak along just below the crests, then move up every so often to peer over. Use the same system when hunting along the edges of clearings, openings and swales. Stay inside the edges of cover where you won't be seen during most of your travel. Limit your inspections of open terrain to momentary trips to the bushes or trees which will offer the best concealment at the very edge of cover. Staying in brush is the best way to conceal your movements during travel, and being in brush helps to dampen noise and contain human scent.

In other places in this book I've mentioned Doug Burris, Jr., the Texan who killed the world-record mule-deer buck in 1972. Doug is a stillhunter who has phenomenal success with the techniques I just mentioned. He has the mounted heads of three mule-deer bucks hanging over his fireplace. The middle one is the world record, yet at first glance it doesn't appear much more massive than the other two. In short, Burris is a master at taking big bucks. He attributes his success to stillhunting, the only system he uses. But he points out that his stillhunting doesn't consist of steady stop-and-go travel. Here's what he told me:

"My system is actually a combination of stillhunting and working from stands. The Colorado oak-brush areas where I do my mule deer hunting are tailor-made for the technique. They offer broken terrain in the forms of canyons and fingers running off the canyons to mesas or plateaus. I like to stillhunt the plateaus and fingers of canyons coming off them, then range back and forth through the canyons and up to the mesas and plateaus.

"This means the deer are often moving at the same time I am, so when I'm stillhunting I'm apt to spot deer ahead or across canyons and draws. If I take a stand on a good vantage point I may have deer working toward me. So I stillhunt awhile, then sit awhile, and just keep going like that from dawn to dusk. The problem is that mule deer may use one area today and vacate it tomorrow. So I pick an area and hunt it out. If there are deer in there I stick with it. If there aren't, I move over to the next area. Stillhunting is the best way of making sure I'm hunting an area holding deer, but if I know the animals are moving, I don't hesitate to take a stand."

Another important point for the stillhunter to consider is that the more he blends into the cover he's working the less apt he is to be seen. This principle takes on added importance if the day is bright. Always keep to the shadows as much as possible.

If you're after mule deer always remember that they love elevation; it's their personal kind of protection. But it can be their downfall because they don't expect danger from above. It's a habit of muleys to bed two-thirds or more of the way up a ridge from feeding or watering areas. So if you still-hunt a bit higher you're far less likely to be seen than if you hunt lower where deer can look down on you.

Hunting high is the ideal way to turn a stillhunt into a stalk in a hurry. It happens when the hunter suddenly spots a bedded buck that's unaware of danger. There are many ways in which stillhunting and stalking are closely related, but the best way I can clarify them is to get into the subject of stalking, which is covered in the next chapter.

CHAPTER
8

Stalking Skills

It is possible for a knowledgeable hunter equipped with the proper modern rifle and cartridge to drop a deer in its tracks at ranges of 500 yards or so. There are a few long-range rifle nuts owning target-type rifles equipped with high-power scopes who have killed bucks a half-mile away. Such shooting leaves much to luck because of poor sighting pictures, but ballistically it can be done.

Now consider that the crafty Indians of pre-firearm eras killed their deer with primitive archery equipment which was almost impossible to shoot with any degree of accuracy. Yet they produced venison for their families year-round by their uncanny ability to get in close to deer. There is no better way to point out that the combination of accurate shooting ability and knowledge of stalking skills can be deadlier today than it ever was.

I pointed out in earlier chapters why hunting from a stand is usually surer and easier, but stalking may be for you if you simply don't have the temperament to sit on a stand for long periods and would much rather be on the move. And success from a stand can often involve a certain amount of luck which may not be appealing to the hunter who wants to score by the exertion of individual ability. The successful stalker makes his own luck. If he fails he usually has only himself to blame. Top this off with the fact that, of the various methods of hunting, stalking sustains interest and excitement the longest.

If you hunt in a mule-deer state, particularly in an area where hunting pressure is low, use of the stalking or stillhunting techniques may be necessary because there aren't enough other hunters to keep deer moving. Mule-deer country is also most appropriate for stalkers since deer are often seen in the distance. Such considerations aren't so readily applicable in white-tail terrain, but times do arise when the success of your hunt may *depend* on your stalking ability.

Throughout much of this book I point out that the modern deer hunter enjoys many advantages the old-timers never dreamed of. In this chapter I want to make a dramatic exception. Let me emphasize that the successful stalker or stillhunter must learn how to hunt *first,* then he can go on with bettering his shooting ability and taking advantage of modern gear. Always remember that before you can kill your buck by stalking you have to approach close enough to get within a certain range. This takes specialized skill of a type the Indians and old-timers had to a far greater degree than does the average deer hunter of today. They specialized in stalking because they *had* to get close. We don't have to get quite so close today. This, again, is why the knowledge of the old-timers combined with the superiority of modern rifles can make stalking so efficient.

Spotting Your Deer

The most important principle in stalking is to see your deer before he sees you. When you accomplish this you have a decided advantage because you can focus all your attention on where the animal is and how to close in on him. The buck, on the other hand, has his mind on something else and is expecting danger only in a general way.

The best times to take advantage of this factor are early morning and late evening when deer are moving about and feeding. After a deer has bedded down his attention is no longer absorbed with getting food. Now, even if you should spot a bedded buck before he sees you, you have to compete with all his senses, which have been turned to hearing, seeing, or smelling an intruder. Not only are deer easy to spot when they're moving about, there's also the chance they may move toward you and make your stalking job easier. Further, you can get away with making some small noises during the early and late hours. When deer are on the move they expect slight disturbances in the woodlands from the movements of other game. But once the woods are quiet you'll be at a disadvantage with every movement you make.

The best way to cut down your odds of alerting deer is to be in a hotspot area before the animals begin moving during early and late hours. In the morning the stalker should be in his hunting area before the stars begin to fade. Take a flashlight to help guide you in, then sit down and wait for the first hint of dawn before you begin pussyfooting about, looking for a buck.

Most modern hunters start the afternoon hunt too early and end it too early. Today's deer, particularly whitetails, do not move out of cover as early in the evening as they did years ago. Now you'll seldom see a deer till just before dark. There's not much sense of getting into the area you want to stalk until the sun is close to setting. When you do start hunting don't give up till the last minute of shooting time passes. The later you hunt in the evening the more deer you'll see. You may not have time to stalk some of them, but there's no chance in the world of stalking a buck you haven't spotted.

One of the greatest errors would-be stalkers make is going too fast and too far while looking for a buck. The hunter who barrels through the brush has almost no chance to spot a deer before the animal becomes aware of him. The trick is to scout for good deer country long before the hunt, then soft-shoe through it while spending about 90 percent of your time looking and 10 pecent walking. Step on solid rocks or firm ground, never put your weight on anything that may snap or crackle. Any deer hears better than he sees, and he's sure to be instantly alerted to any unnatural sound. The beginning hunter often sees these deer because they may wait to make sure the noises are produced by a hunter and not something harmless before they bound away, but he never gets a chance to stalk them. This is why some beginners will say, "Those deer never knew I was there till I got within 50 yards of them. Next time I'll get closer." Nothing could be further from the truth. Deer are well aware of bumbling hunters.

Know Your Quarry

The stalker who has continued success has a thorough knowledge of deer. He knows their habits and how they can be expected to react in various situations.

For example, the expert stalker knows what reactions to watch for in the buck he's closing in on. If the animal throws up his head and stares, he's alerted to something. Obviously you should stop and freeze at this point, but just as important, you should interpret what happens next. If your buck moves his head from side to side he's attempting to see his problem. This usually means he hasn't spotted you yet and probably won't run until he does. You shouldn't attempt a risky shot at this point because if you don't move for several moments the deer may resume his normal routine.

Sometimes such a buck will resort to foot-stamping. This is a sign that he's curious and uncertain and attempting to make a possible enemy reveal himself. He isn't about to run off at this point. When he lowers his head or changes the direction of his gaze he has decided no danger is near. Now you can resume your stalk. If you're up against a whitetail, watch his flag. When the buck gives his tail a switch from side to side he has made up his mind all is well.

However, you'd best get ready to shoot if your whitetail's tail rises and straightens out. This is a sure sign he's alarmed and ready to run. Knowledgeable hunters watch a buck's ears, too. When he becomes suspicious that danger may be near he'll cup his ears toward you, straining to catch any noise that may be out of place. He isn't about to bolt yet, but watch out if he folds his ears back and tucks them under his antlers. This signal

When deer check for danger, they cup their ears and look in various directions while listening. The deer shown here are not frightened yet because the stalking photographer has frozen in his tracks, but a careless movement would send them into flight.

means he's about to depart in a rush. Why does he fold his ears back? Because he doesn't want them vulnerable to the sting of brush as he crashes through cover. When you see your buck's ears go back you're going to have to shoot in a hurry or not at all.

There's one stalking technique that may work for you, but which never has for me. It's based on the knowledge that a deer's eyes, like those of a horse or a cow, are set at such an angle in its head that it cannot see anything not directly under its nose while its head is down for browsing. This is why a browsing deer raises its head every few seconds to look around and assure itself that all is well.

Further, the theory goes that you don't need any stalking cover at all if your approach movements are made only when the buck has his head down. The implication is that a deer cannot distinguish between a stationary object such as a bush or tree and a stationary man even if the last time the animal looked up the bush, tree or man wasn't there. Supposedly, a deer also does not have the mentality to realize that a stationary tree or man is getting closer and larger each time the animal looks up.

The secret of this stalk is in timing the sequences of how long the buck has his head down before he looks up again. Normally, this is about five seconds. The stalker gets into position behind the last available cover and then makes, say, a four-second dash toward the quarry as soon as the deer lowers its head. Then he freezes in a predetermined position, usually holding his rifle in front of his body, muzzle pointing at 45 degrees to the sky and finger on safety. The idea is that you must present the same contour to the buck every time he looks up.

The theory stipulates that if you make your moves soundlessly and only when the buck has his head down, you can get close enough to hit him with a rock. Maybe so, but I've found that making quick dashes in average deer country can't be made soundlessly. At least I haven't been able to make them without alerting my bucks before I got within good shooting range. Every time I've tried this stunt my quarry has heard me coming. Perhaps it would work well in grassy fields or on sandy terrain. However, the theory has its supporters among many knowledgeable deer hunters, and it's claimed that the Indians were masters at making this technique work. Maybe I'm just not enough of an Indian.

In any event, the system is almost limited to the stalking of single deer. When two or three or more are browsing together, you have the situation where each individual deer looks up at different times. It would take a wizard to time all those movements.

Importance of Stealth

A basic rule in stalking is that it's often necessary to get as close as possible to the ground. The man who is willing to get down on his belly and crawl through mud, muck, and brush is going to get far more shooting opportunities than the man who is concerned about comfort or what the stalk is doing to his fancy hunting clothes. The old-timers wore no fancy clothes and they didn't waste a single thought on their appearance; they put up with discomforts that would make many a modern hunter wince. They knew that getting down in the dirt, getting scratched by briers, crawling over rocks, and getting wet could be parts of the game.

In most stalking situations you must move ahead without disturbing the outlines of the terrain between you and your buck. The crown of a cap, a moving shoulder, or even a pair of prominent buttocks can ruin a stalk. In normal stalking you have to get natural terrain features that are higher and wider than you between yourself and the deer, and you have to keep them there. This often means you have to take advantage of various cover features one piece at a time. You have to pick out a bush, tree, rock, or whatever; utilize it to move ahead to a certain spot, then determine another piece of cover that will best shield you for the next part of your advance.

This type of stealth takes time. The old-timers didn't get excited and they never rushed things. I've often thought that one reason they were so successful at stalking and stillhunting was that they didn't have to worry about getting home at 5 o'clock to take the wife out for cocktails, getting to the office Monday morning, meeting the boys for bowling, or any one of dozens of other modern reasons for hurrying up. They stayed in the woods on the theory that impatience invariably scares game. That's still the truth.

Taking your time can mean such things as avoiding the habit of looking up to see your deer too often while you're moving ahead. Instead you should keep your eyes on the ground and have the patience to look for and avoid every twig, stick, or stone that could produce the slightest rustle. Don't look up until you're close behind a concealing piece of cover.

Taking advantage of the wind also takes time. After the game is located you must make your way to a point downwind—or at least crosswind—of the animal before you can attempt a successful stalk. Such an approach eliminates your scent and deadens the sounds of your movements. And once you begin closing in on your deer you should lie motionless when a calm comes on. Wind doesn't blow steadily; it comes and goes with increasing and decreasing velocity. You should move ahead during the increases, which helps drown some noises you are sure to make. Stop as the breeze dies out.

During these stops take the time to note the characteristics of your deer. If it's feeding, get the time intervals (usually about five seconds) between when it lowers its head and when it looks up to scan the landscape. Notice which directions the deer observes most while looking for potential danger. If it spends an unusual amount of time looking in your direction you should go to the bother of figuring out an alternate approach route. In any event, don't try moving ahead through scant cover till your deer's head is down or he's looking in another direction. If he should suddenly look up or turn his head toward you while you're moving, your only option is to "freeze" instantly. Sometimes you'll get away with it. A deer isn't suspicious of an unidentifiable motionless object, but a clever buck invariably will become alert at the first sign of movement.

When I made my first tries at stalking deer years ago, I was never successful. I was ready to give up the technique and I said so to a veteran hunter who killed a buck every year. His comments gave me the determination to keep trying.

"Look at it this way," he began. "If a stalking cat can catch birds you can shoot a deer. The cat doesn't have the benefit of a firearm so it has to get close enough to the sparrow to pounce on him. The bird has wings which enable him to escape easily in a split second if he becomes aware of the cat, yet he gets caught. You have a firearm and your buck doesn't have wings, so you don't have to be nearly as proficient as a cat at stalking. Stalking is an art that's instinctive in cats. Man has to learn it and it takes time. Whenever you have the opportunity to watch a cat sneaking in on a bird you should watch him very carefully. You'll learn a lot, especially how much time the critter uses to make every move perfectly. Knowing when to move and when not to is something no person can tell you. You have to develop a feel for it and, again, this takes time."

One thing that can ruin a stalk is the activity of other creatures of the wild. I refer to certain birds and small animals which, after becoming aware of your presence, may sing out with their particular vocal alarm which will be understood by all game animals. The alarm caw of a crow is more than enough to tell a buck that there's danger nearby. Other offenders that lend a helping hand to deer include red squirrels, blue jays, kingfishers and magpies. Should any of these pests show up while you're making a stalk you'd best freeze or lie low till they have gone elsewhere. This may take considerable time, and it's one more example of why the efficient stalker is never in a hurry.

Any stalker using any system will often encounter conditions when it's impossible to make a successful hunt no matter how skilled he may be. During extremely dry weather when everything underfoot snaps or rustles there's no way you're going to get close to an unalerted deer unless you're able to hunt into winds of gale force. Crusted snow is also an exceptional noise maker. A thin, frozen crust on the ground is another. Skim ice produced by freezing rain is worse yet. On such days you'll be far better off to take a stand somewhere, sit still, and hope a buck will come to you.

On the other hand, rain or snow softens the land and also produces sound baffles. The stalker or stillhunter welcomes a gentle rain as the greatest assist he can get. Not only does rain make the going much quieter, but it also produces natural pattering noises that help cover the hunter's approach. I mention these facts to point out that the best deer hunters don't live by any single system. The successful veterans have learned to master several techniques, and they may use two or three during a single day's hunt. Stalking is no cure-all, but mastering its principles can be most desirable when proper weather conditions present themselves.

If you blunder during a stalk, don't let your startled buck stampede you

Soft new snow enabled the author to stalk this buck silently. Crusted snow, on the other hand, is a noisemaker.

into shooting unless you have a good chance for a killing hit. Once you touch off a rifle in deer country you alert every other deer in the area. Your chance of making another stalk in the same section immediately goes down the drain. If you don't shoot you may be able to walk over the next ridge or hill and spot another buck that is at ease.

Clothing and Scent

When you mention stalking or stillhunting to most hunters, you immediately create the mental picture of a man pussyfooting along while trying to eliminate noise produced by his feet. The smart hunter knows that the clothes he wears also have a great deal to do with the noises he produces.

You should wear clothes that are quiet when you come into contact with briers or brush. Any of the canvas hunting clothes are extremely noisy. They scratch with unnatural loudness in the woods. So do hard-material hats, high rubber boots and plastic rain gear.

Wool is the softest material you can select for general clothing. Leather boots get the nod for footwear, but wear your trouser legs over the outside of your boots to further deaden sound. I'm a nut on Blaze Orange for safety's sake, so I wear a Blaze Orange vest and cap when I'm stalking. These items have become available in soft materials during recent years.

Regardless of the type of boots you prefer, be sure they're soft-soled with foam rubber or crepe. Quiet boots are a must for quiet movement. If you hunt in dry country don't underestimate the advantage of taking off your boots during the last and most crucial part of a stalk. You can move much more quietly in stocking feet than in the best pair of boots ever made.

Human scent is another problem that must be reckoned with. The obvious way to lick it is to stalk into the wind or quartering into it. But sometimes you'll get conditions of wind shift or no wind at all; that's when other tricks of licking the scent problem pay off. Tobacco smoke is particularly offensive to deer. Take two guys with equal stalking ability and you can bet that if one doesn't smoke he'll come home with more game. It's as simple as that because you can't get smoke odors out of your clothing without a thorough washing. Campfire smoke presents the same problem as does the exhaust smoke of automobiles, outboard motors, or other machinery.

One solution is to utilize a set of "stalking clothes" that are never worn except while hunting. At other times (such as traveling to hunting country or relaxing after the hunt) these clothes can be kept in a heavy plastic bag where no man-produced odors can get to them. A trick some of the old-timers used was to rub moderate amounts of pine or sage oil onto their hunting clothes to mask human odor. For an in-the-field substitute, use a handful of pine or sage needles.

Don't figure you can achieve the same objective by using the modern "deer scents" on your person or clothes. They may mask your scent and they may not alarm deer, but they definitely will produce the one situation the stalker must avoid. A deer scent will attract the attention of your buck and he'll focus his senses directly upon your immediate area. This is exactly what you don't want.

A common conception of the old-timer is that of an old woods rat who didn't take kindly to bathing and who wore the same clothes for weeks at a time. The old-time stalkers and stillhunters who were serious about their hunts were an entirely different breed. They bathed (with particular emphasis on thoroughly washing their hair) before every hunt. And they wore clean hunting clothes. The clothes may have been worn and ragged about the edges, but you can bet those old boys wanted them clean and completely washed of human odor. I remember talking with one of these guys years ago who washed his hands and face with some kind of scent-masking solution that he made himself. I've long since forgotten what the ingredients were, but I've always remembered the implication of that washing rite before the hunt. The old-timers had great respect for the cleverness of deer, far more so than does the average modern deer hunter. Perhaps that's one reason they were able to get so close to their bucks. But some of the new-generation hunters hold onto the old traditions, too.

Whenever a discussion comes up on the importance of controlling human scent I always recall the thoughts of Harry E. Troxell III, a young Colorado bowhunter I once worked with on a story for *Outdoor Life*. Troxell's advice highlights how important the control of scent really is.

"My camping equipment surprises many hunters," Troxell told me. "My gear is selected on the theory that the quickest way to spook game is to advertise your presence with human scent. I camp cold. In other words, I never light a fire for cooking or warmth. I pack in canned meats, fruit, and other ready-to-eat items. Cold camping not only eliminates scent but it also eliminates the disturbances of woodchopping, cooking, and other camp chores. A bowman has to get close to his quarry and that's almost impossible if his clothes carry the odors of smoke or cooked food.

"Getting within such bow range is especially difficult if the game already has been alerted by the distant sounds of human activity. Though I can often drive close to my hunting areas, I seldom consider doing it because of the noise. I'll drive into a general area, then backpack into the section I want to hunt. Cold camping may be uncomfortable, but it's a definite help in getting close to game."

The next time you think you're being careful about controlling scent and noise factors you'll do well to remember Troxell's advice.

CHAPTER
9

The Truth
About Rattling

Twenty years ago I read a story in a national outdoor magazine about rattling up bucks. It grabbed my attention because the author claimed that all buck deer will come to the sound of two other bucks fighting, and that any hunter can call in a trophy simply by duplicating the sounds of such a fight. The trick is accomplished by rattling deer antlers together.

The story was very convincing. I tried to rattle up a Michigan buck during that fall's hunting season. I tried several times with zero success.

Since then many stories about rattling have been published. The subject gained national attention among deer hunters. Instruction records hit the market. During my deer hunts in several states I asked veteran hunters, guides, and outfitters about rattling. Many of these men had read about rattling, a few had tried it, none had been successful. I decided that successful rattling had to be one of the biggest mysteries in the entire field of American hunting, or else it was a nation-wide con job.

Some years ago I made a mule deer hunt in the Colorado Rockies. Ken Callaway, producer of the national TV show "Outdoors with Ken," was a member of my group. Callaway, a native Texan, shattered my conviction that successful rattling might be a myth.

"Rattling is *the* way to hunt whitetails in south Texas," Ken told me. "Some of the best TV film I've shot shows many bucks coming to horns. Believe me, it's no myth. It's a sensational way to hunt deer."

Since then I've looked at Ken's movies several times. The bucks in the films were responding to horn rattling as surely as mallards respond to a duck call.

I became so absorbed I decided to make an in-depth study of this myste-rious hunting technique. I wanted to put popular notions to the acid test. I wanted to separate fact from fiction, certify truths, and debunk delusions. I knew that my study wouldn't be meaningful unless I contacted deer biolo-gists and knowledgeable outdoorsmen across the nation. It took me two years to get all the information I wanted. I talked with deer-management officials in nineteen states, and with scores of veteran hunters.

My top priority was personal contact with a horn rattler who rated as one of the very best in the United States. I hit paydirt when I got in touch with Charles K. Winkler, Program Director of Big Game, Texas Parks and Wildlife Department.

"Your man is Bob Ramsey," Winkler told me. "Ramsey has a ranch near Hunt, Texas. He has rattled up hundreds of bucks and he is a trained wildlife biologist. He has the scientific background to explain the facts be-hind his success."

So I visited Bob on his ranch. Listen to what this man told me; it will probably astound you.

"Years ago I kept track of how many bucks I'd brought to horns, but I've long since quit keeping a grand total," Ramsey began. "I remember a hunt back in 1945. I was guiding James Odom, an Austin building contractor. He was a trophy hunter, yet he wasn't interested in anything less than a wide-racked 10-pointer.

"The hunt sticks in memory because I rattled up nine bucks, one after another, without changing position. We were surrounded with bucks for about 10 minutes. Odom wasn't satisfied with any of them, so no shots were fired.

"At the time I figured that I'd brought about 400 bucks to horns during my career. I'm sure the figure is well over 1,000 now. I rattle purely for ex-citement. I haven't shot a whitetail buck since 1956, but I still hunt mule deer."

Ramsey's background explains his success. He graduated from Texas A&M with a degree in wildlife biology. He worked for the Texas Parks and Wildlife Department for five years, then he went into ranching. Now he owns and operates a 5,000-acre spread in the Edwards Plateau region, a re-gion long famous for its enormous numbers of whitetail deer.

Some of Ramsey's convictions emphasize that a lot of what had been published about rattling is pure fallacy. Let's take the subject of mule deer.

"I've read that mule deer will respond to rattled antlers as well as white-tails," Ramsey said. "It isn't true. I have tried rattling muleys many times in Montana, Wyoming, Colorado, New Mexico, and West Texas. I've failed miserably every time. There are biological reasons for these failures.

"Mule deer do not have a home range as whitetails do. They're not terri-torial. They're completely different animals. Whitetail bucks spend most of their entire lives on roughly one square mile of terrain. They hate other bucks during the rutting season, and they'll fight to defend their territories.

"Mule deer have no such ties. They tend to be migrators. Mule deer bucks are often found in groups, even during the rut. Several bucks, with rut-swollen necks often browse and bed together with no animosity. The reverse is true with whitetails. Nature drives them to fighting during the breeding season. Mule deer, except in isolated cases, have no use for fighting.

"Some years ago I made a mule deer hunt in Arizona's Kaibab National Forest," Ramsey went on. "I suddenly became aware of the sounds of two bucks fighting. I found them going at it in a forest-access road. The cause of the commotion was a nearby doe. Both bucks spent a lot of time browsing, but if one made a move toward the waiting doe the other would charge in to fight. The occasional banging of antlers went on for over an hour.

"During this time I spotted eight other bucks in the immediate area. I studied their reactions when the two fighters would slam into each other. The battles produced absolutely no interest in those bucks. Most didn't even bother to glance at the fighting scene. I'm convinced that trying to rattle up mule deer bucks is a complete waste of time."

Ramsey firmly believes that whitetail bucks—anywhere in North America—will respond to the sounds of antlers clashing, but only under very specific conditions. Most important is timing. You *cannot* bring a buck to horns unless the rut is in full bloom.

"Our long hunting season is one reaon why rattling is so successful in Texas," Ramsey says. "If there was a two-week season here, and it was always in October, every deer hunter who tried rattling would come to the conclusion that the technique absolutely does not work. The same hunters could take a pair of horns out on a blackbrush ridge on a frosty morning during the December rut and disprove that theory in five minutes."

I'll get back to Bob Ramsey and more of his insights later, but now let's switch to comments I got in other states. They'll help to take a lot more of the mystery out of horn rattling.

During the early part of my study I got in contact with Hiram Hallock of New Glarus, Wisconsin. Hallock does research work for the U.S. Forest Service. He has hunted deer for many years with Kent McDonald, a fellow researcher. The opinions of these veteran hunters are backed by scientific thinking.

"When the first articles about horn rattling appeared in outdoor magazines we read them with considerable skepticism," Hallock began. "But we decided to try the technique. At that time Wisconsin had just purchased 9,000 acres of private property near Babcock. The area was opened to bow hunters only, even though it was overrun with whitetails. Many were mature, heavy-horned bucks.

"Our first attempt produced no deer. We moved a few hundred yards and tried again. From my position I could see about ¼ mile across a clearing. The second time I clashed the antlers together I saw a buck with a massive rack run into the far end of the clearing.

"I rattled again. The buck immediately began running right at me. He

During the rutting season, bucks engage in battles for dominance. The clashing of their antlers can be heard up to a half mile away. Many hunters are now "rattling" a set of antlers, in imitation, to bring bucks into range.

finally stopped in thickets 100 yards away. When I rattled the third time that big brute came straight on again. It so happened that both Kent and I were in plain view because we hadn't expected deer to come across that clearing. When the buck spotted us he seemed completely surprised and confused to the point of momentary disbelief. Though he was too far from Kent for an effective shot, he didn't leave for at least 10 seconds.

"The next weekend we tried the area again," Hallock went on. "My 14-year-old daughter Suanne went with us. We rattled in a couple of areas with no success. Suanne wanted to try rattling, so we positioned her behind a drainage ditch. After she clashed the horns a few times Kent and I heard a deer behind us. We turned and saw a tremendous buck coming from the west, even though most of the thick cover was to the east. Once again we were caught in the open.

"The buck spotted us at a range of about 80 yards. He acted as though he had been caught completely by surprise, then he turned and walked back in a westerly direction. Suanne was unaware of what was happening, so she started rattling again.

"The 12-pointer practically fell over himself reversing direction. He immediately ran back to the area where he had spotted us. He just stood there trying to figure it all out, then he made an unhurried departure.

"On several other occasions we rattled up big bucks in that same region. In other regions we failed completely. Our backgrounds as researchers prompted us to try figuring out why this was true.

"We think you must rattle in an area where many of the bucks are old enough to have learned the sounds and meanings of buck fights. We think the deer population density must be high enough so that territories of bucks overlap. This situation brings on keen competition for does and sets the stage for fighting. If we hadn't tried rattling in an area that was loaded with deer of all ages we probably would have failed and felt foolish in the process."

That last statement of Hallock's was echoed by several other men I contacted during my survey. Here is an example:

"I have attempted antler rattling during parts of three deer seasons with no results. The only reaction I got was a certain amount of ridicule from my hunting partners who thought I was a little crazy."—Roger Holmes, Chief of Wildlife, Minnesota Department of Natural Resources.

Are there any states—besides Texas—where rattling success has been documented? Read some more comments that turned up during my survey.

"I do not know anyone who has rattled up a deer in Missouri. Our biologists feel it might work, but we just don't know. So we're back to your mystery with no facts for the table."—Ollie Torgerson, Deer Biologist, Missouri Department of Conservation.

"I have checked with our Wildlife Division and can't come up with any information on horn rattling. There may be some hunters in Maine who have tried this technique, but we know of none who have been successful."—William C. Mincher, Director Information & Education Division, Maine Department of Inland Fisheries and Wildlife.

"I'm afraid I can't help you. Rattling apparently is not successful in Georgia. As far as we can determine it is not used as a hunting technique in this state."—David Cranshaw, Director, Georgia Department of Natural Resources.

"To my knowlege horn rattling has never been in common use by California deer hunters. I have no first-hand information on any success with the technique."—C. M. Ferrel, Wildlife Management Supervisor, California Department of Fish and Game.

"I have been fascinated by antler rattling since I first heard of it years ago. I can recollect only one instance where it was tried, successfully, here in New Hampshire. A hunter checking his buck at a check station mentioned that he had rattled up his trophy."—Joseph Wiley III, Wildlife Biologist, New Hampshire Fish and Game Department.

"I have no knowledge of any person who has used the technique successfully in Florida."—Frank H. Smith, Jr., W-35 Project Leader, Florida Game and Fresh Water Fish Commission.

"To our knowledge, no one practices rattling in Oregon. If they do, no knowledge of it has come to any of our deer biologists."—Ken Durbin, Information-Education, Oregon Department of Fish and Wildlife.

"I have not been able to find anyone who practices rattling in our state."—George M. Purvis, Chief Information & Education Division, Arkansas Game and Fish Commission.

Now let's consider some positive reactions. Here's a comment that comes close to duplicating those I received from biologists in several states. "Horn rattling is not a widely used technique in New Jersey. I have not heard of any success, but I cannot believe that it won't work. Broken horns are quite common on many of our bucks. It's obvious that these bucks had been fighting."—David Burke, Deer Project Leader, New Jersey Department of Environmental Protection.

Okay, now let's listen to some men who have had great success far from the brush country of South Texas.

Wayne Atchison of Marion Junction, Alabama, hunts where the limit is one buck per day during a long season. This unusual situation has a bearing on what he told me.

"I rattled up eight bucks during the last two seasons," Atchison began. "I did not take all of them because some had small racks. Each buck that I have killed by rattling had scars both old and fresh from fighting.

"I am currently assisting the wildlife department of Auburn University with a research project on deer. Because of similar projects through the years, I am in the woods at all hours and have access to a great deal of scientific knowledge about whitetail deer. I talk to wildlife groups and have instructed many sportsmen on the technique of rattling. Some of these men reported success, some didn't. In any event, rattling will definitely work in Alabama.

"I'm convinced that the average hunter who tries the system during the rut rattles up five times more bucks than he sees because most bucks are very cautious about approaching a fight. For every buck that rushes to a fight, five will sneak in to see what's going on before they commit themselves. Your eyes are your most important asset.

"Most hunters have been brainwashed by the stories they've read about rattling," Atchison added. "They have visions of bucks coming on the run from all directions. It doesn't work that way. I'm lucky if I rattle up one buck every three or four hunts. Some days it works, some days it doesn't.''

Jack Brauer and Al Hofacker are the organizers of a Wisconsin whitetail study group called "The Stump Sitters." Members exchange ideas and information on all phases of whitetail deer hunting. Brauer and Hofacker put on group presentations which include films, displays, and informative narrations. One of the films is based on successful horn rattling in Wisconsin.

"Al and I have completed a 10-year intensive study with whitetails that involve over 10,000 hours of field research," Brauer told me. "We have rattled up about 50 Wisconsin bucks during the past six years, and we have film to prove it. We teach rattling techniques at our clinics. You can't rattle successfully unless you understand exactly how to go about it."

During our discussion Brauer pointed out that almost 100 percent of his success came on cold, clear, and crisp days just after sunrise or just before sunset. Due to these limitations his group—which now has members in 22 states—concentrates on researching other hunting techniques. If you're interested in becoming a member you can contact Brauer at P.O. Box 1302, Appleton, WI 54911.

After I boiled down my research for this article, several major factors came through loud and clear.

1) Most whitetail states have short firearms deer seasons, and most of these seasons *do not* fall during the rut. Consequently, many gun hunters do not have any chance at all of rattling up a buck. On the other hand, most states have long archery seasons which do coincide with the rut. Rattling could be a lead-pipe cinch for bowhunters.

2) Rattling won't work in heavily-hunted areas because smart bucks have learned to stay hidden by daylight when many hunters are in the woods. These bucks do their fighting and breeding at night. They will not respond to rattling during legal hunting hours.

3) A deer population must be high enough so that there is overlapping of territories used by bucks. If your hunting area does not have a lot of deer your odds on rattling up a buck are slim.

If you're a gun hunter, check with game officials in your state and find out when the rut usually occurs. If it coincides with at least part of your firearms season, you should consider rattling. If you have access to private property which is closed to other hunters you may have a potential rattling bonanza. The technique may also work in very remote areas during gun seasons, but it definitely will not work in heavily hunted areas.

Correct Way to Rattle

Now let's go back to Bob Ramsey in Texas and get his instructions on the correct way to rattle.

"All beginners are too timid," Ramsey told me. "They don't make enough noise. The idea is to get the immediate attention of any bucks

Rattling antlers need not be trophy size but should have at least six points. Note that the tips of the tines have been sawed off and blunted. Sharp tines can produce skinned knuckles while rattling.

Antlers are connected by a short cord for ease in carrying on a deer hunt.

To begin rattling sequence, grasp the antlers firmly by their bases, right horn in left hand and left horn in right hand. Points of both antlers should be pointing to the left.

Initial action begins by holding left hand rigid, bringing right hand up on 45-degree angle, then . . .

. . . clashing the antlers together with as much force as you can muster.

After making the initial loud noise with the antlers, use your wrists to produce clicking and clacking sounds. Allow the tips of the tines to play against each other.

Next, begin scraping and clawing the ground with the antler points. Vigorously attack sticks, stones, rocks— anything that is movable.

Fight nearby brush with the antlers. Smash off twigs and twist branches. Try to imitate two bucks stamping and shoving.

133

Crouched behind a clump of bushes, Bob Ramsey shows how it's done. Note bottle of skunk musk used to mask Ramsey's scent.

within hearing range. Clash the horns together with as much force as you can muster.

"But once is enough. After you made the initial clashing of antlers every buck within hearing distance has your position pinpointed. Now the trick is to make less noise with your antlers. Twist them together with your wrists to produce clicking and clacking sounds, the sounds that two bucks make when they're pushing and shoving. Continue this for five seconds, then abruptly jerk the horns apart.

"At this point begin scraping and clawing the ground with the points of the antlers. Vigorously attack sticks, stones, rocks . . . anything that is movable. Fight nearby brush with the horns, and I mean fight it. Use top strength to smash off twigs and twist branches. Really go at it. Try to imitate two Brahma bulls stomping and shoving each other around.

"After this sequence, wait one minute then gently place the tines together. Twist and turn them so they grate and rasp against each other. Continue this for five seconds. Wait one minute, then continue, but with a minimum of vigor. Allow only the tips of the tines to play against each other, and for only a few seconds. By this time you may already have a buck close by. Study the surrounding terrain for any sign of movement.

"If no buck is near, wait three minutes then scrape the ground again five or six times. Wait another three minutes, then rattle the tines lightly. If there is still no sign of buck coming, pound the ground twice with the base of the antler in your right hand. You have now completed the entire sequence. Wait five minutes and repeat the entire series except for the initial loud clashing of the antlers. Bucks usually arrive at the fake fight scene within 10 seconds to 30 minutes from the time you begin rattling. If no bucks show within 45 minutes it's best to move to a new area."

Rattling antlers should have at least six points. Garage sales are good places to pick up old deer heads or antlers on wooden shields. During deer season you can get antlers for nothing from butchers who process deer.

The first step in preparing the antlers is to saw them off the skull just above or below the burr. Saw off the brow tines—they're useless in rattling—and saw off the tips of each tine. Use a rasp to round off and dull the tips. (Dull tips don't hurt as much as sharp tips if you accidentally hit your hands while rattling. Wear a pair of gloves while rattling for further insurance against skinned knuckles.) Drill a 1/4-inch hole through the base of each antler. Tie them together with a 24-inch cord. Your rattling equipment is now ready.

Always sneak very quietly into the spot where you're going to rattle. No buck will come to the horns if he knows there is a human in the area. Pick a natural blind of brush, one that offers a good view in most directions.

Grasp the antlers firmly by their bases, right horn in left hand and left horn in right hand. You will note that the points of both antlers are pointing to the left. Bring the right hand up on a 45° angle, then clash the antlers together to produce the initial "wham" that begins the rattling sequence.

No matter from which direction a buck approaches he will almost always circle downwind from your position. You can mask your scent by hanging a container of artificial skunk musk on a limb just downwind from your rattling position. Most good sporting-goods stores carry small bottles of this material.

Here are some final tips from Bob Ramsey.

"If I had only one hour to rattle it would be on a crisp, clean day in later afternoon. There would be no wind, the temperature would be about 40°. I would want a freeze the night before and heavy white frost in the morning. Frost really turns on a breeding buck. He may come to horns just after daylight, but he'll be most active just before dusk. Don't try rattling if the wind is blowing more than about 12 miles per hour; bucks seldom come to horns if it's windy."

Now, a very serious word of caution. Imagine the thoughts that go through the mind of the average hunter when he suddenly hears what he assumes is the furious fighting of two bucks. He immediately decides that neither buck is aware of his presence, and that he can rush to the scene and nail the trophy of his choice. He is so positive the fight is real he'll be ready to shoot in a hurry. *Don't ever rattle during firearms season unless you're wearing blaze orange outer garments.*

This safety factor gets us back to the fact that rattling is made to order for bowhunters. The archer is likely to have the woods to himself. He hunts undisturbed deer that are working normal behavior patterns. He can hunt during the peak of the rut. Archers who rattle near fresh scrapes can almost certainly bring a buck to the horns.

Rattling probably is the most overlooked archery-hunting technique for still another very basic reason. A buck coming to the horns always comes very close to the fake fight scene. Bob Ramsey has had many bucks almost run over him while they were rushing to get in on the action. Says Ramsey, "Don't try this game if you have a weak heart. The sight of a big buck running into pointblank range with fire in his eyes can be a stunning experience." What more could any archer want?

Farmlands produce many of the biggest whitetails. This deer with an exceptional rack was taken in Kansas.

CHAPTER
10

Hunting
Farmland Deer

At 6 A.M. that November morning the Michigan farm country was covered with as dense a fog as I've ever seen. My partner and I were sitting in his pickup truck, bemoaning the fact that hunting was impossible. Finally, we decided to head for our stands in hopes the fog would lift. That decision led to one of the most bizarre deer-hunting adventures I've ever experienced.

My stand site, 100 yards from the gravel road where we were parked, was in a brushy fence line that separated a 40-acre picked cornfield from a larger unworked field of high weeds. Charlie's stand was on the opposite side of the grainfield. When we separated, the fog swallowed him as if he were an evaporating ghost.

I was on my stand half an hour before visibility began improving as the fog thinned and formed smoke-like wisps in a developing breeze. It was eerie. In such a situation a man begins to see strange things that may or may not be reality.

When I got my first glimpse of the deer I was positive I'd spotted a whitetail bedded in the weeds no more than 75 yards from me. Then fog covered the scene, and when it reappeared there was no deer. Was I looking at the same spot?

I went through 20 minutes of heart-pounding excitement as I caught recurring glimpses of what could be a bedded deer. Finally my 9X binoculars proved conclusively that it was a deer, and that it wore a small rack. I put the crosshairs of my scope on his shoulder and sent a 100-grain .243 slug on its way. There seemed to be no way I could miss. I was astounded as I watched a deer jump from the spot and instantaneously melt into the fog.

Dejected, I walked over to where the buck had been. There has never been a more surprised hunter than I was when I saw my forkhorn stretched out dead. Immediately I knew there had been two bedded deer even though I had seen only one.

Charlie got his 1981 buck a few days later. He spotted two deer standing in a winter wheat field just as dawn was old enough to distinguish objects at a distance. He focused his binoculars on the animals and determined that the larger one was a six-pointer. The two whitetails began walking slowly toward a bedding area, and Charlie knew where it was. He got there before the deer did, and dropped the buck with his Ruger single-shot .30-06.

The main reason we made those two kills is that we knew there were bucks using the immediate areas. Before I get into why our system is so deadly, some background is in order.

For the last several consecutive years the southern half of Michigan's Lower Peninsula (which is predominately farm country) has shown a far larger deer harvest than the state's Upper Peninsula that once was recognized as offering some of the Midwest's best whitetail hunting. Now listen to game officials in several Midwest states.

"Our largest deer harvest comes from agricultural and mixed wooded sections of southeastern counties," said Leroy Rutske of Minnesota's Section of Wildlife.

From Frank P. Haberland, Wisconsin's Supervisor of Big Game Management: "Our very best deer hunting counties all are ideal mixtures of woodlots and farmland."

From Dave Jensen of the North Dakota Game and Fish Department: "Some great deer hunting is developing in the farming counties having large acreages of sunflowers."

From Lee Gladfelter, Wildlife Research Biologist for the Iowa Conservation Commission: "Some of Iowa's best deer hunting spots are drainage ditches, weedy fencerows, and brushy edge covers in or adjacent to crop fields."

These are just a few of many similar comments I received when I was gathering material for one of *Outdoor Life's* annual September deer round-ups. They are prime examples of the fact that whitetail populations are booming in farm country. The old belief that the big woods offer the best hunting just isn't true anymore for even more reasons.

Farmland deer move more often and travel far greater distances than forest deer. To illustrate this principle, consider the difference between two one-mile-square sections of land. The first section is forested, a mixture of hardwoods and lowland swamps and brushy areas. Deer biologists have proven that many whitetails living in this type of habitat spend their entire lives within one square mile. They don't move far when hunted, they simply hide so well that most hunters never see them.

Now consider another one square mile of farm country. Let's say that 60 percent of the section grows crops, 25 percent is apple orchard, and only 15 percent is covered with brush that's too thick to cultivate. Through summer and early fall all of this section offers ideal food and cover for white-tails, but when the crops are harvested the prime cover area drops to only 15 percent. Deer will feed on waste grain and apples and bed in the small brushy area as long as they're not bothered.

But once these deer are disturbed they evacuate in a hurry. They may cross five or more miles of farm country before they select another home area that satisfies them. All of this highlights three very important principles. First, a farm country section that was loaded with deer last year may not harbor any this year; and vice versa. Two, because these deer move a lot in relatively open country they're far easier to spot than forest deer; three, pre-season scouting is all important. You're wasting your time hunting farm country unless you hunt those precise areas that deer are using.

Charlie and I combine almost all our pre-season scouting with ruffed grouse and pheasant hunting. We jump deer in grouse thickets, we find fresh runways while crossing fields and swales, and we discover places where deer have been feeding on crops. However, unless we jump bucks, we don't know if we've found an area harboring several antlered whitetails or mostly does and fawns. Our next step supplies the answers. We check the animals by actually observing them.

The trick is to slowly drive back roads surrounding chosen areas at the crack of dawn. Dawn scouting—or hunting—is far superior to evening for special reasons. In fall, especially during the rut, deer are moving more than at any other time of year. This is proven by dramatically higher numbers of deer-vehicle accidents during October, November and December. Early fall is when bowhunters invade deer country, and it's also when poaching hits its peak.

Clever bucks quickly become aware of this new pressure, and they react by doing their feeding at night . . . very late a night. Farmer friends tell me that a given field may show no feeding deer at all before midnight, but it may host dozens at 3 A.M.

The later the bucks go out to feed the later they're apt to linger at dawn, especially if they're with does in heat. All of this is why your odds on seeing deer in feeding fields (particularly bucks) are far superior at the crack of dawn than at the falling of dusk.

Dawn scouting has another very positive advantage. Deer leaving a feeding area at break of day are always heading for a bedding area. My partner and I often see deer travel into a particular woodlot, and when we do we have located prime potential for a successful drive.

Driving woodlots is a different ball game than driving forest areas. In big woodlands the best stand sites are along escape routes within the woods the deer are using. This system won't work in small farm-country woodlots because the animals are likely to see, hear or smell standers moving into position. The solution is to take stands in adjacent woodlots the animals are likely to head for.

Another important principle is that it's far easier to drive deer out of small farm-country cover (40 acres or smaller) than large forest areas. The animals know they're vulnerable in small areas so they'll run rather than hide. A two-man team—one driving and one on stand—can be extremely successful in farm country, but woefully ineffective in big woodlands.

Comparative lack of hunting pressure in farm country is still another favorable factor. Tradition tells deer hunters to head for the big woods, so that's where most of them go. Smart bucks in the forests go into hiding as soon as opening-day gunfire alerts them. Farmland bucks hear far fewer gunshots, they're used to normal rural activity, and they're not accustomed to sudden increases in numbers of humans. Consequently they maintain more normal habits, which makes them more vulnerable.

All the things I've mentioned won't help a hunter if he doesn't hunt deer concentration areas. An old-timer once said to me: "Don't look for deer where they've been, look where they are!"

Your first step should be to check potential feeding areas because it's far easier to find deer sign in farm country on feeding grounds than in the much denser cover used for bedding areas. Whitetails have food preferences based on time of year, and they're smart enough to know when various foods will be available.

In my opinion, whitetails love winter wheat and farm crops more than anything else. They also know that when the crops are harvested they have to rely on winter wheat or natural food like acorns.

Let's say that one large area of several square miles harbors well separated corn fields, winter wheat fields, and hardwoods showing good amounts of acorns. During October, the odds are high that the area's deer will feed mostly in standing corn or other crop fields. When the crops are harvested by late October, the herds will shift to winter wheat or grassy areas. Deer in farm country seldom go for acorns and other natural food until the choice man-produced food is gone. The major exception is during wet years, when muddy ground prevents farmers from getting their crops harvested. Find a field of standing corn in late November or during December, and you'll find a prime whitetail feeding area.

Farmland deer use the same runways every day (unless spooked or the food availability pattern changes) because good runway cover is limited. Feeder runways always begin along edges of feeding areas, usually along those edges closest to or bordering woodland cover. I always walk these edges looking for runways showing fresh tracks. When I find lots of fresh tracks I know I've located a feeding area that's being used.

My next step is to find bedding areas by following feeder runways to major runways that lead to thick bedding cover. I don't look for actual beds for several reasons. Often it's difficult to see beds on hard ground. Even when bedding deer make depressions in grass or leaves it's easy to miss seeing them. A well-defined bed in fallen leaves may disappear in a hurry when a strong wind begins blowing. Rain can also destroy visual signs of beds. I know from many hard lessons that a lot of whitetails can bed in a small area and leave few signs of their presence.

There's only one sure way of determining if a potential bedding area actually harbors deer, and that's by jumping the animals. The best time by far to jump them is on a warm, sunny and windless afternoon. On such a day the animals can hear you coming at maximum distance, and they're far more likely to jump and run than hide. Once you actually see deer, you know a bedding area is being used.

There is one distinct disadvantage to farm country hunting. All agricultural areas are private and many landowners post their property. Charlie and I lick that problem with our pre-season scouting combined with bird hunting. Where we get permission to hunt birds we also try to get permission to hunt deer. Consider, too, that there are many abandoned farms these days. Owners of these properties are much more likely to offer hunting permission to responsible sportsmen.

Further, the whitetail population boom in farming areas has led to an all-time high in deer crop damage. Farmers with these problems are welcoming hunters as never before. The picture in Illinois may well by typical.

"Deer forage on a wide variety of crops but they seem to prefer the expensive ones," Forrest Loomis, Illinois' Forest Wildlife Program Chief told me in April, 1985. "We get most of our complaints from farmers who suffer deer damage to high-priced crops such as corn and soybeans. Damage that was tolerated during years of lower market values no longer is ignored.

"In most crop damage circumstances our biologists recommend that landowners should look to intensified hunting (more hunters on their property) during deer seasons to control deer populations. Farmers are getting the idea that controlled legal hunting is the best method of reducing deer damage. Many landowners who wouldn't allow deer hunting years ago now are hoping they can get hunters. It's a great setup for everybody involved."

This is a superb whitetail, but he probably wouldn't qualify for the records. Record heads almost always carry five or more points to a side, unless symmetry, massiveness, and wide spread of over 21 inches drive up the score.

CHAPTER
11

Trophy Hunting

It stands to reason that if a physically healthy man has unlimited time and money he can enjoy the best hunting on earth. Does it follow that if he buys his way into the best game country he is also likely to take a trophy head? Not necessarily, and particularly not if he wants a trophy whitetail deer.

The odds on taking a trophy good enough to make the record book go with the man who hunts big-game other than deer. Consider wild sheep as an example. All but the desert bighorn inhabit the wildest and most remote mountain areas of North America. A sheep hunter has fair odds on downing a record-book ram because he pays top dollar to hunt country that is never seen by the average hunter with average means. He hunts animals that live long enough to grow trophy heads. The same reasoning applies if you go after other wild animals such as grizzly bear, Alaskan-Yukon moose, lion, greater kudu, or what have you.

It's the opposite story with deer, especially whitetails. Most deer live close to man, consequently they are hunted hard by almost anyone who owns or can borrow a rifle. Few bucks live longer than 1½ years. Consider that it often takes a whitetail or mule-deer buck four to six years to grow the best set of antlers he'll ever produce. Such a buck has to make it through at least several hunting seasons before he has the slightest chance of becoming a candidate for the record book.

From what I've said so far you might conclude that it's impossible today to bag a real trophy buck. It's extremely difficult, but not impossible. In another chapter of this book I pointed out that the world-record mule deer was killed in 1972 by Doug Burris, Jr., of San Antonio, Texas. He nailed his monster buck in Colorado. Nearly all of the top twenty typical mule deer

listed in the Boone and Crockett Club record book were taken in the 1960s
and 1970s. Many of the best whitetails were also taken in relatively recent
years. But let me illustrate how difficult it is for you to make the record
book with a deer.

During the last Boone and Crockett Club big-game awards period—
which covered the three-year period from 1980 to 1982—only two whitetail
deer qualified for the record book, in which 312 heads are ranked. Because
there are roughly 1.5 million whitetails bagged annually in North
America—or roughly 4.5 million during that three-year period—the odds
against any one hunter bagging one of those two bucks was 2.25 million to
1. Not only that, but the second-best buck entered in the club's awards
program scored 172⅛ points, a bare 2⅛ points above the minimum 170-
point score required for a typical whitetail's entry into the record book.

Fifteen years ago that magical minimum figure was only 160 points, but
still within range enough to give me the flying twitches for months one season. That fall I killed a typical whitetail buck in Saskatchewan that astounded me. When I approached the downed animal after I shot him I
couldn't take my eyes off his enormous antlers. The beams were so thick
and the tines so long they seemed unreal. At the time I wasn't involved
with trophy hunting as I am now, so I was more impressed than I would be
today. In my mind there wasn't any question that my buck would make the
record book; the question was how close to the top he would rank.

That evening I received an unpleasant shock. I had guessed that the rack
would score over 180 points, but when I scored it with a tape measure I
came up with 166 points. I knew that no big-game antlers or horns can be
officially scored until 60 days after the kill date, to allow for natural drying
and shrinkage. So my hopes of scoring high in the record book were dashed.
Now I knew I'd be lucky if I made the book at all.

I didn't. The final official score was 156 points, just four points short of
the minimum requirement at the time.

I mention this story for several reasons. Even though I was a veteran deer
hunter when I shot that buck, I honestly believed he was one of the best
typical whitetails that ever walked in North America. He certainly wore
the best rack of antlers I've seen on a live whitetail before or since. But he
wasn't nearly as good as he looked as far as the record book was concerned.
Because of my position as editor-at-large for *Outdoor Life* I run into somewhat similar situations every year.

One time in Nebraska I was accused of not knowing what I was talking
about. One of the members of my guide's camp downed a ten-point whitetail. He asked me how high it would rank in the records. The buck had an
immense, impressive rack, but I knew after studying it that it wouldn't
score more than 140 points. The hunter didn't believe me. "That's the biggest buck by far that's been killed around here for years," he said. "They
just don't get bigger than this one. You're wrong. Score him out and we'll
see."

I obliged the fellow. He double-checked each measurement as I made it. We came up with 131 points. He was crestfallen.

Here's another story along the same lines.

After I nailed that Saskatchewan giant I had the head mounted. It hangs in my office where it is seen by many visiting outdoorsmen. Once a visitor from another state studied it closely, then said, "Damn nice buck. But he'll take second place to the one killed by my cousin a couple of years ago."

"Did your cousin have his rack scored by the Boone and Crockett Club?" I asked. "If his buck is a lot better than this one he's a cinch for the record book. And that's a tremendous honor because getting a whitetail buck into the book is hunting's toughest job. You'd do him a great favor by having him get in touch with the Club."

It didn't work out that way. My visitor thought it would be a better idea for me to see the mounted head so he brought it with him on his next trip through my area. When we compared the two heads side by side I felt sorry for the fellow. He stammered when he said, "I can't believe it. Your buck's rack is wider and its tines are longer. It didn't look that big on the wall by itself. Before we matched those racks I thought my cousin's was the best I'd ever seen."

And therein lies a misconception about trophy hunting. A better-than-average whitetail rack coming out of my home area—the northwestern part of Lower Michigan—would be only fair in the big-buck country of northern Michigan. It wouldn't even draw notice in southeastern Saskatchewan where bucks with huge racks are fairly common. The same story holds true with mule deer.

In the foothills of Wyoming I once downed a mule-deer buck which had the best rack I'd seen in four days of hunting. At the time I thought the head was plenty large enough for mounting. It hangs on a wall in my office, too. Three years ago I left the rack of a far larger mule deer buck in the mountains of Montana where I shot him. But then I'd learned how large a really trophy mule deer's rack is. Recently, I brought home the five-point (Western count) antlers of a fine mule deer I killed in the Colorado Rockies. Though it's far more impressive than the antlers of the mounted head on my wall, I didn't even bother to cape the head. I won't pay the expense of another mule-deer head mount until I down a buck that's considerably larger. That accomplishment is possible because I now know the areas where the truly big mule-deer bucks roam.

So trophy hunting can mean two things. If you hunt your local area exclusively, and it's a region that doesn't produce big racks, your goal should be to take a buck that's one of the best ever taken in your surrounding locale. Such an achievement would be a milestone in any deer hunter's career. But if you want to reach for the stars and hit the big-time nationally, then you'll have to hunt the regions where big bucks live. If this is your goal you'll probably have to spend some time and money and hunt hard.

The best key to finding big-buck areas is serious study of the *Boone and*

Crockett Record Book. The book lists the specific areas where all ranked trophies were taken. This is very important because the same areas that have produced big deer with big racks will continue to produce big deer. And the answer isn't all in mineral content of soil, the factor that produces the browse that produces large racks.

Any big-buck area has the right combination of cover, water, escape routes, and the most nutritious browse. If the area is large enough several big bucks will share it. When they die or are killed off other large bucks will move in because the region offers ideal living conditions. This is the precise reason why you sometimes hear of hunters who take trophy bucks quite frequently. These lucky fellows happened to find big-buck country and they hunt it year after year.

But back to the record book. Serious trophy hunters who have studied the book know that many of the best mule-deer racks were taken in New Mexico. Further study shows that a fair share of those bucks came from the Jicarilla Apache Reservation. I once helped a fellow write a story of his hunt on the reservation for *Outdoor Life.* We titled the story "Three Bucks for the Book." That title indicated that all three men on the hunt took bucks that made the record book. They planned their hunt after serious study of the record book.

Colorado produces the most record-book mule deer. You can find the best areas by making a list of the Colorado kill sites tabulated in the book. Mark them with X's on a map of the state. When you're finished with that job you'll find that some of the groups of X's tend to concentrate in specific areas. The next step is to write to the Colorado Guides and Outfitters Association, P.O. Box 983, Glenwood Springs, Colorado 81601. Ask for a list of outfitters operating in the region in which you're interested. (Write the state game agency in any western state for the address of outfitter associations or guides.) Once you make connections with an outfitter or guide in the area, you'll know you're organizing a hunt in big-buck country.

It's a different story if you're interested in trophy whitetails. Most record-book whitetails are taken in the eastern half of the nation, in country that's harder to hunt and is far more heavily hunted than is most of the West. Whitetails are much more clever than mule deer, especially the mature bucks. Also, there aren't as many big-buck areas in whitetail country as there are in mule-deer country. You can pinpoint a few areas such as parts of Arkansas, Ohio, the western end of Michigan's upper peninsula, the southeastern part of Saskatchewan, the northeastern part of Missouri, and southern Texas, but in general an enormous whitetail buck might show up almost anywhere. He'll be an animal that just happened to be a giant, just as our giant basketball and football players seem to come from most anywhere.

Some of these bucks are hunted unsuccessfully for years by hunters who are aware of their presence. A local friend is now in his fifth year of trying for a specific buck he jumped while grouse hunting. He hasn't seen the animal since, though he often has found his tracks. Such stories are common.

Another factor pointing to the cleverness of whitetails is that some of the antlers recorded in the record book are referred to as "pickups." Some of these antlers have been found in the woods, still intact with the skull, long after the buck died. One of the best was found by a farmer on his own property. This guy is an avid deer hunter who thought he knew just about every deer that lived on his place. When you realize that this man had never seen the buck alive, and that the average whitetail's home range is about one square mile, you can appreciate how difficult it is to score on a trophy whitetail. The current world-record nontypical whitetail was found dead of natural causes in St. Louis County, Missouri, in 1981.

There are several general tips that should up your odds on whitetails. First, hunt from a stand. See Chapter 9 for all the details. I'll just emphasize here that the average stillhunter, stalker or driver is trying to match his eyes, ears, and knowledge of his area against an animal whose same facilities and knowledge are far superior. Almost all trophy whitetails are downed by hunters working from stands because the trail-watching hunter is the only one who has the odds in his favor.

Rifle Proficiency

Being an expert with your firearm is all-important. You may get only one chance at a real trophy buck during your lifetime. To blow it because you can't shoot well enough is almost inexcusable. Today the interest in shooting clubs and rifle ranges is higher than ever before. Even if you're a city dweller it's likely there's a place near you where you can practice shooting.

I don't know why, but many deer hunters wait until opening day before picking up their rifles. Except for deer season their rifles are stored away. How proficient would you be with your car, camera, or any other piece of equipment if you used it only once or twice a year? Any firearm is only as good as the man using it.

I'll tell you a little story proving the point, even though it doesn't involve deer hunting. I once knew an Indian guide in northwestern Ontario named Charlie. He told me about the time he had two moose-hunting clients in his canoe. They were canoeing silently along the shoreline of a fly-in lake. Charlie eased his canoe around a sharp point of land and put his hunters almost on top of two bull moose feeding on shallow-water lily pads.

The two Americans shouldered their expensive scope-sighted rifles and began blazing away. The two moose, unhindered by any lead ballast, ran for shore. Water sprayed in glistening sheets as the bulls' hoofs and legs ripped through the water. They dashed out on the beach and melted into thick shoreline brush.

While the shooting was still going on both clients suddenly realized they couldn't hit their targets. One yelled, "Damnit, Charlie, shoot!"

Charlie wasn't normally interested in shooting moose for customers, but this case was different. It was now or never for these guys because it was late on the last day of their hunt. Charlie wanted them to go home happy, but even so he waited till they emptied their rifles and the bulls had disappeared. Then he went into action.

The Indian knew the lay of the land. He figured the animals would run parallel to the shoreline, and if they did they would run around the tip of a narrow peninsula. So he dug in his paddle and rammed the canoe ashore. Then he jumped out and ran up the hill toward the other side of the peninsula. He was almost too late. Just as he cleared the top of the hill he spotted the two bulls running through brush below him. He threw up his old Winchester .30/.30 and dropped both moose. Each took a single slug in the neck.

How can a man with a battered unscoped rifle outshoot two men armed with superior rifles? And how could he do it from an offhand position while panting for breath? Simply because that old Indian was so familiar with his rifle that he could use it as efficiently as he used his canoe paddles and skinning knives. The average deer hunter will never become that fine a shot, but he certainly can improve with practice.

Getting a Good Buck

It seems to me that there are two other major reasons why more trophy bucks *are not* shot each year. When the average hunter gets a chance at an average buck his thoughts are predictable. "I've waited all year for this hunt," he says to himself. "This buck is a good one. I may not spot a better trophy. I may not even get another shot. I'd better take him."

So he shoots. If he is successful his hunt is ended. The larger buck that he might have spotted if he'd kept hunting is therefore safe for the rest of the year as far as this hunter is concerned. The second reason why more big bucks aren't killed is that they're far more clever than average bucks. The average hunter may have the skill to outwit a small buck, but most don't have the skill or patience to compete with the big bruisers.

Recognizing Record Heads

Skill and patience aren't the only things required to nail a trophy. First you have to know what a trophy is. I've already mentioned that most hunters have little understanding of how outstanding a rack of antlers must be to make the record book. Most of us can forget about ever seeing a buck that will qualify for the book, but we're all very interested in taking bucks that will make above-average head mounts for our dens or offices. Any outstanding deer head, professionally mounted, serves to bring back the memories and thrills of a great hunt each time it's viewed. Such memories are what makes hunting so intriguing.

It's very easy to overestimate the size of a rack on a deer before you shoot. I've been hunting deer for many years—I killed my first buck in 1943 when I was sixteen years old—but my heart still tries to jump into my throat when I spot a buck in the woods. My mind seems to shout, "There's a

A trail-watcher's dream come true! Four bucks trot by. A hasty evaluation says that the partially hidden buck at the back sports the best rack. He's a rare ten-pointer with good spread and long tines.

buck." I'm well-convinced this same sort of thing happens to all dedicated deer hunters. If it didn't there wouldn't be much thrill in going deer hunting.

Anyway, when we first sight a buck—if he's wearing a rack of noticeable size—we all jump to the conclusion that the antlers are larger than they really are. I'll be the first to admit that I've shot bucks I expected to be decent trophies, only to run to the kill site and find an animal wearing antlers far smaller than I expected. That's why—when a man spots a buck with an exceptional rack—he's apt to overestimate its dimensions. When such animals are missed they become the basis of the stories that begin with: "Today I missed the biggest buck in the state. I swear that old bruiser would rank near the top of the record book." Well, in reality, the deer probably wouldn't even have qualified for a low ranking.

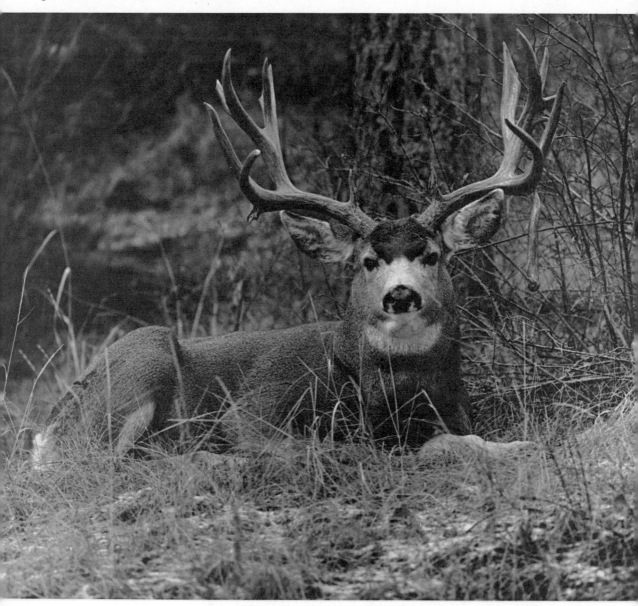

This is an excellent nontypical mule deer. It has an antler spread of about 24 inches, about average for record-book mule deer in both the typical and non-typical categories. As a rule of thumb, if the spread looks about half again as wide as the deer's body, you may be looking at a record.

Again, most hunters just don't realize how massive a buck's rack has to be to be good enough for record-book status. A dramatic realization of this fact came during my 1975 whitetail hunt in south Texas. During this hunt I stopped at Lionel Garza's Texaco station in the town of Freer.

Lionel runs the annual "Muy-Grande" contest which recognizes outstanding whitetail bucks killed in Texas. Garza is dedicated to the sport of trophy hunting. His displays of mounted heads and racks, which were taken by many hunters, cover the walls of his station and a special trophy building behind the station. In addition, he has photos of all the outstanding bucks entered in his contests. Visit Garza's station and you'll be overwhelmed with the evidence of enormous whitetail bucks. Yet, of all those mounted heads, only one was good enough to make the record book.

Antlers and diet. Before I get into telling you what to look for when trying to decide if a trophy buck is good enough to shoot, I want to mention a factor that has an effect on antler development. I've pointed out that deer develop largely on the basis of what they eat. But how much they eat is also important.

How much they eat depends on weather. If a given year in a given area comes up with an early spring, plenty of rain during the summer and a late fall, the area will produce deer with larger than average racks simply because the animals had plenty of nutritious browse during a long period.

In northern states, where deer are subject to extreme physical hardships during severe winters, weather adds another dimension. If the winter is tough and long-lasting, antler development will get a slow start in spring, not only because a buck's physical condition is poor, but also because the new foods he needs are slower than usual in growing. Top that with an early fall and the year simply doesn't produce enough days to promote good growth of browse. Just as farmers experience poor years for crop growth, so a buck experiences poor years for antler growth. This is the reason there are years of good heads and years of poor heads.

Judging heads. There *are* methods of judging the quality of antlers before you shoot. A beginning hunter should keep in mind the difference in size of mule deer racks compared with whitetail racks. As I have pointed out earlier, a whitetail buck boasting antlers measuring 20 inches across the outside spread is really an excellent trophy. But a mule deer's rack measuring 20 inches would hardly rate notice in big-buck country.

If a buck's body is aligned straight toward you or straight away from you, the accepted procedure for estimating antler quality is to compare the width of the rack with the width of parts of the animal's body. The body width of a big whitetail will measure about 15 inches across. This means that even if you manage only a fleeting glimpse of a whitetail wearing antlers wider than his body you're looking at a very good trophy.

But this rule of thumb doesn't hold true with mule deer because a mule deer's rack has to be much wider than a whitetail's to rate as a trophy. The assumption is that a muley buck is a trophy if either antler overhangs the body by at least half the body width.

Here are four young mule deer bucks. Since just-decent mule-deer racks tend to stand higher than those of spectacular whitetails, eastern hunters after record mule deer for the first time tend to be very impressed with the first few mule deer bucks they see. Experience and study of exceptional racks help bring evaluations nearer reality.

Another body feature used in trophy estimation is a buck's ears. With ears cocked the eartip-to-eartip measurement on whitetails is 11 to 14 inches. The same measurement on mule deer is 16 to 18 inches. So if you see a buck of either species with a rack spreading far out beyond his ears you better nail him, especially if he's a whitetail.

The familiar white flag (tail) of a whitetail is also a comparison feature.

Since this flag is often raised when a buck is running it's a dominant feature. If its length is comparable with the height of the buck's antlers the rack is likely to be a great one.

This trick won't work with a mule-deer buck because he has a stingy little tail that he doesn't raise, and also because the trophy rack of a mule deer measures far higher than a whitetail's. The measurement to consider on a broadside muley is the animal's body height from withers to brisket. If the height of the rack approaches the withers-to-brisket dimension he's a beauty.

Trophy Field Care and Mounting

Once the trophy buck is down there are several things that must be done properly before the mounted head will end up as one you'll be proud of. The first consideration is the correct removal of the cape. Don't cut your buck's throat or make any incision in the neck skin. To do so would seriously hamper your taxidermist in preparing a lifelike mount. It's necessary to leave intact much more neck skin than you'd think would be necessary for a full head-and-neck mount. Most poorly mounted heads result because the taxidermist doesn't have enough cape to work with.

Start the job by making a cut through the skin beginning on top of the buck's head just behind the ears. Cut rearward along the top of the neck to a point behind the front shoulders. Then make two vertical cuts—one down each side of the body—to a point where they meet. That point should be at least behind the brisket. Some taxidermists prefer to have these cuts meet just ahead of the forelegs. In any event, when you finish these cuts you'll realize that plenty of skin is required for a good mount.

The trick now is to get the head and cape removed from the rest of the carcass. Start peeling the skin at the point where your horizontal and vertical cuts meet behind the front shoulders. With the aid of a skinning knife, peel the flaps of skin away from the body toward the head. Continue until the freed skin is removed to the base of the skull. Then cut the head free of the carcass by cutting through the neck.

You should get your buck's head and cape to a taxidermist within a few days after the kill to eliminate spoilage. I once found this impossible to do, so I froze the head. I folded the cape, put the works in a cardboard box, sealed the box, and took it to my local meat-packing plant. The box remained in a freezer room for two months.

One definite advantage today's hunter has over hunters of yesteryear is that good taxidermists are far more plentiful. They're far more professional, too. Most old deer heads you see in bars are poor mounts. The majority were done years ago by amateurs who took up taxidermy as a hobby or part-time job. Such shoddy work has been replaced by the extremely lifelike mounts produced by today's professionals who realize that they'll stay in business only if they do excellent work. And it's easier to do professional work now because of modern materials and methods.

Here are the general knife-blade lines for removing the cape, as described in the accompanying text. The key here is to give the taxidermist plenty of neck and shoulder skin to work with.

Even so, you should check out your taxidermist. Look at his displays. Note how realistic they are. If you can't check him out personally, ask for his brochure and a list of references. Contact a couple of those references by phone. They'll tell you in a hurry if they're satisfied with the man's work. The key question to ask is how long it will take to get your head mounted. If the answer is a few weeks I'd advise looking for another taxidermist. The good ones tan their hides before mounting them, and tanning takes time. You won't get a good mount unless the hide is tanned. Tanning is expensive, too. If a guy offers to mount your head for less than $250 you can expect a poor job.

One other thing to consider is where you're going to hang your mount. It's likely there will be one best spot on your office or den wall, and that the mount will look most dramatic if the head is turned either right or left with a curve in the neck. The old-fashioned way of mounting deer so the heads were high and looking straight forward is out. You have to decide which way the head should be turned, and you have to be sure to give these instructions to your taxidermist.

Still another detail to discuss with your taxidermist is how lifelike you

This is Doug Burris, Jr. and some of his mule deer mounts. The head in the center, taken in 1972, ranks as the world record in the North American Big Game Awards Program. With only one abnormal point on its right antler, the head shows excellent symmetry, long points, good mass, and an extraordinary inside spread of 30 6/8 inches. The score: 226.

want your buck to appear. Many taxidermists have beauty in mind more than reality. If you nail a real old buster of a buck he isn't going to be very pretty. Likely he'll have a torn ear, a grizzled snout, and a thick neck. Many taxidermists have a tendency to pretty up rugged features and make the finished job looked more like the bucks you see in paintings. It's up to you to decide what you want. Personally, I perfer deer heads that are more on the rugged side. But be sure to discuss this point. If you don't the odds are your taxidermist will lean toward a pretty deer.

The vast majority of deer hunters are not trophy hunters. Most have little or no knowledge of the Boone and Crockett Club records or the official scoring system. Consequently, many big bucks are shot and never scored because the hunters aren't aware of the excellence of their trophies. The most dramatic example of this is the current world-record typical whitetail. The antlers were discovered hanging on the wall of a bar near Sandstone, Minnesota. Some interested citizen noticed the enormous rack and had it officially scored. It totaled 206⅛ points. Much investigation finally determined that the buck was killed in Burnett County, Wisconsin, in 1914 by James Jordan.

So if you do come up with an enormous rack you owe it to yourself to see if you're due some recognition. Some states have big-buck clubs that recognize outstanding bucks taken within the state. Minimum score totals for state clubs are always lower than those specified by the Boone and Crockett Club. For information on state clubs write to the information-and-education division of your state's conservation department or department of natural resources.

For information on obtaining score charts and on how to get your trophy buck scored write to the Boone and Crockett Club, 205 South Patrick Street, Alexandria, VA 22314. By return mail you'll get the name and address of the official scorer living nearest you. Then it's up to you to contact him.

Here are the current world-record nontypical whitetail deer antlers. The buck that wore them was found dead of natural causes in St. Louis Co., Missouri, in 1981.

Gun Talk

Cartridges

Because of my profession as an outdoor writer and editor I find myself in the fortunate position of being able to make two extended deer hunts each year. During the last fifteen years I've taken an average of two whitetails or mule deer each season. All of those animals were downed with 100-grain .243 slugs. One big mule deer managed to run off 60 yards after being hit just back of the lung area, a bad shot. One whitetail made it 30 yards before piling up, another whitetail buck struggled about 10 feet before caving in. All other deer (plus some antelope) I've shot during the fifteen-year period dropped in their tracks. So the main reason I shoot a .243 is that it's just plain amazingly deadly on deer. I don't have to have anybody tell me it's deadly; I know it's deadly from plenty of personal experience.

Why is it so deadly? Because its high-velocity, rapidly expanding bullet hits and reacts with an enormous degree of shock. Deer hunters are finally coming to realize that heavy, round-nose, controlled-expanding bullets just aren't the best medicine for deer because these animals aren't very big. A lot of big-caliber gunners lose their venison because slugs weighing much over 150 grains can go right through a deer while expanding very little unless they hit solid bone. A 100-grain .243 bullet—or others of comparable weight and design in such calibers as the 6.5mm, 6mm, .264, .270, .257 Roberts, .280, .284, 7mm Magnum, and the .30/06—begin expanding soon after contact. By the time they reach the inside of a buck they're really blowing up, and that's why they're so deadly. Quick-opening bullets hitting at high-impact velocity are by far the best for deer hunting.

Another advantage of the modern high-velocity cartridge is its flat trajectory. With such a cartridge, should a long-range shooting opportunity present itself, you have a bullet that will handle the situation. For example, if you sight in a .243 rifle to hit dead-on at 25 yards the bullet will hit only two inches high at 100 yards and only four inches low at 300 yards. This means you could aim for the lung area of a buck standing anywhere from 25 yards to 300 yards away and be reasonably sure of a fatal hit. In other words, you wouldn't have to worry about holding high for the 300-yard shot as did the old-timer with his .30/30. Today's high-velocity flat-shooting cartridges enable you to hold the same point of aim every time on any deer within reasonable range. Just get a sight picture on the lung area and touch off.

These days, deer hunters often make trips to relatively distant areas for mule deer and whitetails, and long-range shooting is much more common than it was years ago when most gunners stuck to their local areas where shooting ranges held to a norm.

The trouble with long-range work is that most hunters don't have the shooting experience to handle it. We all hear about the guys who nail mule deer across canyons with 500-yard kills, but it's best to take those stories with more than several grains of salt. Consider that 500 yards is the length of five football fields placed end to end. You could hardly see a deer that far away in most terrain conditions.

Then consider how far a bullet drops from line of sight at extreme range. Even a .243, sighted in at 200 yards—which is a fairly long range—will drop its bullet more than 40 inches out at 500 yards. In my opinion successful 500-yard shots are pure luck unless the shot is wide-open at a stationary target; even then, the rifleman has to be blessed with good fortune if he even hits the deer at that range, let alone puts his slug into a vital area.

Add to all this that the average hunter's range estimation can be pretty sloppy. It has to be. How much range estimation practice have you done in your lifetime? Most of us would have to answer, "darn little." But we can help ourselves. Practice range estimation whenever you take a walk or while hunting small game. Pick a spot ahead that you guess to be 200 yards. Pace it off. You'll probably be surprised to find it's far closer to 150 yards. An estimated distance of 400 yards will be more likely to measure closer to 300. That's why you hear those stories of 500-yard kills. If the guys who made them later paced the range off, they'd most likely find they'd been toying with the truth.

Best choice for deer hunting: fast-opening bullets in the 100- to 150-grain class. In the bullet-expansion photos shown here, a Remington Core-Lokt pointed bullet enters gelatine and begins expanding almost immediately. The mushrooming of the lead core continues until the thickest portion of the metal jacket resists further mushrooming and helps hold the bullet together.

These cutaway drawings show the relationship of lead to jackets in the Rem-ington Core-Lokt soft-nose and soft-point bullets. Many hunters using rifles of .30 caliber or larger favor the soft-nose bullet because it provides maximum mushrooming and shocking power. The soft nose loses velocity and energy more rapidly than the flatter-shooting pointed bullet.

Top that off with the unusual light conditions commonly confronted while you're deer hunting. Things look farther away than they really are at dawn and evening. Your buck will also look farther away in snow or fog. So practice range estimation with the pacing-off technique during the off season. This will help you improve your percentage of hits when actually shooting at deer. The guys who shoot the most deer at long range are good at judging distance.

Some experts become proficient at estimating distances by dividing the ground between the shooting position and the target into 50- or 100-yard segments. I once estimated the number of football-field lengths between my stand and a mule deer buck in Wyoming. I came up with 3½, which equated to 350 yards. When I paced off the killing shot I came up with 326 yards.

Rifles

I don't believe in the theory that eastern whitetail hunters should use a light, fast-pointing rifle and western hunters a heavier, flat-shooting rifle. For one thing, there are some opportunities for long-range shooting in the East, and there are a lot of mule deer shot at short ranges in the West.

In fact, North American deer are hunted in more places and over more types of terrain than any other big-game animal by far. This fact suggests that it's simply impossible to conclude that any one deer rifle is the "best" anywhere. If one rifle in one caliber was the best in a given area most deer hunters in that area would be using a specific gun and cartridge combination. You just don't see this in deer woods today.

What you do see is more and more hunters going to bolt-action rifles shooting high-velocity cartridges. This modern trend is noticeable everywhere in deer country, East, West or in between. I think the reason is that the "brush-buster" myth has been exposed, that such supposed truths as the advantages of the semiautomatic have not proved to be realistic, and that many of today's traveling hunters want a rifle and cartridge combination that works reasonably well in the East or West.

The important point is that the ease-of-use offered by modern rifles, and the ballistics offered by modern cartridges, have significantly narrowed the advantages and disadvantages long claimed in the East-West controversy. It's a controversy that just isn't very important anymore. And one of the main reasons, one I mentioned earlier, is that any rifle can be a good deer rifle if the man who is using it is a good deer hunter. Go with a modern rifle shooting a modern high-velocity bullet in the 100- to 150-grain bracket and you'll be well-armed wherever you hunt deer.

Shotguns

Another subject I haven't mentioned in this chapter is the use of shotguns loaded with slugs or buckshot. I've never hunted deer with a shotgun, but I've talked with a lot of hunters in farm country who are limited by law to the use of these firearms. The serious ones tell me that the specially barreled slug guns equipped with low-power scopes are quite accurate out to 100 yards. They claim that regular-choked shotguns shooting slugs lose accuracy at about 50 yards, and that the use of buckshot ought to be outlawed.

The thing with buckshot is that it's extremely dangerous. A shotgun shooting buckshot sprays lethal balls in several flight patterns. Your chances of hitting someone are far higher with nine or more balls than with one slug. Further, you can aim a slug. Your chance of hitting a deer at point of aim with buckshot is practically zero. Nobody can tell where buckshot will hit a deer so the odds of crippling zoom.

If you want to be a serious deer hunter and you hunt where rifles are legal don't even consider using a shotgun. Your investment in a good rifle and scope will average out to very few dollars per hunting season if you have a reasonable number of hunting years ahead of you. If you're limited by state or county laws to the use of a shotgun for your deer hunting, you'll be wise to invest in one of the specially barreled slug guns and a low-power scope.

Scopes—And How to Use Them

Though there's no substitute for deer-hunting experience when it comes to knowing how to shoot a deer, at no time in history have modern rifles, ammunition, scopes and equipment been so reliable as they are now. The so-so deer hunter of today is going to eat a lot more venison than his counterpart of years ago because he has the opportunity of hitting his buck with modern equipment. Let's develop this thought a bit further.

Years ago the Winchester Model 94 .30/30 was a famous deer rifle. Winchester has sold more than 3 million of them, practically all to deer hunters, since the rifle was introduced in 1894. Twenty-five or more years ago when you saw another deer hunter in the woods he probably would be carrying a .30/30. How many of those rifles do you see in today's woods? Not many, and here's why:

The muzzle velocity of 170-grain factory loads for my .30/30 is 2,220 feet per second, and their energy at 100 yards is 1350 foot pounds. The muzzle velocity of 100-grain factory loads for my .243 is 2960 feet per second, and the energy at 100 yards is 1620 foot pounds. Obviously the .243 slug, and others comparable to it, steps out faster and hits with more shocking power.

Sight-in a .30/30 to hit at point of aim at 100 yards. If you have to shoot at a deer 300 yards away your bullet will drop 29.6 inches from point of aim. My .243 slug will drop only 12.2 inches. Again it's obvious that, given the same shooting opportunity, the man firing the .243 or a comparable modern caliber is much less likely to miss than the man with the .30/30 if both men have the same shooting skill.

Going a step further we can say that the old-timer with a .30/30 would have no business shooting at a deer 300 yards away because his iron sights and beer-belly bullet trajectory would give him a very bad combination of sight picture and bullet-placement estimation. The same guy shooting my .243 would have a most reasonable shot because he would be shooting a flat-trajectory bullet and he could turn my variable scope up to 9x and be presented with a very good sight picture. Also, if shooting light happened to be poor, iron sights would be difficult to line up. A scope gathers light, so it offers a far better sight picture and will allow a hunter to shoot earlier in the morning and later in the evening, especially on the dull days which are common in deer country everywhere. This is crucial in whitetail woods because deer begin moving at the first hint of dawn, and again at dusk.

Consider another important point. Most whitetails are shot in thick brush, which means the hunter must shoot through openings in the brush so his bullet won't be deflected before it gets to his buck. A scope, because of its magnification, often makes it possible for a hunter to pick a clear path for his bullet. Iron sights of any type lack this advantage.

Also, a scope has more of a built-in fail-safe system for accurate shooting than does an iron-sight setup. With iron sights you have to line up two different sighting points at different distances from the eye. With a scope you have only one sighting point, normally the intersection of the crosshairs.

I believe that many shooters, especially inexperienced deer hunters, tend to line iron sights on a deer's vital section and then look up as they pull the trigger. This tendency results in shooting high and is due partly to buck fever and partly to the fact that it's difficult to keep two sights lined up, especially on a moving deer. You can't fall victim to this problem with a scope because you must have the crosshairs (or post) on the buck to get a sight picture. If you look up for any reason that sight picture is gone immediately. So, with a scope, you either have a good sight picture or none at all. This is not true with iron sights. Also, a scope is superior on running shots because you can try to keep the horizontal crosshair along the deer's body. It's a sighting reference line that you don't get with iron sights.

The biggest problem with using a scope is its comparatively narrow field of view. The average hunter thinks he should close his left eye as he mounts his rifle for the shot so that he can pick up his target through the lens with his right eye. This is *all wrong*.

You should get into the habit of keeping both eyes open as you shoulder your rifle. Use the same technique you use with a shotgun. In this way you can see both the deer and his surroundings with both eyes until you get roughly on target. This eliminates the problem many scope users have when they suddenly see a deer against the wide landscape, then have trouble finding him through the scope. This happens because the field of view from natural eyesight becomes abruptly narrowed.

You should get roughly on target with both eyes open before you close the left eye and lay the crosshairs exactly where you want them for the shot. The reverse is correct for left-handed riflemen. The both-eyes-open technique will greatly help the sight-picture problem that many unknowing scope users complain about.

Most hunters who have trouble finding game through a scope bring it on themselves because they never look through their scopes except during deer season. Practice makes perfect in anything we do, so it's just common sense to practice with your scope during the off season. The both-eyes-open technique can be used for dry-firing practice any time and anywhere. You could take a few moments right now to pick up your rifle and do a little scoping practice through a window in your home. Do this several times a year and you'll become familiar enough with your equipment to find an instant sight picture.

A good trick I've always promoted is to get plenty of practice with a scoped .22 rifle. I use one for small-game hunting before deer season and for plinking year-round. When you get to the point where you get pretty good with the .22 you won't have any problem finding game with the larger scopes used on deer rifles. Any shooting practice with any type of scope helps lick the sight-picture problem.

What scope is best? There's no specific answer, but much depends on where you hunt. If you hunt in densely wooded whitetail country where brush is thick and shots are short you'll want a scope with a wide field of view. Most modern scopes have a very wide field of view, which is the main reason they have become so popular in recent years. The scopes of years ago had such narrow fields of view that most old-timers figured they were nearly worthless. They were right, but that's all changed now.

An average modern scope of 2½x will present a view circle of 42 to 44 feet at 100 yards. A 4x covers 30 to 34 feet. As the power increases the view-circle coverage decreases. Short-range whitetail hunters will limit their ability for quick shooting in thickets if they go beyond 4x.

However, if the same hunters mix their deer gunning with occasional trips west to mule-deer states where shots are often long, they'll be limited with their 2½-to-4x scopes because of lack of target definition at long range. One answer for these men is a variable scope which will adjust from, say, 2 to 7x or 3 to 9x. I have scopes on my deer rifles in both categories, so I'm set to hunt whitetails in the East or mule deer in the West with no problems concerning scope power.

There's one problem with scopes that seems to be a holdover from the old days. During those times it was common practice to come in out of the cold and stack rifles in the corners of cabins or tents, perhaps near blazing-hot wood stoves. This habit caused no problem because the rapid change from cold to hot temperature had little effect on iron sights. It's a different story when glass optics and mounts are involved. Too-rapid temperature changes can expand or contract scope mounts and stocks, and cause them to shift sufficiently to change the point of aim.

My most telling experience of this sort of thing occurred during a hunt for mule deer in the West. We were in a tent camp during a blizzard. The temperature plummeted. We stayed in camp for a day and a half, and my rifle happened to be placed near a hot stove. The next day I was on a stand when a fine mule-deer buck trotted up and stopped in front of me. I lined up on his lung area and touched one off. He piled up on the spot.

I was very proud of that shot until I examined the carcass. I couldn't believe my eyes when I found that my slug had broken the buck's back. The situation confounded me till I realized that my scope had to be lined off my point of aim. I test fired the rifle later and found that it shot high and to the right. And that was a mystery because it had shot exactly on target when I tried it the day before the hunt. The rifle hadn't been dropped or abused in any way. I finally came to the conclusion that the rapid temperature change was the culprit.

Since that day I've been careful not to make the same mistake. If I'm hunting my local area I store my rifle away from heat runs in my house or in my locked car after I have sighted it in. If I'm on a trip I store it in the coolest and safest place available. (Fogging, either on the inside or outside of a scope, can be caused by rapid temperature changes, too. Storing my rifle in the coolest place available also licks this problem.) And, if I'm on a trip, I always resight my rifle after I reach my destination. Often this can't be accomplished before I reach the hunting area, but I'd much rather risk spooking game than shooting at a fine buck with a rifle that doesn't shoot where I think I'm aiming it.

When scopes first became popular with deer hunters there was the tendency to feel that they were fragile and could easily be knocked out of line, particularly in vehicles and airplanes. Such concern is understandable, but most scopes and mounts manufactured today are far more rugged than the early models. With normal care you won't have to worry much about your scope's vulnerability.

You'll be a lot better off worrying more about the condition of the optics. The average automobile driver wouldn't think of driving with a dirty windshield, yet few hunters seem concerned with the fact that a scope's lenses can easily become dusty, water-spotted, dirty, finger-marked, or oil-smeared. Trying to aim through such neglected lenses dramatically increases the odds of missed shots. If you don't have protective caps for the ends of your scope you should buy a pair. Keep caps on your scope at all times except when actually hunting. While in the field I keep a few sheets of camera-lens tissue in my wallet. It takes only a moment to clean my scope's optics whenever they become dusty or dirty. Camera-lens tissues can be purchased at any photo shop, and they won't scratch a lens as will your dry shirttail or handkerchief.

Where to Hit Them

Regardless of what caliber rifle or sighting setup you use the object of the game is always to put your bullet where it will make a clean kill. Since bullet placement is the critical factor it logically follows that the biggest vital area of a deer will be the easiest to hit. The lung area is very vulnerable since lungs are filled with blood vessels and protected by only a thin rib cage. Hit a deer in the lungs with any expanding bullet or suitable caliber and he's yours. He may go a few feet or yards, but he's going to go down in the immediate area and he's going to stay down.

As long as there are deer hunters there will be arguments about this premise. Many veterans say a deer shot in the heart, brain, neck, or spine will drop in his tracks. This is true in most cases, but my contention is that the guy who can hit these small areas consistently has the shooting ability to make the Olympics. Shooting at deer under normal hunting conditions is too tough a job to permit hitting the smaller vital areas with any degree of success.

During my forty-two years in the deer woods I've seen so many bucks shot in the guts, back quarters, or legs that I long ago concluded that many hunters don't have the shooting ability to consistently hit a deer, period, let alone in a specific area. Even among good rifle shots there are few who can

The lungs make up the largest vital area on a deer. A shot for the lungs that goes high may hit the spine; forward, it may smash the shoulder; low, it may enter the heart—each shot capable of downing a deer. Aiming for the lungs will give you the optimum record of kills over the years.

keep all their offhand shots in a one-foot circle at 100 yards or a two-foot circle at 200 yards. So what sense is there in the advice of many so-called experts who promote heart, head, spine, or neck shots? The average guy simply can't hit targets that small under hunting conditions. I lost a couple of bucks years ago because I gambled on shots I should not have tried.

Just before the 1958 deer season my family and I moved into our new home. I had a beautiful den with a wall perfect for hanging a head-and-neck mount of a trophy buck. I had a couple of buck mounts but neither seemed to do justice to that new den wall. I decided I was going to try for a really fine Michigan whitetail.

The first day of that deer season I passed up an average six-pointer. A week later I got my chance at a bigger buck. I was on a stand near a narrows in a small lake. Deer often used that narrows as a swimway when they were pushed by drivers. This particular buck swam across from the north side of the lake. I was on the south side. After looking at him through my binoculars I was sure his rack had four points on one side and five on the other. A fine specimen for my den. I decided to try for him as soon as he stepped into the point of woods 70 yards in front of me.

But he didn't come ashore where I expected him to. Instead he swam closer to me and stepped into the woods only 30 yards away. I decided to try for a spine (backbone) shot because I knew I wouldn't ruin much meat, the head, or the cape. For some strange reason I figured the shot would be easy because the buck was broadside and standing still, and I was aiming from the relatively stable sitting position. So I touched one off.

That fine buck blasted out of there under full power with his flag high. I took another desperation shot but I knew I'd goofed. My first bullet must have gone over his back by not more than an inch. When I realized this and the fact that the same amount of sighting error would have produced a kill had I aimed for the lung area, I was beside myself with disgust. As it turned out I didn't get a head mount or vension that year.

One time I was stillhunting along the edge of a small pond in northern Wisconsin. A new fall of fluffy snow was on the ground. It was so soft that my movements were practically silent. Because of the ideal stillhunting conditions I practically walked on top of a spikehorn buck. He was drinking out of the pond, unaware of me, and I spotted him as I came around a bank. He was no more then 30 yards away. I thought I had a perfect opportunity for a heart shot.

When I fired, the buck wheeled and bolted into thick cover. I didn't have time to squeeze off a second time, but during the instant it took for the whitetail to disappear I noticed he was dragging his left front leg. I knew in a flash my bullet had gone a bit low and to the left and had broken the deer's foreleg. I mentally kicked myself all over the creek bottom for not having shot for the lung area where the near miss would have been a fatal hit. As it turned out another hunter got the wounded buck after I'd tracked him for an hour, so I didn't feel as bad as I would have if I'd been convinced I'd left a wounded animal in the woods.

Why do so many hunters discount the deadliness of the lung shot? A good question, and I can only guess at the answer. It seems to me that a good many riflemen feel that if a high-powered slug hits bone it will blow up something and create sudden and violent shocking force. This may be okay if you're after dangerous big game but it doesn't hold true when you're after deer. If you put a properly expanding slug of good construction and weight into a deer's lungs, it's a physical impossibility for him to go far because an expanding bullet will produce profuse hemorrhaging and the animal has to drown in his own blood in moments. It's as simple as that.

Check Results of Every Shot

Last fall during the second weekend of our Michigan deer season, I was attempting to drive deer out of streamside thickets toward my son who was on a stand. While fighting my way through a particularly thick clump of brush I spotted a dead deer only a few yards ahead. It proved to be a fine forkhorn buck that had been shot through the heart. The animal had probably died the previous weekend because it was now bloated and partially spoiled.

Through the years I've found other dead deer in the woods, and every time I've come upon the sight I get mad as hell. A lot of prime meat is wasted every fall by deer hunters who shoot at bucks and assume they have missed when they actually haven't. There are various reasons for this. As I mentioned above, many hunters go after deer with rifles and ammunition which combine far more firepower than is ideal for killing deer. The guy shooting a heavy slug in, say, a .30/06, is likely to put his bullet straight through a deer before it has a chance to expand.

Expanding bullets that blow up inside a deer produce the extreme shock that kills. Bullets that don't do their expanding jobs usually produce fatal wounds if the animal is hit in a vital area, but he may run a considerable distance before dying. And even a buck that is hit properly with a proper bullet may show no immediate sign of being mortally wounded. I once shot at close range a mule-deer buck in Montana which didn't even flinch when my slug blew up in his lungs. I couldn't believe it when he turned and ambled toward some thickets. I put another 100-grain bullet into his lungs just as he was walking into cover. That one didn't seem to phase him either.

The buck didn't go very far before caving in, but from all appearances it seemed as if I had missed him with both shots. The same thing happens all too frequently with deer hunters, especially on long shots. Never take it for granted that you missed. Deer have amazing stamina. If you haven't heard stories of bucks running off with their hearts exploded from bullets you haven't been deer hunting very long. Some deer, especially those frightened before the shot, refuse to go down. They'll run off and die while running before they'll drop. This is common when a deer is hit in a vital area with a bullet not appropriate for the job. Such bucks don't go far before piling up, but they can begin a dash with strength enough to convince you that your bullet missed.

So it's common sense to check the results of every shot. Carefully mark the spot where you last saw your buck. Go to that spot and look for blood or hair. If you find no indication of a hit it's best to cut 20- to 30-yard arcs across the last direction the animal was headed. Look for blood as well as looking for tracks. If you find nothing return to the original spot and repeat the search through bigger arcs. If you still find no signs of a hit you can be reasonably sure you missed.

The reason this system should be employed is that deer do not always drop blood immediately upon being hit. Often they'll move off some distance before the bleeding starts. When you do find blood you can often tell where your deer was hit. Bright frothy blood with visible bubbles indicates a heart or lung shot. A buck hit in these areas won't go far. Dark beet-red blood usually means a bullet through the liver. A liver shot usually puts a deer down quickly, too. If the blood contains bits of yellow or green matter you're faced with tracking a gut-shot animal. Such a wounded deer will often travel a considerable distance before dying. Clear, uniform blood of medium color almost always means a muscle wound that does not penetrate the body cavity. Animals so wounded are usually not found and generally recover.

Sometimes a mortally wounded deer will drop no blood at all. In this case his tracks may be a clue that he has been hit. A wounded deer will usually leave game trails and other deer he may have been with at the shot. He wants to be alone and will go off by himself. If a deer's tracks suddenly deviate from his original course it could mean that he's been hit. Be especially suspicious of deer that head for nearby water. It's instinctive for wounded deer to go to water. They feel that water will cool and heal their wound. In any event, smart hunters consider as wounded every deer that moves away after the shot. Only after careful checking should you conclude that your shot actually missed.

The Box Your New Gun Comes In

A new gun today may be well-traveled by the time it reaches the hands of its ultimate owner. Along the way from manufacturer to wholesaler to retailer to customer, it receives rough handling. Yet your gun must survive this journey in factory-fresh condition—unscratched, unmarred, undamaged in any way. Otherwise it can't be sold. This is accomplished because quality guns leave the factory packed and recessed in form-fitting styrofoam or cardboard constructions which do an amazingly effective job of protecting them from damage. Surrounding the gun inside its contour-hugging form is a heavy-duty cardboard box. This is further protected by a cardboard shipping sleeve. Unfortunately for some guns, they may be the best—and sometimes the last—protection they'll ever have.

The safest way for you to transport a gun is inside one of the hard, foam-lined modern carrying cases made specifically for this purpose. But the next-best method, and one that's free, is to use the original protective shipping box.

So, when you buy a new gun don't leave its box with your dealer. Ask for the original box, bring it home, and keep it. If, for some reason you ever wish to return your rifle to the factory, your shipping carton is right at hand. Did you ever try to improvise a package for shipping a gun? It's a tough job.

Because of modern design, today's rifles require less care to keep them in working order than their counterparts of years go. They're designed so that the parts regularly needing special attention can be reached or removed quickly and easily. Actually, a modern rifle can be as ruined by too much care as by too little. Most grit and grime builds up on a gun because it has too much oil and grease to stick to. An over-oiled gun operates stiffly in freezing temperatures, too. Don't lubricate your rifle any more than is necessary to keep the parts operating efficiently. Stubborn gunk is easily removed with a rag dipped in gunpowder solvent.

Many hunters think they should oil the trigger mechanism to get a smooth trigger pull. The opposite is true. Modern rifle trigger mechanisms are quite complex and function best when they are absolutely clean and dry. If you oil them you beget crud which, in turn, makes trigger-pull rough and inconsistent. So not only should you avoid oiling your trigger mechanism, but you should be very careful to keep oil out of it when you oil other parts of your rifle.

All you need to clean your rifle is a cleaning rod with a bronze-bristled brush, solvent, an old toothbrush, oil, some clean rags, and barrel patches. Start by giving the bore a good wetting with solvent. Let it soak for a few minutes and then scrub it clean with the rod and brush. Run the brush completely through the bore before reversing direction. Repeat about ten times. This will remove streaks of lead and powder deposited in the barrel. Start from the breech if your rifle is a bolt-action. This will eliminate possible damage at the end of the muzzle, which could result in loss of accuracy. If your rifle is not a bolt-action, you'll have to clean from the muzzle end, but be careful. Be sure your rod and brush are clean; a good barrel can be ruined with a gritty cleaning rod.

After you finish the brushing operation, run a couple of clean patches through the bore. Then clean powder residue and grit or dirt from the various contours and slots of other metal parts with the toothbrush. Follow by wiping with a solvent-wetted rag, then wipe off all parts with a dry rag. Now rub a light coat of oil over everything and run an oily patch through the bore.

At this point your cleaned rifle is ready for storage, and this is the point at which a great mistake can be made: don't store a rifle in a gun case because gun cases often create and hold condensation which can cause rust and corrosion. One dramatic episode taught me how fast such storage can ruin a rifle.

Some local crook decided he wanted a good deer rifle. He decided my house would be the place to get one for free, so he broke in while my family and I were away on a winter vacation. In addition to stealing the rifle he stole a gun case in which he stored the rifle during anticipation of the following fall's hunting season. Small-time burglars usually get caught, as this one did. The police nailed him on another charge in late summer, searched his residence, and found my rifle. (I had reported the serial number when it was stolen.) The metal parts were almost completely covered with rust.

Store your guns in a dry, well-ventilated place such as a gun cabinet or part of a closet. Don't store them in the open where dust can accumulate on them. Guns in racks on open walls make great exhibitions, but guns stored in this manner collect dust in a hurry.

CHAPTER
13

Modern
Hunting Gear

Some years ago I was on a deer hunt in which hunting from tree stands was almost mandatory because of thick ground cover. In this situation, a hunter on the ground could see only a few yards through the thickets, but had good visibility from a vantage point in a tree. My problem was my fear of climbing trees. I had to climb up into a big pine tree and sit on a branch. I didn't like any part of the deal, and when the hunt was over I told myself I was all finished with climbing trees. But thanks to modern gear I've changed my mind.

My new attitude developed after *Outdoor Life* published an article of mine about how to hunt from stands. One of the letters I received from readers came from Jim Baker, President of Baker Manufacturing Company (P.O. Box 1003, Valdosta, Georgia 31601). Said Jim: "Our Baker Tree Stand is the only patented tree stand that will actually *climb* a tree. It offers a firm, secure platform on which to sit or stand. I'd like to send you one for field testing and evaluation."

I took up Jim's offer for two reasons. First, if the contraption would climb a tree safely I could forget about my fear of climbing. Second, if it really offered a firm and secure platform I wouldn't have to worry about falling off a branch.

When I got the unit I discovered that it's light, folds up easily for carrying on a shoulder strap, needs no steps, does no damage to trees, and works as easily as Jim claimed it would. You merely put your feet in its platform stirrups, grasp the tree trunk with a bear hug, and walk the stand up the tree. An accessory, which works on a lever principle, eliminates the bear hug. Through a mechanical-advantage system you merely lever yourself and your stand up a tree with a series of easy arm and leg motions.

The Baker Tree Stand is a good example of how modern gear gives today's hunter advantages the old-timers never had. There are many such advantages.

Wet and cold feet are a thing of the past when you place your trust in top-quality modern boots. Browning, for example, makes a boot crafted from heavy-duty, silicone-impregnated Boulder leather. The top is hydrodynamically sealed to sure-footed crepe lug soles. These boots are guaranteed waterproof when given recommended care. In addition they are fully insulated from top to toe, incorporate German speed lacing, and offer the comfort of glove leather lining and cushioned insoles. Even the tongue is uniquely contoured for comfort and unencumbered lacing. Strong Taslan laces complement all the other features.

The hunter of years ago would have drooled over such boots. Alas for him, the materials and manufacturing processes needed to produce them were unknown in those days. Many other companies beside Browning make top-quality boots for hunters, as well as a myriad of other clothing items. You can get a Browning catalog by writing: Browning, P.O. Box 500, Morgan, Utah 84050.

The Browning "Sportsman's Check List" is the most complete I've seen. You'll find it, with minor changes, on accompanying pages. It lists equipment used by all outdoorsmen.

Are you still using the old-time tent that weighs a ton, takes four people to pitch and strike, is subject to leaking, and smells of mildew? If you are you're way behind the times. Today's tents made of such materials as nylon taffeta and cotton drill are practically condensation free. As well, they don't leak and are lightweight. I have a two-man 5x7 tent that weighs only five pounds including poles, stakes, and stuff bag. The rigging is simple and quick. The tent includes elastic shock cords at each corner which allow them to give in a strong wind. It also has coil zippers, a tough waterproof floor and a waterproof rain fly. In short, it's a far cry from the two-man tent of the old days. Today's tents incorporating modern design with modern materials come in all sizes from one-man to big wall tents suitable for a party of hunters.

One of the most dramatic examples of how hunters' gear has changed over the years is the compound bow now being used by many archers. These bows combine space-age technology with the age-old art of archery. They shoot your arrows as much as 50 percent faster than a recurve bow of equal weight. Yet they're shorter and easier to shoot. They incorporate a system of pulleys and cables that work somewhat like a block and tackle. The mechanical-advantage system enables you to hold an arrow at full draw without tiring. Even many of today's conventional bows would make the old-timers stare with disbelief. They never heard of fold-down bows, adjustable draw weight, bow sights, stabilizer rods, sure-fold arrow rests, aluminum arrows, and other modern developments.

And how about propane-powered camping equipment such as lanterns, heaters, and stoves? The advantages of a lightweight, easy-to-operate pro-

This tree stand can be backpacked until needed for climbing a limbless tree trunk. The hunter attaches his feet to the stand and, using the climber, pulls himself up the trunk (above). Teeth on the stand and climber prevent slippage. When the hunter reaches desired height, the climber becomes a seat (left).

pane stove over firewood are numerous. For example, with firewood rain can turn camping into a drab world of cold meals. Without a fire you're also subjected to shivering in the darkness. A propane stove isn't the least fazed by rain, nor is a propane lantern or heater. They'll burn on right through the heaviest downpours. With such equipment the old days of chopping wood, putting up with smoky campsites, and huddling around a fire for light or heat are gone. Deer-hunting campers of past eras might feel there is something almost immoral about the ease and convenience of camping today. They'd probably feel that things ought to be a little tougher. Maybe so, but modern equipment enables today's hunter to spend more time actually hunting, more time being comfortable, and less time doing camp chores.

Even such minor items as sunglasses can be of extreme benefit to the modern deer hunter. Today's polarized sunglasses can reduce glare, eliminate squinting, and help to discern game that tends to disappear into backgrounds. A hunter can stretch his day by using amber or yellow shooting glasses during early morning and late evening. Such glasses intensify light and contrast. They enable you to pick out detail in poor light conditions.

How to Choose Binoculars

In the next chapter I'll point out why binoculars can be a tremendous aid to spotting deer, but here I'll discuss choosing the right pair.

The first decision to make is what magnifying power is best for you. The basic reason for using binoculars is to make things look closer. This is accomplished by magnifying the image. A glass that makes an object look six times closer is termed a six-power glass and is marked 6x. In addition to power you should also consider light-gathering ability, field of view, size, weight, and cost.

A glass anywhere from six to eight power is preferred by most deer hunters. If you go beyond 8x you should remember that increased power has its drawbacks. The larger-power glasses are heavier and therefore less steady to hold and have reduced fields of view and poorer light-gathering qualities. When you're trying to focus in on deer in brush or at long distances, the problem of holding a high-power pair of glasses steady is important. This is one reason why it makes little sense to go beyond 8x.

Remember that each little tremor or shake is multiplied in direct proportion to the power of your glass. Six-power binoculars will multiply each shake six times, so it's obvious you'll get a clearer picture in terms of shake with a 6x glass than you will with a 10x.

Field of view—the amount of landscape you can see through your glasses without moving them—decreases as power increases. An 8x glass has only three-fourths the field of view that a 6x has. Increased magnification also cuts down relative brightness. A 6x pair of binoculars has four times as much light-gathering brightness as a 10x. Since deer hunters often find their best action in poor light conditions (early and late in the day) it again makes little sense to choose binoculars beyond 8x.

If your glasses are marked with the numbers 6x30, the "six" is the power and the "thirty" is the size of the objective lens in millimeters. The size of the objective lens has a big effect on performance. The larger the objective lens the brighter the image will be. So it's obvious that a 6x15 wouldn't serve you nearly as well as a 6x30.

From my experience I'd say that most of the deer hunters I know who have had a lot of experience with glassing use either 6x30 or 7x35 binoculars. Maybe I have odd eyes, but my favorite pair is 8x40. Anyway, this is the range you should choose from. You can buy binoculars for as little as $50, but you won't get much quality for that price and you won't get fully optically coated lenses. Expect to pay about $200 for a good pair.

Until recent years, good binoculars have been pretty much standard in size. Now you can get good-quality glasses that weigh as little as six or seven ounces. They're so small they fit into a shirt pocket.

How to Choose a Hunting Knife

The more experienced the hunter, the smaller the knife he carries. Why? Because you don't need a blade longer than four inches or so to perfectly execute the gutting, skinning, quartering, and caping of your deer. A good knife is small, sharp, and handy. Those Bowies with the 10- and 12-inch blades may look good swinging from your belt, but when it comes to field dressing a deer they are nothing except awkward.

Further, all you need is a sharp blade. You don't need long finger guards, blood grooves, saw backs, finger grips in the handles, double edges, double hilts, or any of the other gimmicks which range from silly to downright dangerous. Get a top-quality knife with a blade of four inches or so and you'll be perfectly equipped. Anything bigger is excess weight.

Short Tip on the Compass

A compass should always be carried in wild country for the obvious reason that it may prevent you from becoming lost. Strange as it may seem, some hunters don't lose their way—but they lose their deer after they have killed and field dressed it. This happens when they leave a deer in the woods to get help in dragging it out.

Remember that a compass does nothing more than point north. It won't tell you where your deer is and it won't lead you back. You must take a compass reading on the direction you're going when you head out. Note all the major features of terrain where your deer is, and all the major features on your way back to camp or vehicle. Base your return trip on compass heading and observance of the familiar terrain features. Nothing is more discouraging than to lose a prime field-dressed deer simply because you can't find it. This compass trick is even more important during changing weather conditions. Snow or rain can change the looks of even familiar country in a hurry.

Clothing

All-wool underwear is best for cold-weather hunting, but I can't use it since woolen underwear irritates my skin. I prefer two-piece dual-layer cotton suits so I can change either or both halves as I choose. These insulated suits were developed during World War II. They offer plenty of warmth except during the very coldest weather. Another fine bet is wool mixed with cotton, nylon, dacron, or silk. This type of underwear is warmer than an all-cotton garment and is favored by hunters who are sensitive to wool.

For socks, wool is again best. Wool absorbs perspiration and it has the ability to "breathe." Wear nylon socks underneath the wool if you have sensitive skin. All hunting socks should have thick cushioned feet. Such socks are more comfortable and offer added protection against the cold ground. Many hunters make the mistake of buying their socks too short. Short socks have a tendency to work down and bunch on the feet—an exasperating situation. Knee-length socks are best for comfort and for turning down over short boots.

I can get all sorts of arguments over my choice of hunting pants. Personally, I don't like many of the pants that are designed for hunters. They don't fit well and they have too many useless giant pockets and other encumberments, which is why they don't fit well. Many of these pants are reinforced with rubber in the knees and seat. Well, I prefer my pants to perform their basic function. I can't see the logic in using them for gear carriers and rain suits. I wear plain trousers of hard-finished, water-repellent fabric. In extremely cold weather woolen pants are best, but most deer hunting is done in temperatures in which proper underwear provides plenty of leg warmth. Poplin or army cotton duck are pretty hard to beat for pants. These materials shed dew, briers, and branches and remain in fine shape. They also fit well without binding in the seat or chafing in the crotch. Remember to buy hunting pants large enough to fit easily over underwear. If they're too tight they'll bind in the cramped quarters of stands, or when you're kneeling and crawling.

There are two important things to look for in shirts: they should be full-cut and they should be light. A short-tailed shirt won't stay put where it belongs. Heavy shirts weigh you down. It's better to wear two light shirts than one heavy one. Two lightweight closely woven woolen shirts will be warmer than one heavy shirt because of the insulating layer of air between the fabrics. For my first shirt I prefer fine-grade, thickly napped cotton flannel that resembles chamois cloth. Such a shirt is softer and more comfortable than wool, though not quite as warm. Another advantage of wearing two shirts is that if the day warms you can take one off. With a single heavy shirt you're stuck with all-day discomfort.

I buy outsized quilted underwear shirts for an oddball reason that I find very practical. These modern down-insulated suits are extra-warm, ultra-light, and have knit cuffs to hold in body heat. For very cold weather I use the upper part of one of these suits as an extra shirt worn over my other shirts. In effect, I use it as a jacket instead of underwear. If the day gets warm, it's far easier to slip out of my insulated shirt if it's on the outside instead of the inside of my other clothing. The same thing holds if I enter a warm room or cabin.

In cold weather I wear a snowmobile suit or a long-cut coat that keeps my hips warm. A down-filled coat is hard to beat, as is the modern design that mixes wool, polyester, and acetate. Such coats trap millions of air cells which hold body heat. Be sure your coat is water-repellent and includes a hood. When buying a coat insulated with down or synthetic materials, always check the manufacturer's tag giving you the temperature rating. Thus you can get a coat that ideally matches your hunting conditions.

The last items of clothing a deer hunter may need are gloves and mittens. If the weather is mild I prefer the ordinary, cheap cotton working gloves since they fit tight and don't interfere with gun handling. In colder weather the modern gloves combining thin capeskin with foam insulation and nylon linings are the best bets I've found. For very cold weather it's hard to beat leather mittens worn over woolen liners.

I feel that my selection of clothing offers the ultimate for the deer hunter's needs. Unless I'm on a stand in a snowmobile suit my outfit is without bulk, permits free body movements, is light in weight, keeps me dry, and fits me properly.

Here are just a few more modern items to consider:

Unbreakable vacuum bottles. They're built like a battleship. Stainless-steal construction won't rust or stain. No glass to break. Vacuum insulation keeps contents hot or cold for many hours.

Hot-seat cushions. They use no electricity, fuel or chemicals. A scientifically developed space age filler radiates body heat from the cushion. Belt clip attached for easy carrying. They cost about $4 each. I like a hot-seat when sitting on a stand in very cold weather.

Anti-foggers. A stick-type material that steam-proofs and fog-proofs any glass or plastic. One quick smear with the stick, a follow-up buffing with a soft dry cloth, and your glasses or scope won't fog up in wet or damp weather. I once had an excellent shot at a trophy whitetail during a drizzle. When I shouldered my rifle my scope was so fogged up I couldn't find the target. That buck got away. He wouldn't have if I'd been able to use the new fog-proofing material.

Hand warmer muff. Attaches to the buttons on the front of a coat or through a belt. An inside pocket holds a conventional hand-warmer. It's lightweight, detachable, and can be folded and carried in a pocket. It's made of quilted nylon on the outside and polyester fill inside. It's water-resistant. The unit is ideal when you're sitting on stand because your bare hands can be withdrawn in an instant from the lap-located muff.

Electric boot dryers. They dry all types of footwear from shoes to waders. Damp boots dry in one hour, wet boots dry overnight. Light, compact and rugged, a pair of dryers plugs into any 110-120 volt AC or DC outlet, draw only 8 watts, and will do no damage to any type of boot.

Freeze-dry foods. If you're backpacking or camping, the saving in weight of freeze-dry foods over fresh or canned goods is no less than amazing. No refrigeration is needed and freeze-dry foods last for a year or more. There's no waste and everything is portion-packed and tailored to the size of your group and your plans. Each meal is plastic-packed in strong, feather-light, and waterproof containers. Preparation and cooking requires only a fraction of the time required for fresh food. Simple and easy cooking instructions are printed on every bag. One feature that's often overlooked is that there are no skins, peels, or other debris to dispose of. The bags are burnable.

Emergency signal kit. Eddie Bauer, 1737 Airport Way South, Seattle, Washington 98134, sells a kit that works in any terrain or any weather. It contains a 10-mile signal mirror, a red smoke flare, a fire starter kit with matches, tinder and instructions, and two red Skyblazer Flares. These flares are self-contained. Just unscrew the safety cap and pull the release chain. Each flare reaches an altitude of 400 feet with an intensity of 20,000 candle power that is visible up to 20 miles. The beauty of the kit is that it weighs only five ounces. You can attach it to your belt and never know it's there. If every back-country deer hunter had one you would never see all those "lost hunter" stories that hit the front pages of newspapers every fall.

Down-filled gear. It gets better all the time and ranges from underwear and socks to shirts, vests, coats, hats and sleeping bags. The heavy clothing of years ago can't come close to down for warmth, comfort and convenience.

Four-wheel-drive vehicles and pickup campers. Back when I began hunting deer as a teenager I used to drive my mother's car to the end of a dirt road, then hike for miles back into remote country where whitetails herded each fall. Ten years ago I got into the same hotspot with practically no walking. It was a simple matter to drive in there with a four-wheel-drive (4WD) via a two-track trail. Two years ago the area—which is National Forest land—was closed to vehicle traffic because too many 4WD's loaded with hunters were putting too much pressure on the deer.

Many years ago I camped in those woods with old-fashioned camping gear. Later, when vehicle traffic was permitted, hunters would base in the area with modern pickup campers and tent trailer-campers loaded with propane equipment, portable generators, and all the conveniences of modern camping. The area held some of the best whitetail hunting I've ever experienced but it went downhill fast when the hunting pressure increased. I was glad when vehicle traffic was prohibited. Now that it's limited to hunters on foot the deer herd has bounced back.

I believe that 4WD's and pickup campers loaded with modern camping conveniences can be too efficient in some areas. In my opinion the 4WD's and pickup campers, and perhaps even house trailers, should not be allowed in certain areas where they make the hunting too easy. Some state game departments have outlawed vehicle traffic off established roads and trails. This is as it should be in those areas where these units are the cause of too much pressure on the game.

On the other hand, these modern vehicles—in places where they are properly and legally used—can make a camping-hunting trip a delight that was far beyond the imagination of the old-timers. Such vehicles offer so many comforts that some hunters owning such equipment take their families along on their hunts. The wife and kids often don't hunt at all; they just go for the camp life because it's almost as comfortable as staying at home.

In this chapter I've mentioned only a few of the modern conveniences available to deer hunters. You'll find scores of others in top-quality sporting-goods stores. Some of the best sources of information on what's available are the many free catalogs offered by such sales outlets as Eddie Bauer, Browning, L. L. Bean, Cabela's Incorporated and Orvis. There are many others. Check the advertisements in the outdoor magazines and you'll find the sources for dozens of free or inexpensive catalogs. Send for these catalogs and you'll get a wealth of information about modern gear.

Sportsman's Checklist

(Courtesy of Browning Arms Co.)
While planning your trip make a "/" in the boxes opposite the items you'll need. Then as you pack the item, finish the "X."

BIG-GAME HUNT—BASIC ITEMS

Rifle Season

☐ Rifle (sighted in)
☐ Spare rifle
☐ Rifle cases
☐ Pistol w/holster
☐ Ammunition
☐ Belt cartridge case
☐ Rifle cleaning gear with gun oil

☐ Spotting scope
☐ Hunting regulations
☐ Check state Hunter Orange
   Safety Requirements
☐ General license
☐ Special tags
☐ Deer call/rattling antlers

Archery Season

☐ Bow
☐ Extra bow string (with nocking
   point marked)
☐ Hunting arrows
☐ Spare broadheads
☐ Broadhead cement
☐ Broadhead sharpening file
☐ Field arrows

☐ Bow sight
☐ Bow quiver
☐ Bow string silencers
☐ Brush deflectors
☐ Bow string wax
☐ Bow tip protector
☐ Armguard
☐ Shooting glove or tab

☐ Camouflage bow or tape
☐ Camouflage stick or cream
☐ Camouflage outfit

☐ Archery regulations
☐ Archery license

Include on above hunts

☐ Binoculars
☐ Compass
☐ Hunting knife
☐ Buck scent
☐ Topographical map of hunt area
☐ Block and tackle/Game hoist
☐ Bone saw
☐ Meat sacks
☐ Bulk salt (to preserve hide & cape)

☐ Plastic bag for heart and liver
☐ Rope
☐ String or wire (small piece to tie tag to carcass)
☐ _____
☐ _____
☐ _____
☐ _____
☐ _____

PERSONAL GEAR

Clothing

☐ Boots
☐ Camp shoes
☐ Hat
☐ Gloves
☐ Coat
☐ Jacket
☐ Vest
☐ Sweater
☐ Shirts
☐ Trousers
☐ Underwear
☐ Long underwear
☐ Socks

☐ Rain gear (camo, green or orange)
☐ Belt
☐ Handkerchief (bandana)
☐ Silicone boot dressing
☐ Spare boot laces
☐ Duffle bag
☐ _____
☐ _____
☐ _____
☐ _____
☐ _____

Toilet Articles

☐ Comb
☐ Fingernail clippers
☐ Hand soap
☐ Razor
☐ Shaving cream
☐ Small mirror
☐ Toothbrush
☐ Toothpaste

☐ Towel and wash cloth
☐ Tweezers
☐ _____
☐ _____
☐ _____
☐ _____
☐ _____

Other

☐ Alarm clock
☐ Canteen

☐ Camera w/spare film/flash bulbs

- ☐ Cigarettes
- ☐ Glasses
- ☐ Pocket knife
- ☐ Pencil/Notebook
- ☐ Pillow
- ☐ Pipe & tobacco
- ☐ Pipe cleaner
- ☐ Safety pins
- ☐ Sewing kit
- ☐ Sleeping bag

- ☐ Sunglasses
- ☐ Walkie Talkie
- ☐ Wallet
- ☐ Watch
- ☐ _____
- ☐ _____
- ☐ _____
- ☐ _____
- ☐ _____

FIRST AID, DRUGS, SURVIVAL

- ☐ Stomach balms
- ☐ Antihistamine
- ☐ Aspirin
- ☐ Band-Aids
- ☐ Chap stick
- ☐ Coke syrup (for upset stomach)
- ☐ Cough syrup
- ☐ Eye drops
- ☐ First aid kit
- ☐ Insect repellent
- ☐ Laxative

- ☐ Merthiolate/Iodine
- ☐ Nose drops
- ☐ Prescription drugs
- ☐ Survival kit
- ☐ Snake bite kit
- ☐ Suntan lotion
- ☐ _____
- ☐ _____
- ☐ _____
- ☐ _____
- ☐ _____

CAMPING GEAR

Shelter

- ☐ Tent (check poles, ropes, pegs)
- ☐ Tarp
- ☐ Tent stitcher
- ☐ Sleeping bag

- ☐ Mattress/Cot
- ☐ Tent heater & fuel
- ☐ Portable latrine

Cooking

- ☐ Camp stove & fuel
- ☐ Pocket stove & fuel
- ☐ Matches
- ☐ Grill/Grate/Griddle
- ☐ Skillet
- ☐ Dutch oven
- ☐ Pressure cooker
- ☐ Coffee pot
- ☐ Dish pan
- ☐ Dishes
- ☐ Knives, forks, spoons

- ☐ Spatula
- ☐ Can opener
- ☐ Butcher knife
- ☐ Dish cloth & towel
- ☐ Firewood
- ☐ Cooler
- ☐ Vacuum bottle
- ☐ Water cans
- ☐ Table
- ☐ Chairs
- ☐ Camp stool

Lighting

- ☐ Camp lantern & fuel
- ☐ Extra mantles
- ☐ Flashlight w/spare bulb & batteries
- ☐ Flares

Tools

- ☐ Axe
- ☐ Broom
- ☐ Buckets
- ☐ Hammer/Nails
- ☐ Pliers
- ☐ Rope
- ☐ Saw
- ☐ Sharpening stone
- ☐ Shovel
- ☐ Wire

Permits

- ☐ Fire permit
- ☐ Golden Eagle permit to federal lands
- ☐ Local permits

Other:

- ☐ Pack frame
- ☐ Backpack
- ☐ Day pack (for lunch, etc.)
- ☐ _____
- ☐ _____
- ☐ _____
- ☐ _____
- ☐ _____

CAMPER OR TRAILER

- ☐ Broom
- ☐ Propane
- ☐ Ice
- ☐ Spare tire
- ☐ Extension mirrors for vehicle
- ☐ Spare keys
- ☐ Spare fuses
- ☐ Spare mantles for propane light
- ☐ Jack crank (camper)
- ☐ Hitch lock (trailer)
- ☐ Levelng jacks (trailer)
- ☐ Fill water tank
- ☐ Check turnbuckles (camper)
- ☐ Check tire pressure & lug bolts (trailer)
- ☐ Check running lights
- ☐ Charge battery (trailer)
- ☐ Check propane gas fittings
- ☐ _____
- ☐ _____
- ☐ _____
- ☐ _____
- ☐ _____

BOAT

- ☐ Approved life jacket (one for each person)
- ☐ Anchor
- ☐ Line (tow)
- ☐ Lights
- ☐ Horn
- ☐ Paddle(s)
- ☐ Fire extinguisher
- ☐ Signal flag
- ☐ Bail bucket
- ☐ Boat registration
- ☐ Fuel

☐ Cushions
☐ Charge battery
☐ _____
☐ _____

☐ _____
☐ _____
☐ _____

VEHICLE

☐ Spare fan belt
☐ Spare radiator hose
☐ Spare heater hose
☐ Spare fuses
☐ Spare keys
☐ Spare oil
☐ Spare brake fluid
☐ Chains
☐ Jumper cables
☐ Shovel
☐ Tools
☐ Tow chain
☐ Road maps

☐ Check oil
☐ Check water
☐ Check antifreeze
☐ Check tire pressure (also on spare)
☐ Check battery water
☐ Fill spare gas cans (transport externally *only*)
☐ _____
☐ _____
☐ _____
☐ _____
☐ _____

DOG EQUIPMENT

☐ Leash
☐ Brush
☐ Whistle
☐ Dog food
☐ Kennel crate
☐ Collars and identification tags
☐ Tie out chains
☐ Feed and water pans

☐ Extra water
☐ First aid kit for dogs
☐ Health certificate (if interstate)
☐ _____
☐ _____
☐ _____
☐ _____
☐ _____

HORSE EQUIPMENT

☐ Halter & lead rope
☐ Feed bag
☐ Oats, grain, or conditioner
☐ Salt or trace mineral
☐ Curry comb and brush
☐ Saddle blankets
☐ Saddle pad
☐ Saddle
☐ Saddle bags
☐ Scabbard
☐ Bridle/extra bit
☐ Extra rope

☐ Utility axe & saw
☐ Chaps
☐ Spurs
☐ Panniers, pack bags, pack boxes
☐ Mantie (canvas pack cover)
☐ Lash rope & cinch
☐ Hobbles
☐ Bell and strap
☐ Tether rope
☐ Horse cover blanket
☐ Feed & water buckets
☐ Feed—hay* or pellets

☐ Horse shoes & nails (#5 city head)
☐ Anvil (rail) & 4 lb. hammer
☐ Shoeing equipment (rasp, hoof pick, hoof knife, shoeing hammer, hoof nippers, clinching bar)
☐ Horse cut spray/iodine
☐ Horse insect repellent
☐ Brand inspection certificate*

☐ Health certificate*
☐ Check horse trailer
☐ _____
☐ _____
☐ _____
☐ _____
☐ _____

* Check state regulations if interstate travel is involved.

FOOD STAPLES

Accessories

☐ Aluminum foil
☐ Charcoal
☐ Charcoal lighter
☐ Dish washing soap
☐ Garbage bags
☐ Facial tissues
☐ Matches
☐ Cups

☐ Napkins
☐ Plates
☐ Towels
☐ Plastic bags
☐ Plastic eating utensils
☐ Scouring pads
☐ Toilet paper

Baking Items

☐ Baking powder
☐ Baking soda
☐ Biscuit mix
☐ Cornmeal

☐ Flour
☐ Pancake flour
☐ Shortening

Canned Goods

☐ Baked beans
☐ Chili

☐ Chili beans
☐ Fruit (also dehyd.)

Juices:

☐ Grapefruit
☐ Orange

☐ Tomato

Meats:

☐ Deviled ham
☐ Sardines
☐ Spam
☐ Tuna

☐ Milk (also dehyd.)
☐ Soups (also dehyd.)
☐ Stew

Vegetables:

☐ Beets
☐ Carrots
☐ Corn
☐ Lima beans

☐ Peas
☐ Potatoes (also dehyd.)
☐ String beans
☐ Tomatoes

Hot drinks

☐ Bouillon cubes   ☐ Hot chocolate
☐ Coffee   ☐ Tea

Relishes

☐ Horseradish   ☐ Peppers
☐ Ketchup   ☐ Pickles
☐ Mustard   ☐ Relish
☐ Olives

Sauces & Dressings

☐ Applesauce   ☐ Steak sauce
☐ Bar-B-Q Sauce   ☐ Vegetable oil
☐ Mayonnaise   ☐ Vinegar
☐ Salad dressing   ☐ Meat sauces
☐ Soy sauce

Spices

☐ Celery salt   ☐ Pepper
☐ Chili powder   ☐ Rosemary
☐ Onion salt   ☐ Salt
☐ Oregano   ☐ Seasoning salt
☐ Paprika

Spreads

☐ Honey   ☐ Peanut butter
☐ Jam & jelly   ☐ Syrup

Others

☐ Noddles   ☐ _____
☐ Rice   ☐ _____
☐ Sugar   ☐ _____
☐ _____   ☐ _____

FOOD PERISHABLES

Bakery

☐ Bread   ☐ Hot dog buns
☐ Crackers   ☐ Cookies
☐ Hamburger buns   ☐ Pastries

Beverages

☐ Soft drinks   ☐ _____
☐ Hard stuff   ☐ _____

Dairy

☐ Butter   ☐ Eggs
☐ Cheese   ☐ Milk

Fruit

☐ Apples   ☐ Oranges
☐ Apricots   ☐ Peaches
☐ Bananas   ☐ Raisins

Meats

☐ Bacon   ☐ Hot dogs
☐ Chicken   ☐ Lunch meat
☐ Fish   ☐ Sausage
☐ Game   ☐ Pork chops
☐ Ham   ☐ Steaks
☐ Hamburger

Vegetables

☐ Celery   ☐ Peppers
☐ Corn-on-the-cob   ☐ Potatoes
☐ Lettuce   ☐ Tomatoes
☐ Onions

Miscellaneous

☐ Candy   ☐ _____
☐ Cereal   ☐ _____
☐ Chewing gun   ☐ _____
☐ Choclate bars   ☐ _____
☐ Dessert items   ☐ _____
☐ Potato chips

And last but not least . . .
tell someone exactly where you're
going! It could save your life.

CHAPTER
14

Maps for
Deer Hunting

A few years ago, in wild tangled country in northern Michigan, a deer hunter walked away from his camp on an overcast morning. He jumped and followed a deer in an area heavily tracked up earlier by other members of his party.

Several hours later, worn out from hiking through swamps and across ridges in deep snow, he lost the deer track and started back to camp.

He was no beginner. He had hunted deer for the better part of twenty years and knew his way around the woods. But he was in country he had never seen until that November, and he had made the grave mistake of not looking at a map at the start of his hunt. He was carrying a compass, but had only the vaguest notion of where he was and which way to go.

He ran out of matches the first night, slept under logs after that without a fire, circling, wandering, lost in swamps and beaver ponds. He staggered out of the woods onto a road at the end of seventy-two terrible hours. He came out only six miles from camp, but had traveled more than thirty miles to get there. He came very close to freezing to death, all for want of taking a good look at a map in the beginning.

That ordeal serves perfectly to illustrate the most common and urgent reason deer hunters need maps if they are planning a trip in unfamiliar territory. Similar stories are read in newspapers each fall. But not getting lost is far from the only reason for utilizing good maps. Consider the following letters I've received because of my position as staff editor of *Outdoor Life:*

"I've heard about the great deer hunting near the Marais des Cygnes waterfowl area and I'd like to hunt there next fall," writes a Kansas reader. "Some of the area is closed to hunting. I've never been there. Where can I get a map of the area?"

Here's a similar letter from a Minnesota reader.

"I've read that Minnesota's northeastern counties harbor a lot of deer. I want to hunt there next fall. I've heard that the region is rugged wilderness and I'll surely need a good map of the area. Where can I get one?"

Here's another inquiry from a reader that is almost word for word like dozens of letters in my files:

"I've dreamed for years of going deer hunting in Colorado. My two partners and I have decided this is the year. We want to hunt the western part of the state. Where are the best locations and where can I get maps of the areas?"

That deer hunter's problem is typical of an ever-growing segment of outdoorsmen, especially deer hunters, who want detailed information on where the action is outside their home states. Letters flow in asking for information on map sources in many states and provinces.

I can get accurate answers to most where-to-go questions because I work closely with state fish-and-game officials throughout North America. But answers to questions regarding availability of specific maps often stumped me.

Recently I decided that I knew far too little about the subject. I wondered just how many types of maps are available to outdoorsmen. How good are they? Who distributes them? How much do they cost? What's the latest word in maps that will benefit deer hunters?

To find out, I conducted an in-depth investigation. I sent lengthy questionnaires to state, federal, and private agencies in the United States and Canada. I asked for specific information on various types of maps that are of value to hunters, and where outdoorsmen could get those maps.

My mailbox was soon loaded with maps of all descriptions. A resulting study of the piles of material revealed that there are far more maps available (many for free distribution) than I had imagined. You should know about these maps. The facts I dug up are so interesting that I'm devoting an entire chapter to the subject of maps.

The Overall Picture

I was surprised to learn that many state fish-and-game departments have taken a new attitude on maps, an attitude that you'll be happy to hear about.

"Everyone seems to be map-conscious these days," one official in a western state told me. "Our department is well aware that we haven't been able to supply the outdoorsman with the specific type of maps he needs. Frankly, we've just never had the money to publish all the maps, directories, and charts that the public wants.

"The answer is for state game-and-fish departments to cooperate with federal and private agencies in map production and distribution. We can supply hunting and fishing information—the other agencies can supply engineers, artists, and map-making facilities. The results would be maps that sportsmen would have real use for. That's the direction we're heading in."

So are other states. Here's what the Chief of Information and Education for South Dakota's Department of Game, Fish and Parks told me:

"Our department is currently working with the U.S. Forest Service and the Bureau of Land Management on a series of nine recreation maps. The maps are scaled at a half-inch to the mile. They'll cover approximately 3.5 million acres of state and federal public land. With the exception of obvious places like the Black Hills, most South Dakotans are unaware of these holdings. The maps are a boon to deer hunters looking for new places to hunt. They are available from our department office in the State Office Building in Pierre, 57501."

An official from another state said to me:

"Right now there isn't any substitute for the U.S. Geological Survey quadrangles when it comes to helping the deer hunter. These maps show topography (relief features and surface configuration) like no other map shows. But our game-land maps (hotspot areas) show the best hunting and game-concentration lands, again something no other map shows. We're superimposing game-land maps onto topo maps. These maps are ideal because they show the best hunting areas and exact terrain conditions."

Private enterprise also is recognizing the ever-growing demand by outdoorsmen for accurate maps. Here's what C. Ross Anderson, President of AAA Engineering and Drafting Company in Salt Lake City, Utah told me:

"After years of preparing relatively useless recreation maps for various government agencies, our company launched a private mapping program. We cooperate with every private, state and federal agency that can supply information that answers real needs for the sportsmen. We are working very closely with park services, forest services, U.S. Geological Survey, Bureau of Land Management, state highway departments, tourist and publicity councils, chambers of commerce, snowmobile associations, etc.

"We have produced several maps of areas in western states. These maps are indexed to show best action areas, campsites, public lands, accommodations, boat ramps and just about everything a sportsman wants to know. We hope to produce similar maps covering other areas of the nation. A lot of the information on these maps is excellent for deer hunters."

Another map producer, Clarkson Map Company, produces special recreation maps designed for outdoorsmen in the Midwest. The company has produced several different books of hydrographic (depth contour) lake maps covering the most popular fishing lakes in Michigan, Wisconsin and Minnesota. Another of their productions is a book of maps covering every county in Michigan. These maps show dozens of legends including campgrounds, roads, trails and conservation department units. Similar books of maps cover Wisconsin and Minnesota. You can get details by writing the company, Kaukauna, Wisconsin 54130; or phoning 414-766-3000.

Government agencies are also publishing special-use maps. A good example is the U.S. Bureau of Sport Fisheries and Wildlife map of Waterfowl Production Areas in the Midwest. That agency is responsible for the purchase and easement of 300 areas totaling 103,516 acres of wetlands in North Dakota. The areas are managed to provide the most favorable conditions for duck reproduction and to provide hunting opportunities for waterfowl, upland birds and deer. The areas are open to free hunting and are not to be confused with refuges. You can get these maps by writing the Division of Wildlife Refuges, Federal Building, Fort Snelling, Twin Cities, Minnesota 55111.

Why Are Good Maps So Important?

Obvious examples are state highway maps. You wouldn't think of driving your automobile through unfamiliar states without road maps. Yet many deer hunters head into areas where they've never been and they don't even think about getting maps that would help their hunting activities. That's a major mistake. I learned the lesson well many years ago while hunting deer in Saskatchewan.

My partner Bob and I found that our hit-and-miss hunting of woodlots and swales wasn't very productive. One day we drove into a tiny town to find lunch and we walked into the hamlet's only restaurant. We sat down next to a booth holding four exuberant stateside hunters. Their luck with whitetails had been great. Bob and I couldn't help wincing as we overheard their talk of seeing lots of deer.

Finally we could stand no more. We introduced ourselves and hinted that we sure would like to know where we could find some bucks.

"No problem," grinned one of the hunters. "We found a hotspot this morning that's loaded with deer. We didn't spook those animals much because we only needed one buck to fill our take-out limits."

"Great," exclaimed Bob, "where do we go?"

"About 10 miles northwest. You might have a problem getting there because it's off the highway, way back in over a series of back roads. I'll draw you a map."

A few minutes later it was obvious that the hunter couldn't draw a reliable map because he couldn't recall the locations of many crossroads and landmarks. We asked the proprietor of the restaurant for an area road map. He didn't have one. I went across the street to a gasoline station and found no maps of any kind. We were licked.

Our new friends did their best to explain how to get to the area. But Bob and I never found it though we spent hours in the search. For the lack of a simple map we probably missed out on a great adventure.

Another time I was in Manitoba on a camping deer hunt when my Cree Indian guide decided we should follow some fresh deer tracks. We paid a lot more attention to those tracks than to the direction we were going. An hour later we jumped the animals but they crashed away unseen in the thickets. The guide decided to take a short-cut back to where we had parked our canoe along the bank of a small creek.

Two hours later we hadn't found the canoe and I figured we were lost.

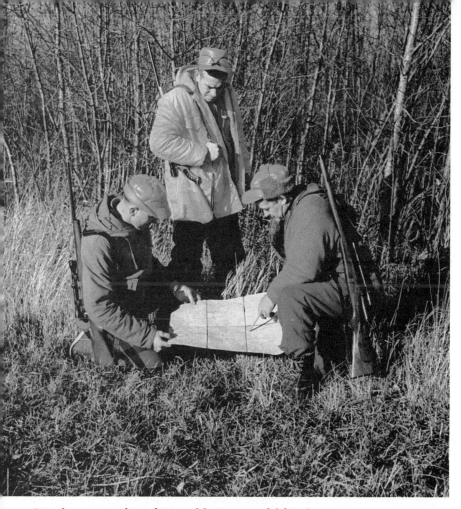

Deer hunters need good maps. Maps are useful for planning a trip into unfamiliar territory, for planning deer drives, or for discovering backcountry regions that look like feeding, bedding, and runway areas.

Three hours after that the guide finally admitted he didn't have the slightest idea of where we were. The only thing I knew for sure was that we were at least 10 miles from the closest road and 20 miles from the nearest town. We knew we would be in serious trouble if we didn't find that canoe.

Late in the afternoon we stumbled out of the bush onto the bank of a large river. The guide breathed a grunt of relief and said, "That's our river, but current going wrong way."

Soon he decided that the current was going the same way it always had, but that we had been traveling west instead of east. We walked downstream along the bank for a mile before the guide suddenly recognized a landmark. We were out of trouble then and we walked almost straight to the canoe. I've often wondered what would have happened if I'd been by myself in that totally unfamiliar wilderness.

I later obtained a topograhic map of the area, and I was able to trace the progress of our misguided journey. If I'd had that map when we became lost I could have saved a day's anxiety, with a simple compass reading. I've never gone into any wilderness since without a map or maps covering the area I was going to hunt.

That logic was emphasized in many replies to the questionnaires I sent out asking about the value of maps. Denton H. Hartley, Chief of Information and Education for the New Hampshire Fish and Game Department, was particularly impressed with the lost-hunter problem. Here's what he said:

"Just ask a natural-resource warden or conservation office in any state or province whether he wished sportsmen knew more about maps and listen to the answer. Lots of deer hunters get lost in the woods, but their number is small compared with those who are lost before they ever enter the woods. Plenty of gunners drive down old roads running in various directions, see a likely looking spot, get out, and start hunting. They don't know what road they're on, where it goes, or which way is north. It's amazing to me that many outdoorsmen don't even carry highway maps."

Maps are especially efficient in planning deer drives. I once joined a group of Wisconsin hunters who consider their topographic maps indispensable, not only for a successful hunt but also as safety tools.

Before a drive begins a map of the area is spread out. Each hunter is shown (by landmark features on the map) where the drive will originate, where it will end, and where each posted hunter will be standing. Because of the map each member of the group knows exactly where to go and what area he should cover. The military-type planning pays off with lots of venison.

Good maps are also perfect tools for deer hunters trying to discover back-country regions that are naturals for feeding, bedding, and runway areas. Whatever your reason for getting off the beaten track you'll find that maps are your best planning aids.

Another great advantage of carrying maps is that local people can point out hotspot locations. Many times I've had filling-station attendants, farmers, and resort operators pinpoint choice hunting areas when I pulled a map out of my pocket.

Maps also have a value as souvenirs of hunting trips. They're great for helping to explain to friends where you were, what terrain conditions you found, and where you killed your buck. A map brings back memories in a hurry and helps you relive all of the excitement.

Finding an all-purpose map covering a specific area is practically impossible. But several maps of the same area obtained from various sources can supply you with a wealth of valuable details. George A. Kaminski, Information and Education Chief for Wyoming's Game and Fish Commission, summed it up well when he told me this:

MAPS FOR DEER HUNTING

"Our commission is obligated to put out maps that clarify deer-hunting regulations and the areas of the state to which they pertain. They are economically designed for mass distribution and they show little more than where a sportsman may hunt.

"But once a man selects his area he can turn to other agencies for detailed terrain information. The Bureau of Land Management, the U.S. Geological Survey, and the U.S. Forest Service are the best bets for maps showing topographic features and public ownership boundaries.

"Highway department maps emphasize all types of roads, driving distances, and locations of towns. County maps go into detail on local trails, streams, and woodlands. If a sportsman has all those maps he has the finest information available."

Federal Maps

The topographic sheets are sold for a small sum by the U.S. Geological Survey. These maps are approximately 16½x20 inches and are drawn to scales from one-half inch to two inches per mile, depending on the character of the country charted. Bodies of water are printed in blue, man-made features in black, and features of relief (hills, mountains, and valleys) are indicated by brown contour lines. Woodlands show up in green. These maps are the best available for sportsmen wanting to know the lay of the land.

Topographic maps are produced for all areas of the U.S. that have been surveyed. Begin by requesting free index maps on the states of interest. These indexes will show areas covered by quadrangular maps and prices of each. To order maps east of the Mississippi River, including Minnesota, write Branch of Distribution, U.S. Geological Survey, 1200 South Eads St., Arlington, VA 22202. For maps west of the Mississippi, including Alaska and Louisiana, write Branch of Distribution, U.S. Geological Survey, Box 25286, Federal Center, Denver, CO 80225.

The U.S. Forest Service publishes maps of lake and forest regions in the various national forests. Write the U.S. Forest Service, Washington, D.C. 20250 for a key map that shows areas covered. That index lists regional offices where you can obtain the detailed maps that interest you.

The Bureau of Land Management (B.L.M.) is a top bet for maps showing lands open to public hunting. Most of the maps are printed in colors denoting public lands, Forest Service lands, state lands, game-and-fish department lands, national wildlife refuges, and private lands. These maps are a boon for sportsmen looking for action areas in the midwestern and western states holding large acreages of public-access lands.

Many of the B.L.M. maps cover entire states, but some are limited to sections of states and these maps carry an amazing wealth of detail. They show all roads (by special symbols), from paved highways down to trails suited only for seasonal travel by four-wheel-drive vehicles. They show power lines, creeks, marshes, township boundaries, railroad tracks, and just about anything else that can be identified. One of these maps, combined with a Geological Survey map of the same area, would give a deer hunter a better picture of the land than an aerial photograph. Write the U.S. Department of Interior, Bureau of Land Management, Washington, D.C. 20240 for details and an index of available maps.

Canadian Topo Maps

To order Canadian topo maps in various scales from one inch to ¾ mile and from one inch to about 4 miles, request instructions from the Canada Map Office 615 Booth St., Ottawa, Ontario, Canada KIA OE9.

Specific Hotspot Maps

Although topographic and other terrain-feature maps give you a clear picture of the physical characteristics of a given area, they can't give you any information on hunting hotspots. That information has to come from local sources or game-and-fish officials who are close to the scene in their individual states or provinces. Some conservation departments have done a remarkable job of reducing their best hunting information down to maps and charts.

An official in Nebraska's Game and Parks Commission told me:

"Hunting maps are exceedingly difficult to keep up to date because of the fluctuation of prime hunting areas from year to year. But we do publish pamphlets showing general hotspot areas. The pamphlets include maps of the state showing which sections harbor the highest numbers of deer. With this map a hunter could pinpoint one of the best counties for his hunting area."

Some of the best aids to Minnesota hunters are fire-plan maps. What's a fire-plan map? It's a map drawn from aerial photos and designed primarily to aid in fire prevention and control. It shows all roads, lakes, streams, trails, railroad grades, ponds, and other details including power-transmission lines. Most of the maps cover a 36 square-mile area. The scale is two inches to one mile.

Minnesota's Departments of Natural Resources and Administration are cooperating to make these maps available to sportsmen. You can get an index of the maps by writing: Documents Section, 500 Lafayette Road, St. Paul, MN 55146.

Several excellent maps are available covering Minnesota's famous Boundary Waters Canoe Area. A map folder listing canoe routes and other useful information on the entire Superior National Forest is available free from: Supervisor, Superior National Forest, Box 338, Duluth, MN 55801.

"In Kansas we have a good number of maps on public hunting areas," said Thayne Smith, a veteran deer hunter from Wichita. "We get maps from various agencies—U.S. Army Corps of Engineers; Bureau of Reclamation; Kansas Park Authority; the Forestry, Fish and Game Commission; and others.

"Our commission game-management area maps, designed principally for hunters, cover most of the state's thirty-plus areas. They're very detailed, showing open-hunting lands, roads, streams, camping areas, and so forth. The back side of these maps carries text explaining best hunting techniques, pertinent regulations, and other details that will help the sportsman enjoy himself."

From the foregoing statements it's obvious that it's a good idea to direct all your questions about maps to the Information and Education Division in the Conservation Department of the state you're interested in. If they don't have a particular map in supply they'll know where to get it. Here's another example of what I mean:

"We keep a batch of material that falls under the heading of maps," says Joel Vance of the Missouri Department of Conservation. "Some of it is published by other organizations such as the U.S. Forest Service, the U.S. Army Corps of Engineers, and the Upper Mississippi River Conservation Commission.

"I'd say that Missouri is very well mapped from a deer hunter's standpoint. Outdoorsmen can obtain any of the maps I'm talking about by writing to: Information Department, Missouri Department of Conservation, P.O. Box 180, Jefferson City 65101."

Here's still another viewpoint from a western state:

"Our Game and Fish Department publishes very few maps because so many good ones are available from other sources." That's the word I got from that agency's public-relations chief.

"Whenever someone asks for the best deer hunter's map available I tell them to contact the State Highway Department," he told me. "I'm not talking about road maps. I'm referring to individual county maps that the highway people publish. These maps show remarkable detail, down to seldom-used trails and abandoned farm buildings. They're far more complete than regular highway maps. They sell for one to two dollars depending on size.

"A good bet for particular areas is the state forest maps put out by several colleges and forestry schools in the West. They contain symbols denoting public lands open to hunting, parks closed to hunting and refuges. Lakes, roads, creeks and boundary lines are all detailed.

"Another fine map (published by the U.S. Department of Agriculture in Missoula, Montana) shows public hunting areas in most western states.

"In addition to those publications I'd suggest the Geological Survey, and B.L.M. maps. They're hard to beat. Any state conservation agency can tell you where to get maps."

Local Maps

No matter where you go it's a good bet that chambers of commerce, guide associations, and sporting-goods stores will have maps offering great detail on local areas. They're often extremely accurate because they cover small localities. Often they pinpoint hunting hotspots, little-known trails, and other very valuable details that are seldom included on state and federal maps. When you get into new country always ask if such local maps are available.

How to Carry Maps

For the sportsman who makes full use of maps and carries them on hunting trips, protecting them from wear and weather and keeping them in usable condition can be a problem. A map not taken care of has a short life. Properly protected, it will last a long time.

I used to think maps should be rolled and carried in tubular cases. But after fighting those rolled maps with cold hands in semidarkness for years, and having them flap like runaway window shades just as I was about to see what I wanted, I changed my mind.

My maps are folded now to make neat, flat packages. For instance, I fold topo maps to 7x11, with the name of the quadrangle exposed on both sides. Folded this way, any map is easily carried in the field in a waterproof envelope, and easily unfolded for use.

Some hunters eliminate the waterproof envelope by reinforcing their maps with a cloth backing, such as a piece of muslin sheet. Here's how to do it:

The basic trick is to glue your map to the cloth with wallpaper paste. To insure overall contact between map and cloth the cloth should be stretched and tacked to a flat surface such as a plywood board. The cloth should be larger than the map to allow for trimming after the paste dries.

Small maps can be pasted in one piece. Large maps should be cut into sections to eliminate bulky folds. Fold the map so that it fits your pocket, unfold, and cut into sections along the fold lines. Paste the sections (in their proper relationship with each other) to the cloth. Leave a space about 1/16 inch between the sections so the finished product will fold easily and compactly.

To insure complete contact between the map and cloth it's necessary to wet the map—or sections of it—for a moment in warm water. Then apply the wallpaper paste to the back of the map with a paint brush. Pressure by hand will insure contact between the cloth and map. Wipe off excess paste with a damp rag. Let dry for at least one day, then trim the edges with a pair of scissors. The reinforced map is now ready for years of use.

An outdated map may show a road that no longer exists, or it may not include new roads, trails or other features. It's not a good idea to use maps that somebody gives you. They could have been stored in closets for years. Note the publishing date on any map of questionable accuracy. If it's old, order a new one from its publisher. Address information is contained on most maps.

Plat Maps

My partner and I were executing one-man drives through small woodlots. It was my turn to take a stand along the north end of briar thickets near a gravel road. I had walked within 50 yards of my destination when I glimpsed four whitetails sneaking through the briars. I was sure that Charlie had jumped the deer but the brush was too thick for me to see if any of the animals wore antlers.

The dilemma was over in seconds. The whitetails bounded out of the briars and onto the road where they were in clear view. The largest one wore a six-point rack that glistened in the late afternoon sun. The last deer in line was a fine spike buck. There was no time to shoot, even if they hadn't paused in a public road. The animals no more than hesitated before they began running. I'm sure they were unaware of me because none had looked in my direction. I watched them run across a clearing then melt from view in another wood lot 300 yards to the north. When Charlie arrived on the scene I told him what had happened.

"They didn't even notice me," I said. "I saw all four white flags clearly as they reached the edge of the woods, then they disappeared instantly. I think those deer stopped as soon as they hit cover. I'd bet they're standing there watching us."

Charlie didn't even bother answering me. He turned and began trotting toward his truck. I knew exactly what was going through his mind. First, we didn't have permission to hunt the property where the deer were. Also, we had less than two hours to get that permission, make another drive, and shoot a buck before it got too dark to hunt.

There wasn't a farmhouse in sight, but there was a quick and easy way for us to find out who owned the property. We checked our plat book that we always carry in the truck. In moments we found that the woodlot we wanted to drive was part of 116 acres owned by Ralph Berndt. The book also told us that there were buildings on the north side of the property, and we surmised that one of the buildings would likely be the house where farmer Berndt resided.

Within 15 minutes our assumptions proved correct. As soon as we introduced ourselves we got good news. "Yeah, you guys can try for those bucks," the farmer said. "Partly because you had enough courtesy to ask before charging into those woods, and partly because I'm getting too much crop damage from deer. Now I'll tell you something. I see deer coming out this end of those woods all the time, and they almost always walk out through the same gulley. I'll show you right where to stand."

About 40 minutes later I was making my zig-zag drive through the woodlot when I heard Charlie's Winchester .243 roar. When I reached the scene of the shot he was field dressing the six-pointer. He looked up, grinned, and said, "Thank the Lord for plat books."

Plat books (sometimes called land atlas books) are books of plat maps. Each full-page map covers one township. A full book covers all the townships in any given county. My plat book covers Mason County, Michigan. It has detailed plat maps for the county's 16 townships. In effect, my plat book gives me land ownership details on over 100 square miles of potential hunting country.

All plat books detail and depict specifics relating to many factors besides land ownership. All data in the books are gathered from official public records at county courthouses and elsewhere. An index map in each book shows townships as they are located geographically. Numerals on each township indicate the page number where particular maps appear in detail.

Each individual map will give a surprising number of facts. Each parcel of land shows the name of the owner or owners, the exact location, the area and shape of the parcel, and its size in acres. Also shown on each map are towns and villages, creeks, rivers and lakes, locations of buildings on each parcel, all roads and highways (including their names), railroads, section numbers and section lines. Each book also includes a list of land owners. This index is an alphabetical listing of every landowner in each county whose name appears on the book's township maps.

Here's how the alphabetical listing can help you. Suppose somebody mentions that he heard there are a lot of deer on Fred Johnson's property in Branch Township, but he doesn't know where the Johnson property is. Just get out your plat book and look up Fred Johnson in the index listing. Following the name you will find the section and page number of his land. Then it's a snap to find the property on the map and get all the details I mentioned.

The normal use of a plat book develops when you see a piece of property you want to hunt, but it can be used in other ways too. Strange as it may seem without an explanation, we used my plat book twice last fall to get permission to hunt lands we had already been hunting for many years.

The first instance developed when we decided to work our one-man drive in a wooded area that always held a lot of deer. When we drove up to the place we noticed that it had been freshly posted with new "No Trespassing" signs. This is always a touchy situation because it often means that the land has been sold. In other words, the hunting permission you received from a previous owner is now obviously worthless.

Fortunately, in this case, our plat book was a brand new issue that had been updated. It did indeed show that the land had a new owner. There were no farm buildings on this property, but that's never a problem. We drove to a country store, looked up the landowner's phone number in a telephone directory, and gave him a call. We got permission to hunt the 120 acres, but as it turned out we didn't see a single deer that day.

The other instance concerned a new gate across a two-track road on property that had never been posted. We had been hunting the lowlands for so many years we couldn't remember the landowner's name, but we did recall that he taught school in a nearby village. Our plat book immediately revealed the man's name. It took only minutes to call the school and get in touch with him. "I put that gate there because I'm getting too much traffic on the two-track," the landowner told me. "But if you fellows want to walk in, go right ahead. You can still hunt my land."

Our most surprising access to hunting lands through use of our plat books came in a very unexpected way. The experience is a good lesson to keep in mind.

One fall several years ago we found two well-traveled deer runways during our pre-season scouting. We suspected that they very likely merged on property that we didn't have permission to hunt. We tracked down the landowner and found that he was in his mid-forties, about the same age as my partner Charlie. The two men hit it off right away, so we didn't have any trouble getting hunting permission.

One evening several days later we were studying a plat book when we came across the same landowner's name on a different piece of property. Then we found that the same man owned two more 80-acre parcels in the same area.

Over the weekend we visited him again. "All told I own almost 400 acres and rent another 200," our new friend told us. His name was Brad, and he added, "You fellows can hunt on all the land I control."

That's still not the end of the story. It turned out that Brad did quite a bit of hunting himself, and he happened to mention that the cost of ammunition was getting so high that hunting was becoming too expensive. It so happens that Charlie hand-loads all of our shells and cartridges. The next time we visited Brad we left enough .30-06 and 12-gauge loads to last our farmer friend for years. He thanked Charlie and said, "My uncle owns a lot of land in this area too. His name is Robert Lundberg, and I'll tell him that I've given you two permission to hunt it. Feel free to hunt any Bob Lundberg land you can find on your maps."

In that case our use of a plat book gained us hunting access to almost 1,000 acres of land.

We had another similar experience that should help to emphasize the point. Charlie and I were going grouse and woodcock hunting one day before firearms deer season opened. We always leave home about dawn so we can look for deer feeding in crop fields on our way to bird-hunting spots. It's not unusual to see one buck in a picked corn field, and it's relatively common to see two together. Rarely do we see more than two, so you can imagine our astonishment when we spotted five mature bucks in one bunch.

We naturally figured we had chanced upon a great place to hunt deer. So we forgot about gunning birds until we tried getting deer hunting permission. Out came the plat book. We discovered that the bucks had been standing on property owned by a Charles Holden. There were no buildings on the 80-acre parcel, so we resorted to a trick we often use when we're in a hurry. We check names on mail boxes in the immediate area while driving slowly down nearby roads. The stunt worked that day. Within minutes we found a roadside mail box showing the name, C. Holden.

Mr. Holden turned out to be another one of an increasing number of farmers suffering too much crop damage by deer. Not only did we get permission to hunt his land, but we got the okay to hunt his brother's adjoining 80 acres. Further, we received permission to hunt the Holden family homestead that covers 120 acres in the same area.

And how many of those bucks did we get? Charlie and I failed to even get a shot, but his son nailed a six-pointer. That was the only buck any of us saw during three days of hunting. We just don't have any idea of where those whitetails went. It's another prime example of how crafty today's deer can be.

This is a good place to make another point, too. Though plat books can be a tremendous help in getting hunting permission, they're certainly no guarantee of positive results of any kind. Some landowners will consider giving permission, others won't and we'll never change that.

But keep in mind too that there are some parcels of land that are open to public hunting that you may not have thought of.

In many states public utilities own rights-of-way for their power lines. Often these routes are about 200 yards wide by hundreds of miles long. I hunt lots of those rights of way. They're clearly marked in my plat book.

Other top bets are paper-company lands. In many cases they're open to hunting by anyone and, of course, they're clearly mapped in plat books. Still another possibility is tax-advantage land. These are privately-owned lands, but their owners get tax breaks if they open them to public hunting and fishing. If your state offers these property-tax advantages your plat book can offer you still more benefits.

Everything I've written so far will help you only if plat books are available for the counties you want to hunt. There is one sure way to find out. All privately-owned lands in any state are taxed, and tax assessors must have totally accurate land descriptions. Such descriptions are always kept in county courthouses. Any one of three sources, in any county courthouse in the nation, will have information on whether or not a plat book (or county land atlas) is available for the county you're interested in. Visit or phone the county clerk, register of deeds, or treasurer.

Plat books are produced by private concerns, usually map publishers. I know of only three, there are probably more. Of the three publishers I'm aware of (one each in Colorado, Indiana, and Illinois) the largest is Rockford Map Publishers, Inc., 4525 Forest View Ave., P.O. Box 6126, Rockford, IL 61125. This concern publishes county plat books for at least some counties in 18 states. It has maps for over 100 counties in Illinois. The picture is similar for Indiana, Iowa, Michigan, Minnesota and Wisconsin.

Ron Baxter, of Rockford Map Publishers, had the following to tell me: "We start from scratch on every plat map we produce. We begin with aerial surveys and regular highway maps. We have our own crews check out all important facts about land descriptions, then they draw our maps. There often is little uniformity from state to state on how land parcels may be mapped for tax purposes. But the bottom line is that plat maps always show who owns what and precisely where it is. I doubt if there is a better tool for a sportsman who is serious about finding new lands to hunt on."

Plat maps are no more difficult to read than standard highway maps. A few of the legends are a bit unusual, but the explanations for them are found on a general-information page in the beginning of each plat book. Most of Rockford's plat books sell for $15.00 each. Some sell for higher prices because they cover more than the average number of townships.

CHAPTER
15

Are Deer
Really Smart?

The subject of this chapter causes heated arguments among the best and most experienced venison-chasers. It's a simple question: How smart is a deer? Is an adult buck, particularly a whitetail, the craftiest quarry you'll find anywhere in outdoors? Or are deer in general really pretty stupid?

All any hunter can do is develop his own ideas. I can reflect only the sum of my own observations tempered with what I've read and what I've learned from other hunters.

Just recently I spent an evening talking over the subject with a hunter who has killed many deer in Texas. He came up with a statement that condenses my thoughts.

"My opinion is that deer are not smart, but they can be fantastically clever," the veteran hunter began. "Look up the two words in a dictionary and you'll see what I mean: The *American College Dictionary* offers one definition of smart as meaning shrewd or sharp, as a person in dealing with others. Note that your inference here relates to human beings who deal in facts. There are two definitions of clever that are not restricted to human activity. One means to be dexterous or nimble with the body. Another means showing adroitness or ingenuity. Both meanings could apply to animals as well as humans. I think a wise old buck can be extremely clever, but I've seen a lot of them pull stunts that sure weren't smart, stunts that put them into somebody's freezer."

Whenever I get into an argument on the subject I ask: "How come so many deer are killed on highways by cars?" It's a fact that about half a million deer are killed on highways each year. Now if deer were smart they'd know enough not to run into a vehicle they see coming and have every chance to avoid. A deer has to be pretty stupid to get knocked off by a car, especially in daylight.

That's one example of plain stupidity. Let's consider another that would seem to indicate an even greater lack of brains, at least where whitetails are concerned.

In northern states, during winters of heavy snow, whitetails herd into cedar swamps or other lowland thickets to escape the worst effects of blizzards and extreme cold. These areas are termed "yards" and they are used traditionally year after year. The problem is that herds are confined to very small areas where available food is rapidly consumed. If the winters are hard and long many of the younger and weaker deer die of starvation.

The horror of all this is that in many instances there would be no starvation if the deer were smart enough to reason things out. Game biologists tell us that in many starvation areas deer die only a few hundred yards from lowlands harboring plenty of browse that isn't utilized. Why weren't these deer intelligent enough to travel a short distance and save their lives? Biologists claim it's habit for the animals to yard in specific areas regardless of the consequences. That's certainly not being very smart.

But being clever is something else. Let me mention some examples of just how clever deer can be.

A bowhunter friend of mine spent four days last fall hunting a section of local woodland. During those four days he saw sixty-seven deer, thirteen of them bucks. During the rifle season he spent another four days hunting the same area and he saw only four deer, all does. A month after the rifle season closed he was back in the same area hunting rabbits.

"John," he told me, "you wouldn't believe the number of deer in there. "Snow was pawed up everywhere under the oaks where whitetails were turning up acorns. I saw more than twenty deer and I wasn't even looking for them. Now where the hell were all those deer during rifle season?"

To find a possible answer let's turn to another fact from deer biologists: on good range a whitetail may live its entire life in a one- or two-square-mile area. Most deer select a relatively small home territory and stay in it. So, to answer my bowhunter friend's question, his disappearing deer probably remained in the same area he hunted, but they were clever enough to stay out of sight during the firearms season. Why just during the firearms season?

All wild birds and animals react dramatically when somebody starts hunting them. In all the whitetail states most of the deer harvest is taken during the first few days of the gun season, then the kill drops drastically. Mule deer that fed in valley fields close to ranch houses all summer are gone shortly after rifles begin roaring in fall.

It seems to me that wildlife which survives in proximity to man has learned there are times to avoid human beings, and those times come with the echo of gunfire. For instance, deer are frequently almost tame in summer, exhibiting entirely different behavior patterns than in fall.

I'm writing this in my office which is on a lakeshore backed by several hundred acres of woodlands. These woods are loaded with fox and gray squirrels. Most of the year they raise havoc with my bird feeders. They become almost brazen, refusing to retreat more than a few yards up the closest tree even when I run outside in efforts to chase them away so the birds can feed. In fall, however, when I hit the woods with my .22 rifle in search of the makings of a squirrel dinner, those little varmits become very elusive.

The lake outside my office window is a good area for attracting a few diving ducks in fall, but you should see the enormous flights of ducks that pile in during April while the spring migration is under way. The fall ducks raft in the middle of the lake and will flush a quarter-mile away from an approaching boat, the spring birds swim along shorelines and pay much less attention to human activity. Why?

Is wildlife getting smarter? Can it be that through recent generations of ever increasing gunning pressure our hunted species have developed built-in alarm systems that say "be clever" in fall?

It seems to me that as the years go by our heavily hunted game is becoming increasingly clever all the time. The easily killed birds and animals don't last long enough to breed. The ones that stay alive do the breeding and they pass on their own genes.

A few months ago I brought up the subject with Lyle Laurvick, the gunsmith from Superior, Wisconsin, who I've mentioned elsewhere in this book. Lyle is a deer-hunting addict. He has hunted whitetails almost every day of each Wisconsin season since 1946. He doesn't quit hunting when he gets his buck; he puts aside his rifle and helps other hunters by participating in drives. A man with that much experience is worth listening to.

"No question about it, deer hunting is a different ball game today and is played by an entirely different set of rules than years ago," he began. "The older bucks with the big racks didn't get that way by being stupid. The stupid ones have all been through meat grinders. These modern bucks are of a much more clever strain than the ones we hunted years ago.

"This is one of the hardest things for today's hunter to accept. But I can tell you dozens of personal experiences proving that today's bucks don't make the mistakes made by the bucks of yesteryear. It seems as though there can be only one explanation: today's deer are much more clever because of heredity. Their basic trick today is to hide instead of running.

"I'll tell you a story that should convince some skeptics. I had a buddy, Bob Gainey, a pilot who flew two or three months of each year, mostly crop dusting. He wasn't much of a hunter, but every day during deer season when he could fly he was in the air. In the evenings we would sit down over a pot of coffee and discuss how the deer were outwitting hunters. Bob watched all sorts of goings-on from his very high vantage point.

"Time after time Bob told me about big bucks he saw bedded in sunny weeds close to a jungle of cover," Lyle went on. "He'd circle slowly and watch when he'd spot hunters moving toward the deer. Most of those bucks never budged an inch, even when hunters passed within 30 feet. The clever old boys would watch the men till they walked past, then resume napping as if nothing had happened.

"As I mentioned, Gainey wasn't much interested in hunting. But he'd buy a deer license and keep a rifle in his car just in case an easy opportunity presented itself. One afternoon he had the manager of our airport along for a ride. They were heading home when they spotted an enormous buck bedded in thick alder brush no more than 40 yards from a gravel road and less than three miles from the airport. Bob decided that nailing that buck in his bed would be a cinch.

"He put his plane down on the runway, then headed for the buck's hiding spot in his car while the airport manager flew back upstairs to watch the show.

"Gainey figured he knew exactly where the buck was lying. All he had to do was drive to a spot opposite the deer's bed, find him with his riflescope and shoot him on the spot. He parked his car, shoved a cartridge into his rifle, climbed to the top of his vehicle and searched in vain for the enormous rack.

"He then crawled down very quietly and tried sneaking toward a particular poplar tree near which he was sure the buck was bedded. When he got to the tree he looked for the bed that had to be a few feet south of the poplar. No bed. It then entered his mind that he had chosen the wrong poplar, so he attempted to climb it for a better look into surrounding brush. The 180-pound man and the skinny tree didn't go well together and Bob put up quite a commotion.

"About that time the buck had seen enough. He exploded out of the brush near a similar tree and bounded toward the road. Gainey was disgusted that he'd picked the wrong tree, but he was even more upsest when he got back to the airport and heard the manager's story of the episode.

" 'Bob,' Bill said, 'you could have killed that buck easily after he jumped. He hit the ditch on the side of the road in a few bounds and he froze right there because he spotted a woman walking toward him down the road. He waited till she walked by, then carefully tip-toed across behind her. She never knew he was there. If you had hurried after him you would have had an easy shot.' "

It depends on how you analyze this incident whether you'll claim that buck was smart or clever. I'll contend that the whitetail wasn't smart at all. If he could reason like a human, he wouldn't have wasted one second trying to avoid being seen by an unarmed woman when he knew there was a man with a rifle just three jumps behind him. He simply reverted to cleverness to avoid a new situation that suddenly presented itself.

It's not the purpose of this chapter to tell you about the hunting techniques necessary to cope with the traits of modern deer. You'll find all that information detailed in other chapters. My purpose here is to mention the changed reactions of today's deer so you'll understand more readily why the how-to tricks work as well as they do.

I've harped on the theory that modern bucks have learned it's much more clever to hide than to run, but I can't resist mentioning another of Lyle's stories that may do much to cement the theory. Here's the way Lyle tells it:

"One recent fall there were few deer shot in my area because of extremely poor hunting weather which, in my book, is the Number 1 reason for a low harvest. My buddy Bob Gainey was shook up about the fact that so many hunters were positive the herd had declined. He had been flying all season and he had spotted plenty of deer from the air.

" 'You know, Lyle,' he said, 'you could make a pile of money betting disgusted hunters that you could show them twenty deer in twenty minutes. I'd take them up in my plane and we'd see deer by the dozens.'

"Well, a while later George Constance walked into my gun shop. I got him all shook up by saying that anybody who couldn't spot deer couldn't call himself much of a hunter. He was hopping mad when I bet him $10 I could show him twenty deer in twenty minutes. He about broke his arm reaching for his wallet. He figured he had been conned when I told him Bob Gainey was waiting at the airport, but he drove out there.

"When he came back he was amazed. Not only had he seen a lot more than twenty deer, he had seen at least twenty big bucks. And Bob never did fly more than fifteen miles from the airport, which is in the huge Superior, Wisconsin–Duluth, Minnesota metro area."

When Deer Act Dumb

We can only draw conclusions from the actions of deer in different situations. If a buck were smart he would never lose all of his instincts for caution. With man or animal it's possible to be clever one day and not so clever the next because cleverness isn't an instinct. I doubt if there's a veteran deer hunter anywhere who won't agree that a mature buck can exhibit the heights of stupidity during the rut. That's not being smart, but it is instinctive.

I shot my best whitetail buck, a Saskatchewan giant, because that fool deer wouldn't leave three does. My guide and I spotted the four deer in broad daylight in a willow swale and we made a successful stalk. I fired my first shot at the buck while he was still unaware of our presence. The range was only 150 yards, but my .243 slug hit a willow branch and deflected.

The four whitetails lit out on a run straight away and I missed two more shots. In the prairie country you can see a long way so after the animals were out of reasonable range I ran to the top of a knoll and watched them run in the distance. Through my scope I saw that buck break away from the does several times and head for heavy cover. But each time he noted the does weren't staying with him and he rejoined them. Eventually they trotted into a small pocket of brush. They didn't come out the far end.

"Okay," my guide said, "it'll be quite a walk but we've got that buck dead to rights if he stays with those does. We'll circle around a couple of miles then come in on that brush from downwind."

That's what we did. When we got close to the brush my guide walked around to the south end and I stationed myself near the north end. As soon as my guide began crashing through the cover that giant whitetail exploded out with a rush. He ran right in front of me and I piled him up.

That buck did a lot of things that weren't smart at all. First, he allowed himself to be caught out in the open where he could be seen in daylight. Mature whitetail bucks just don't do that except during the rut. Second, though he wanted to escape to heavy cover where he would have been safe, he couldn't resist staying with the does. He still could have saved his skin if he'd had enough sense to watch his back track from just inside that pocket of cover where his lady friends decided to stop. He didn't even do that, which is a common stunt pulled by bucks during seasons other than the rut.

There's one trick deer try that makes me wonder if they have any reasoning power at all. That's their idea of trying to escape notice by freezing motionless even if they are in scant cover. I've had many experiences with this act; one yielded my best mule-deer buck, a real bruiser that I nailed on the western slope of the Colorado Rockies.

Why have modern deer developed the strong tendency to hide rather than run when confronted with approaching hunters? Usually this is a clever tactic for two basic reasons: Because of ever-increasing numbers of hunters, a running deer is likely to blunder into more trouble ahead. Also, if he jumps and runs the hunter who jumped him is suddenly aware of his presence and may get a shot. This is especially true in mule-deer areas where the country is relatively open. So a clever deer doesn't jump and run. He freezes and hopes to go unnoticed.

My guess is that this tactic works exceptionally well when there is no snow on the ground. I'd bet that for every deer a hunter sees there are at least twenty more that see the hunter but are unseen themselves. Deer are so successful with this trick that they use it year-round. If they had real mental ability they'd realize most of their camouflage is gone when there is snow on the ground.

Anyway, I was on horseback that morning in Colorado when I happened to spot the big buck silhouetted against a snow background in some aspens. The buck was watching me, and if he'd had any common sense he'd have run over the top of the ridge he was standing on as soon as I made my first move to dismount. But he didn't. He stood still as a statue all during the commotion I made yanking my rifle out of its scabbard and dismounting. By that time I realized the buck figured he was hidden. I took my time with my shot and dropped him in his tracks.

Some hunters to whom I've told the story claimed that buck didn't move because mule deer are used to horses. Well, they shake their heads when I tell them another story. It concerns the time I was coming down a mountain in Montana during an elk hunt.

It was late in the afternoon and turning dusk. A group of us were in two four-wheel-drive vehicles. We were driving slowly down a winding snow-covered trail. Suddenly my guide said, "Look at that fool buck standing over there in that sagebrush. He thinks we can't see him. You might as well take him. He's a good three-pointer."

Our casual attitude about shooting the deer was born of the fact that many hunters don't bother with deer when concentrating on elk. My general big-game license that year included two permits for deer, and I intended to fill at least one. Since we were finished elk hunting for the day my guide thought I might as well nail that buck.

I stepped out of the vehicle, jerked my rifle out of its case, jacked in a cartridge, took aim, and knocked the buck flat. Can anybody convince me I outwitted a super-smart animal? No way. But it could be that I shot a clever buck who was too clever for his own good. If he'd been smart he'd have known he couldn't hide against a snow background even though he was standing motionless in brush. He'd have been safe if he'd bolted as soon as the vehicles stopped. The reason he didn't is the same reason that thousands of deer are killed every year after snowfall. You will hear about similar incidents any time deer hunters discuss their success stories.

My guess is that deer will freeze motionless against snow backgrounds because the seemingly clever stunt works so well when there is no snow on the ground. In any event today's deer use it so extensively that the art of seeing deer—or parts of deer—is one of the most important abilities the modern hunter can develop. For that reason I devoted a long chapter in this book to the subject of seeing deer.

The frequent reaction of a deer shot at and missed is another reason to question his mental ability. If you're a veteran you probably, at one time or another, missed a shot at a buck and had him stand right there as if nothing had happened. One time years ago my brother fired five shots at an eight-point whitetail buck standing broadside less than 70 yards away. They had no more effect than if he'd been shooting blanks. The sixth slug from the old rifle took that buck in his lung area and dropped him as if he'd been sledged.

Why will a mature buck occasionally do such a crazy thing? Perhaps it's partly because he's not smart enough to recognize gunfire for what it is. My gunsmith friend Lyle Laurvick has some theories about this.

"In today's woods there is a lot more gunfire than there used to be," he told me. "I'm convinced that deer have no fear of noises that they hear frequently. I've been on hundreds of stands in trees, places where I've been able to look down on deer and watch their reactions when rifles roared nearby. Invariably they'll look immediately in the direction of the shot, then go back to whatever they were doing before the noise occurred.

"The incidents that really convince me of their lack of fear of gunfire have been my experiences on my rifle range. I fire hundreds of rounds through my customer's rifles on that range, and it happens to be located in good deer country just outside town. I've had scores of deer feeding within 200 yards upwind of me while I'm shooting. They'll look up when I start a new round of shots, then go back feeding with an apparent 'so what?' attitude.

"Two days before our season this year I'd just finished firing a string of twenty-one shots," Lyle continued. "Right then I happened to spot a six-point buck standing 150 yards away. One of the customer's rifles lying on my bench was an H&H Magnum equipped with a 15x scope. I viewed that deer through the scope and he didn't seem the least bit frightened or alarmed. It's obvious to me that it takes more than gunfire to spook a deer."

I believe that Lyle is right when he says, "It takes more than gunfire." It's my guess that deer depend upon more than one specific sense to detect danger. Of the three senses, sight, sound, and scent, it's likely that scent is the most important because deer seldom tolerate human scent. It would appear that no deer would stand still and let a man shoot at him if he could detect human odor unless the animal was sure he was hidden. But caught by surprise a buck is not likely to try being clever. He may not bolt till he sees the hunter or smells him, but add one of those senses to the sound of gunfire and the animal probably will panic. I'd bet that a buck shot at and missed isn't unusually alarmed until he sees or smells the man shooting at him. Many fine bucks have been bagged because they waited too long to make sure they were in trouble, and that's not being very smart.

Add to these thoughts the knowledge that deer behavior is often controlled by habit and curiosity to the point of stupidity. Deer are extremely curious about unfamiliar sounds. They will not hesitate to investigate when something new and unusual happens in their home area. Though I've never tried calling deer with a varmint call I've heard and read that the technique is quite successful in some parts of the country. Why a deer, supposedly smart, would be curious enough to run to a varmint call is beyond me. A fox or coyote will respond to a call because he thinks he will get something to eat; what does a buck think he will get?

As to being controlled by habit, deer habitually use the same runways, feeding and bedding areas, and they favor certain watering spots. One of their most stupid habits is their tendency not to expect danger from above. They seldom have the sense to look up, and that's precisely why tree stands can be so effective.

Most hunters claim that whitetail deer obviously are super-smart because their populations are higher now than when the Pilgrims landed in America. They say that an animal smart enough to survive the drastic conditions of modern civilization and greatly increased hunting pressure has to have a great amount of brains. Serious students of the principles of game management know better. They're aware that the original whitetail populations in many of our states were virtually wiped out by overhunting back around the turn of the century. Even the mule deer in our western mountains were nearly exterminated by meat and hide hunters.

We don't have more deer today because the animals know how to take care of themselves; we have our millions of deer because of controlled hunting and the knowledge applied to deer-management programs by modern game biologists. The principle is basic: Give a wild animal the habitat he needs and his populations will multiply as long as he gets the required protection.

The reason the majority of hunters don't bag a buck seems to me to be fundamental. Every hunt is a contest of wits with only two possible outcomes: either you get your deer or you don't. Usually the hunter loses the game because he is a lot smarter but far less clever than his quarry. The odds highly favor the deer because they know every inch of the relatively small area they live in year-round. The hunter is in the same area only a few days each fall. He normally doesn't score because he makes mistakes, does something wrong, and doesn't hunt hard enough.

We can be thankful that deer make mistakes too, and I hope this chapter has convinced you of that. Perhaps it will make you hunt harder next fall. If you hunt the way you should you may very well cash in on a small error made by your buck. Many hunters go at the game of wits half-heartedly because they figure they're no match for a "smart" buck in the first place. That is a mighty stupid attitude to have.

CHAPTER
16

How Weather
Affects Deer

If you successfully hunt deer enough times from the same spot you're bound to learn a lot about how the animals react to weather conditions. Much of this knowledge can be the key to putting venison into your freezer. Lack of understanding of the principles involved can lead to hours or even days of wasted hunting effort.

For example, during the past 15 years I've shot seven whitetail bucks from the same spot that's on my property in Michigan. I just happened to be standing on that knoll when I killed the first of the seven. A couple of years later I was sitting there with my back to a beech tree when I dropped the second buck.

By then I realized that the spot was a natural place for a stand. For the next several years I made temporary blinds there from cedar and oak branches. After I killed two more bucks I built a permanent blind from weathered boards so I wouldn't have to bother with rebuilding each fall. The spot produced again last year when I got my buck the first morning of our November deer season.

I keep notes regarding weather conditions during all of my outdoor activities. Some years ago I was really surprised to discover that I'd never seen a deer from that knoll whenever the wind was from the north, whenever a very strong wind was blowing from any direction, or when heavy rain or snow was falling. Now I never waste my time hunting there under such conditions.

To help explain the first discovery I'll give you a verbal picture of the lay of the land. The knoll is the highest place on a series of east-west running hardwood hills and ravines that slope down to a large inland lake. The shoreline of the lake is 300 yards downhill from my blind. Behind my stand relatively level woodlands of mixed hardwoods, aspen and hemlock run south several hundred yards to typical Michigan farm country. The area's whitetails feed in or near the crop fields and bed in various thick edge covers, or in the woodlands near the lake.

Consider what a deer realizes when confronted with a north wind blowing across the lake and into the woods surrounding my stand. Of most importance, the animal knows that hunters are almost bound to approach from the south and not from the lake to the north of my woods. The north wind takes away the deer's ability to scent danger coming from the south. Also, all deer normally won't bed on north-sloping hills when there's a north wind.

An opposite situation applies when a south wind is blowing. Then the deer want to bed in my woods because they will be downwind from the danger areas and they can bed in comfort.

My notes, plus my deer-hunting experiences over many years, have enabled me to draw many conclusions on how deer react to given weather conditions. Last winter I organized my notes and thoughts by category, and came up with weather-related information that I considered most important for deer hunters across the nation. Then I cross checked my conclusions with some expert deer hunters. Following is a boiled-down version of what we agreed upon.

Bruce Brady, for many years *Outdoor Life*'s southern field editor, has hunted whitetails in almost every southern and southeastern state. "The absolute worst time to hunt deer anywhere is when a very strong wind is blowing," Brady emphasized. "During such conditions the animals will lay up and won't move. All deer rely on the senses of sight, sound and scent to warn them of danger. When a strong wind is blowing, bushes, tree branches and loose bits of ground cover are moving. Strong winds make noise, and produce crosswinds that temporarily blow from various directions. In short, deer won't move in high winds because their three most important senses of survival are at least partially destroyed. Most hunters hunt when they have the time, but statistics show that they almost never kill deer during strong wind conditions."

Heavy Falling Rain or Snow

Brady, along with many other experts I talked with, agree that deer seek shelter whenever precipitation is heavy. The animals much prefer umbrella-type protection, such as stands of thick pines. Most deer biologists feel that deer do not seek such protection because they get chilled, but rather because heavy precipitation limits their ability to hear, see or smell danger. If you have to hunt when strong winds are mixed with heavy rain or snow you should hunt in the thickest cover you can find.

Light Rain or Mist

Many years ago a veteran deer hunter told me that rainy days are by all odds the best times to hunt whitetails. I thought he was putting me on until I met Paul Mickey. He's emphatic about how good deer hunting can be in light rain. Mickey has taken over a dozen outstanding trophy whitetails. His best, a non-typical giant scoring 238-2/8, is the best non-typical ever taken in Michigan; and the 35th best ever taken in North America. Mickey killed that buck on a rainy day in 1976. Many of his other big bucks have been taken in rainy or misty weather.

"Most serious deer hunters know that rain dramatically reduces use of the two senses that deer rely on most heavily for safety—hearing and scent, but many aren't aware that it also disturbs a whitetail's travel schedule to such a degree that it abandons normal caution," Mickey once told me. "When a night is clear, it takes up to an hour for full darkness to turn into dawn. On a rainy night the period of darkness to dawn is much shorter, sometimes as short as 15 minutes. There isn't any gradually lightening sky. Instead, shooting light seems to come on very rapidly.

"On rainy mornings deer tend to stay in feeding fields much later than usual," Mickey went on. "Then, when daylight comes on fast, they suddenly realize they have to hurry to reach daytime security cover in bedding areas. This situation makes even the wariest deer much less cautious. A buck that would normally stop every 20 yards or so to test for danger with his eyes, ears and nose now may travel over 100 yards between stops. And when he does pause, his senses are drastically dulled by the rain. A man on stand never has as many odds in his favor as he does when he hunts on a rainy morning."

Mickey also pointed out that in really nasty weather—freezing rain or wet snow—bedded deer get very uncomfortable. Because of this they'll begin moving toward feeding areas much earlier in the afternoon than normal. Nasty weather urges deer to move later in the mornings and earlier in the afternoons, and both situations offer the hunter longer periods of shooting light than on clear days when deer hate to leave security cover until near darkness prevails.

Light Snow Vs Heavy Snow

Jim Zumbo, a long-time *Outdoor Life* staff editor, lives in Vernal, Utah. His home-base location is relatively close to several other Rocky Mountain states. Because of this, he often hunts mule deer in as many as five states each fall. But he originally lived in the East where he put in many years hunting whitetails before switching to mule deer.

"We seldom get rain in the mountains after October 15, so we're usually dealing with snow during deer seasons," Zumbo told me. "Light snow has about the same effect on mule deer as light rain does on whitetails. It doesn't repress normal deer activity, but it does make the animals much more vulnerable to knowledgeable hunters. Several times, after I first moved to Utah, I heard veteran still-hunters and stalkers say that they always try to hunt when light to medium snowfall is occurring. They claimed that falling snow bothers a deer's ears and interferes with his hearing. It also cuts down on his vision and helps to cushion the sounds of a hunter's approach. I also believe that any precipitation tends to drive a human's scent into the ground.

"In any event I like to stillhunt and stalk alone, and I'll guarantee that these methods work best when a light snow is falling. But the very best mule deer hunting in the mountains comes after a heavy snowfall that stays. We get early heavy snows that soon melt, but the first one that doesn't melt drives migrating mule deer crazy.

"High-country muleys can be extremely susceptible to heavy snow because some sort of sixth sense tells them that it's extremely dangerous," Zumbo continued. "They know they have to get down to lower elevations to survive, and when they begin migrating they don't stop for anything. Any hunter who knows of a mule deer migration route, and can be there the first day after the first heavy snowfall that stays, will get hunting that can simply be incredible.

"The most dramatic example of this I've seen involved a group of 14 hunters who were tent camping near a migration route. They killed 14 mature mule deer bucks in a single day, and that was the first day after the first big blizzard. I could hardly believe my eyes when I saw all those big bucks loaded into three pickup trucks."

Zumbo's statement is easy for me to understand. Some years ago I hunted out of Collbran, Colorado, with outfitter Ray Lyons. He told me several times while we were riding horses into our hunting area that I should definitely hold out for at least a fine 4-pointer. "There are lots of migrating muleys on the slopes we'll hunt," Lyons emphasized. "You'll see more big bucks in one day than most hunters see in a lifetime. Wait for a really big bruiser."

I did. I dropped a massive 4-pointer in his tracks with a 100-grain slug sent on its way with my Winchester Model 70 .243.

Warm, Calm and Sunny

Despite all I've written so far about weather, many seasoned deer hunters will claim that they see more deer on nice days than on nasty days. They're right. Deer are definitely most active on nice, clear days. Some of the most convincing proof of this fact comes from Al Hofacker, a record keeper for the nationwide group of deer hunters called the Stump Sitters. The group's data comes from many thousands of hours of observing deer by hundreds of members. According to Hofacker, hunters averaged seeing 41 deer per 100 hours of observation on partly cloudy days; 45 per 100 hours on overcast days; and 59 per 100 hours on clear days. "I was surprised at how the figures added up," said Hofacker. "Until I studied our data I had assumed that deer moved best on cloudy days. Now I know that our members are seeing 40 percent more deer on clear days."

A few years ago the Stump Sitters cooperated with the University of Wisconsin-Stevens Point on a research project involving deer activity in relationship to weather variables. Results showed that, in general, whitetails are fair-weather creatures. Hunters observed the most deer during periods of clear skies, light wind, and no rain or snow.

All of this seems logical because under such weather conditions deer can take maximum advantage of their superior senses of hearing, sight and scent to alert them to potential danger. It also follows that although hunters see more deer in nice weather, they'll be much more successful in bagging them if they hunt when weather conditions dull the animals' abilities to sense danger. Weather variables can up your odds in other ways too.

Depth of Snow

Jim Zumbo told me that mule deer may move completely out of one given area as soon as snow depth exceeds one foot, but that deer in another given area may not migrate until snow depth reaches 18 to 20 inches.

"I have no idea why this is true," Zumbo said, "but it's a fact from my years of observation in many mule deer areas. One of my very best hunting areas becomes worthless as soon as the snow gets over a foot deep. It took me a few years to discover that fact. The hunter who keeps accurate records of his observations can eliminate hunting in the wrong places."

In general, deep snow will force deer to change their feeding locations. Stump Sitter data, according to Al Hofacker, indicates that whitetails will continue feeding on ground foods such as acorns or waste grain in snow depths up to six inches deep. The animals can paw the snow away from such foods without a great deal of trouble, but when the snow gets considerably deeper the deer will switch to brushy browse. Choice browse may be far away from choice ground food. A harvested corn field that attracted dozens of deer in November could very well attract none in December.

However, it's well to keep in mind that there can be exceptions to any rule. Several years ago in my area of Michigan, we had a very hard freeze before the first snowfall. During the first few days of deer season I hunted from a stand near a harvested corn field. I saw a few deer each day, but not nearly as many as I watched a few days after our first blizzard hit. Official depth of snow on the ground was over a foot. Fierce winds produced drifts over four-feet deep, but the strong winds also blew that frozen field almost bare of snow. The easy to get waste corn drew deer like a magnet.

Clear Vs Dark Nights

The long-held belief that deer feed heavily on clear—especially moonlit—nights apparently is more myth than fact. Deer biologists point out that a deer's night vision is so good that the animal can feed actively on the darkest of nights. In fact, deer are likely to feel safer in the open during dark nights. In any event, the degree of light intensity at night will probably have little bearing on the success of your hunt the next day.

Storm Fronts

One popular belief that isn't a myth is that deer usually go on feeding binges the day before major fall storms hit most anywhere in the nation. Rapidly falling barometric pressure precedes these storms. Deer biologists agree that deer activity picks up significantly as the barometer drops. Whitetails, particularly, tend to roam wide and feed heavily before storms; so this is obviously an excellent time to be on stand near feeding areas.

The very best place to be on stand the day a storm hits is near dense cover. As I noted earlier, deer want to move into heavy cover when a bad storm arrives. So when the storm is close, get on a stand overlooking a runway (or runways) leading to the thickest cover you know about and wait for deer to move to you.

The worse the storm the thicker the cover the deer will seek. Lyle Laurvick, the gunsmith friend of mine who lives in Superior, Wisconsin, hunts with a group that has a very high hunter success ratio; especially when they hunt a certain area at a certain time. "The place is close to the very remote Lake Superior shoreline, and it's so jungle-like thick in there that we cut some trails before each deer season," Laurvick says. "There are few deer in that big swamp during normal weather conditions, but that changes fast when big storms hit. We hope for a major blizzard before deer season ends. If we get it we know we're going to take a lot of venison out of that place."

But Laurvick and other experts are quick to emphasize that there are three phases to hunting storm fronts and storms. During the front—prior to the storm itself but when the barometer first begins tumbling—deer are most interested in feeding heavily and are still little concerned about cover. Hunting from a stand in or near a good feeding area is the way to go. But as the front passes and the storm begins, take your stand near cover areas. When heavy rain or snow is falling, the animals want to be holed up until the precipitation passes.

"We go into action after the blizzard passes," Laurvick explains. "We know the thickest pockets of cover where the deer will be, and we know the escape routes they'll take when they're jumped. We're so familiar with how the animals will react that we know exactly how we should drive our area and exactly where the hunters on stand should be. We execute our drives with military-like precision, but the real key to our success is knowing what the whitetails are going to do when a roaring blizzard hits."

There are many other bits of knowledge that can help the weather-oriented hunter. Most sportsmen have been indoctrinated with the idea the deer always travel upwind so that they can scent danger ahead. The expert hunter knows that the animals must sometimes travel downwind, and that this usually happens when the best travel route to a preferred feeding area runs downwind from a bedding area.

When whitetails are faced with this situation, they'll almost always travel along ridgelines because air currents tend to swirl over uneven land contours. By routing through such air currents the animals are offered some security because they can use their noses to scent danger from all directions. The hunter who is aware of this principle hunts along ridgelines whenever the weather dictates that he should.

All deer—being very hardy creatures—don't pay nearly as much attention to temperature changes as humans do, but temperature extremes can put some odds in the hunter's favor. Most deer seasons aren't open during extremely hot periods, but many hunters have to cope with extreme cold weather. From what I've heard from many veteran hunters, and from my own observations over more than 40 years of deer hunting, I don't think deer want to move before full dawn after a very cold night.

A deer can curl up into an extremely small circle and maintain body heat in the coldest temperatures if he doesn't move. It follows that he won't want to move until full sunlight is shining on him, and that he will most likely bed in an area where the day's first sunlight will hit him. So the weather-wise hunter expects deer to bed on southern exposure ridges or slopes during very cold nights, he expects them to be still feeding during late morning hours, and he expects them to favor sunlighted areas that are out of the wind as long as extreme cold temperatures hang on. And he knows he should be patient on stand because deer won't move as often or as far as they will on warm days, so he dresses warm enough to stay comfortable.

This is the type of thinking that takes the success of your hunt out of the "luck category" because you're depending on good basic hunting knowledge. You can't use weather-related knowledge to tell you when to hunt, but you can definitely use it to tell you how to hunt. When you know how deer react to weather you'll know where they're likely to be at any given time and what they're likely to be doing. With that kind of knowledge you'll know whether it's best to take a stand, try stillhunting or stalking, or organize a drive.

CHAPTER 17

Hunting Away from Home

Because I'm a full time outdoor writer, much of my job involves hunting away from home. I've been on deer hunts over much of North America. In recent years these trips have been very successful because I've learned how to plan them. But I'll never forget some of my early hunts.

Years ago I made a trip into Minnesota that turned out to be a complete flop. A casual friend told me he used to hunt in a certain area of the state that was loaded with deer. Being a greenhorn I had visions of driving into the area, picking a hunting spot and waiting for a buck to walk by.

It turned out that it had been many years since my friend had hunted the area. Much of the woodland he had described in glowing terms had been lumbered and cleared. The game warden he told me to look up was retired. The youngster who had taken his place seemed more interested in wearing a shiny uniform than helping deer hunters. I never saw a deer in two days of hunting. By then I realized I was up against a hopeless situation. I was in strange country without local contacts and without any idea of where to get advice. I got into my car and made a very depressing journey home.

This sort of thing happens all too often to inexperienced hunters. They read glowing reports of great deer hunting in outdoors magazines, they note the area hunted, and they decide to travel out there next fall and get in on the action. This type of planning will lead to disappointment.

The Importance of Contacts

On any hunt in an area unfamiliar to you it's necessary to have a contact who knows the area and how to hunt it, and you must be assured he will hunt with you. This is the precise reason why good guides or outfitters can charge high rates and be worth every penny you pay them. A good guide in average game country is much more likely to get you a shot at a buck than is a poor guide in top game country. I'm not saying you have to hire a professional guide to insure a good hunt in unfamiliar country, but it's almost mandatory to have a contact who can perform many of the functions of a guide. Some incidents come to mind that illustrate the point.

A friend has hunted in Montana for the past five years. His first trip was a washout because he simply climbed into his car and drove out West to go deer hunting. The next year he tried a different area with the same results, until he got smart. He decided to quit hunting, drive to various ranches, strike up conversations with ranchers, and offer to pay a guiding fee. One rancher took up the offer and showed my friend a big buck after only a couple hours of hunting. The two men struck up a fine friendship and my buddy has been going back to the same ranch every year since. Now, he never has much trouble getting his game. The system this fellow used is a great one for any hunter who has the time to scout around, knock on a few doors, and develop contacts.

My major rule when hunting a new area is go with a man who knows the area, and go when he tells me to go. If you go earlier or later because of personal preference you'll seriously hamper your odds on bagging a buck.

Hunting Partners

Because hunting is also my job I often have to leave for hunts alone, but it's certainly more enjoyable if I have a companion along. I make darn sure it's a companion who is going to add pleasure to the hunt, not take pleasure away. I've seen too many hunting parties in the field having a lousy time because one or more members of the group made life miserable for their companions. When you spend a lot of money for a hunting trip nothing is more disheartening than having the fun ruined by some guy who doesn't get along with the rest of the group.

It seems to me that some hunters select their partners at cocktail parties. It's almost as if a couple of casual acquaintances meet and the talk swings to hunting. One guy might say, "Why don't we plan a deer hunt in Wyoming? I'll bet Jack and Pete would go. We'll have a great time."

Well, a man may act a lot differently in the field than he does at home. You don't know how a friend feels about hunting until you've been out with him a few times when the going is rough and the game doesn't cooperate. The middle of an expensive hunting trip is not the time to find that you and your buddies don't see eye to eye. Game hogs, bemoaners of not getting meat, and complainers about weather or accommodations can ruin the best of trips. The time to find out if you want to make an extensive trip with a man is after you know him well enough to be sure he enjoys the outdoors the same way you do.

Before planning a hunt away from home, you should consider the following factors:

Creature Comforts

Do you want to hunt big country, but also want creature comforts at the end of the day—a bed in a motel and nights in town?

Being a Michigan flatlander, the thrill of hunting big country—mountain ranges or foothills—offers a special appeal to me. Being in my late fifties, I'm not really as excited about roughing it as I used to be. If I can find creature comforts at the end of the day after hunting in good deer country I'll take them. There are a couple of ideal ways of doing this. They are advantages the old-timers didn't have.

The boom in motels across the country during the last decade or two has reached into the boonies. Some of the little towns boasting populations of only a couple of thousand or so have surprisingly nice motels, especially if they're in vacation country. I've based in motels during several deer hunts in the prairie and intermountain states, and they worked out fine. A town that has at least one decent motel generally has at least one good eating place. The thing to remember about motels in good hunting country is that they fill up fast. Some hunters returning to the same area year after year make their reservations a year in advance.

Another excellent way of enjoying creature comforts at the end of a hard day of hunting is to base in one of the newer fold-out trailer campers. I well remember a deer hunt four of us made in Wyoming a few years ago. One of my partners and I decided to drive to our host's ranch, pull a rental fold-out trailer, park it near the ranch, and enjoy life. Our two other partners decided on different transportation, and they accepted our host's invitation to base in one of his outbuildings that had been used as a bunkhouse years earlier.

Warren and I were extremely cozy in our rented trailer. We had good heat, lights and plenty of room. Our two companions shivered because of inadequate heat, and they put up with mice and cobwebs in the run-down bunkhouse. For my money fold-out trailers are great. They're compact, easy to tow, and you can get them into almost any back-country that's open to cars or trucks.

Plusher accommodations are more readily available to deer hunters than they are to most other types of hunters and fishermen simply because deer can live close to man if good habitat is available. One of the finest small-town inns I've stayed in is in Chamberlain, South Dakota. There were four of us on that trip, and we all downed fine bucks within a few miles of town. We lived about as well as you can anywhere and still enjoy good hunting. Such a hunt would be ideal for elderly, out-of-condition, or physically handicapped hunters.

Do You Want to Camp Out?

A few years ago my conception of the ideal deer hunt was to camp far from the crowd. Getting away from other hunters usually means pack trips with horses or backpacking trips. Recently I was on a December pack-trip hunt in the Colorado Rockies. I figured our group had to be the only hunters on the mountain because we were 11 miles up from the nearest road. I was really surprised when one of our guides told me he had met two young deer hunters who had backpacked up that mountain. When he had come upon the two men they were boning out a big four-point buck.

The best way to get some solitude and enjoy spectacular scenery is to book a pack-trip hunt with a good outfitter. Backpacking trips can get you into lonely country, too, because most hunters won't walk more than a short distance from their cars. If you take a day to backpack into a remote area you'll leave the great majority of hunters far behind. A couple of my deer-hunting friends go this route. They select their hunting areas by studying topographic maps. They pick regions far from roads. They hike in and hunt where there are large chunks of public hunting lands. Most guides have no more control over access to those lands than you do.

Another good bet is to contact state game departments and ask specific questions concerning where you'll find the type of hunting you want. If you're just interested in meat you should ask which sections of the state produce the most deer and which sections have the highest harvests. If you're interested in a trophy you should ask which sections produce the biggest bucks. I've asked the game departments of every state in the nation these questions. It was surprising to discover that in most cases the biggest deer are not found in the same areas that produce the most deer.

Though I've mentioned it in other places in this book, I want to emphasize that game departments in most of the better deer states no longer try to attract nonresident deer hunters with the enthusiasm that they used to years ago. Many state game officials are now worrying about too many deer hunters rather than too few. Many of these officials no longer have any problems selling their high-priced nonresident deer licenses, so it makes sense that they have cut down on the reams of deer-hunting information they used to supply to prospective nonresident hunters. But it's a different story with tourist associations, state travel agencies, and outfitter or guide associations. Such organizations want your dollars, and they spend a lot of promotional money to get them. If you ask, most state game departments will give you the names and addresses of the organizations that will be of most help to you.

Because of the factors I've mentioned and because most modern hunters have more leisure time and more money than ever before, and because of the advantages of modern camping equipment, the possibilities of camping and hunting where you can be alone are far better now than in the so-called "good old days."

Hiring an Outfitter?

If you prefer to hunt deer country with a top outfitter who can provide you with shooting opportunity and take care of all camp chores, dressing game and so forth, your opportunities have never been better. Most of these opportunities are in the West where increased numbers of hunters have led to increased numbers of outfitters and guides.

The easiest way to make contact with top outfitters is to get the names and addresses of the organizations from their advertisements in outdoor magazines. Of course, not all outfitters advertise, so another good bet is to ask state game departments for addresses of guide and outfitter associations. Then contact such outfits, mention what type of hunting you want to do, and you'll get more information than you need.

Still another approach is to go to your newsstand and pay $2.50 for the magazine *Deer and Big Game,* an annual published by *Outdoor Life.* In it you'll find deer-hunting forecasts for each state, details on license costs, permit quotas, permit application deadlines and many other details. The magazine also contains addresses and phone numbers for all state fish and game departments. It's on sale each year by July 1.

My first rule is to contact several outfitters or guides in the area I want to hunt. When I get replies I examine them carefully. Those that promise the moon are automatically rejected. It seems that too many nonresidents have the wrong idea that game in the western states is so plentiful they'll find big bucks stepping out of cover all over the place. Unscrupulous guides and outfitters prey on this false belief. They assume that if they promise exceptional and easy hunting they're sure to book plenty of clients. They worry about producing, later.

It's simply impossible to consistently produce what they promise because deer hunting isn't that easy anywhere. Sure, some hunters are lucky, but by and large it takes a lot of work and knowledge on an outfitter's part to get his clients reasonable shooting opportunities. And there are many contributing factors an outfitter can't control. Bad weather, game populations that may be up or down, and heavy or light hunting pressure all have good or bad effects on a client's opportunity to bag a buck. The good outfitters are aware of these things, and they're aware they'll get some clients who can't hunt hard enough and can't shoot straight. These men don't promise you great trophies and easy hunting. Instead they'll tell you how long they have been in business, what facilities and services they can offer, and that they'll do everything possible to make your hunt safe, comfortable and rewarding. When you get replies along those lines you're usually dealing with honest men.

The next step is to get references. The reputable men will be more than happy to supply the names and addresses of hunters they have guided during recent years. Your letters or phone calls to a few of these hunters will get opinions as to whether the men they dealt with produced a satisfactory or unsatisfactory hunt.

Another system can work, too. I often get letters from gunners who read my deer-hunting stories in *Outdoor Life.* In the stories I always mention the names and addresses of my guides and outfitters. Quite often readers will ask me if I'd recommend the men I hunted with. You can use the same system. When you read the story of a deer hunt that intrigues you, why not follow up on it? Write the author in care of the magazine's editorial offices and ask whatever questions you want answered. Many authors reply to these letters.

Once you make firm contact with the man you want it's time to ask some specific questions. As I mentioned earlier you should know what types of gear to bring along. Little things like knowing whether insulated boots would be more suitable for the hunt than regular hiking boots could make a world of difference in comfort. The one thing that ruins many hunts is boots that don't match the type of hunting that's required.

You should know what type of shooting opportunities you're likely to get so you can sight-in your rifle to meet them. You should know what the weather conditions will probably be so you can pack clothing that will be most comfortable and efficient.

You should also know what type of personal gear you'll have real use for. A lot of hunters expect an outfitter to pack half their worldly goods into the back country for them. There's no sense in bogging down a hunt with equipment that won't be used. How can a hunter make good use of a month's supply of clothing, six pairs of boots, and a lot of unnecessary stuff like tape players and other convenience items? A few changes of clothes, some for warm or dry weather, some for cold or wet, are all a man requires. Check with your guide or outfitter on what he recommends.

One situation that's a modern trend, but which varies from state to state, is the use of Blaze Orange outer garments. Most states require them, others don't. Check with your guide on such items so you won't waste time shopping before the actual hunt begins.

Long before the hunt, arrange the meeting place with your man and when you'll meet him. It's best to try picking a time that's most convenient for both of you. A guide who has been working all day doesn't take kindly to meeting a plane in the middle of the night. Attention to such details always makes hunts run smoother.

Meat or Trophy?

Short hunts with the primary purpose of just getting venison is what many hunters have in mind. If this is your idea of how to go your first decision should be to travel to one of the states showing a high hunter-success ratio, as mentioned in Chapter 17. Write to the game department in the state of your choice and ask for information on which area of the state shows the highest deer harvest. Most of these states are in the intermountain area, which means they contain guide and outfitter services. Check guide and outfitter names and addresses through one of the systems I've mentioned. Then write for information on rates, services, and best times to schedule hunts. When you get the dope you can make your decision on where to go.

If you want to score on a trophy mule deer, the odds are you'll have to make arrangements with a guide or outfitter who operates in trophy country. As I've mentioned, the best heads taken from each state seldom come from the same areas that show the highest hunter-success ratios.

If you're really serious about the subject I'd suggest purchasing a copy of the book *Records of North American Big Game.* The last edition, published in 1981, sells for $29.50 plus $2.00 shipping costs. It's published and sold by the Boone and Crockett Club, 205 South Patrick Street, Alexandria, Virginia 22314.

The book lists hundreds of the best trophy deer taken in North America, the precise areas where the animals were killed, and the year they were killed. Study the book carefully and you can make a list of the major areas producing trophy bucks. Then, if you're interested in mule deer, you can contact guides or outfitters in the areas you select. I'd suggest picking an outfit that recommends a pack trip back into remote areas. Few big muley bucks are killed in areas easily reached by the average hunter. Most of the big brutes don't grow those enormous racks by being dumb enough to try surviving in heavily hunted areas.

From my experience, your best chance of downing a trophy whitetail is in southeastern Saskatchewan. I've never seen as many big bucks in other areas. There are some guides there, but in general you won't find guides and outfitters in most of North America's whitetail country.

Mule Deer or Whitetails?

There are several things to consider when you're trying to decide whether you want to hunt mule deer or whitetails. If you want an outstanding trophy it's best to go after mule deer for the reasons I just mentioned. Hook up with a good guide or outfitter and your chances soar because those fellows know where the deer are and they know how to hunt them.

Also, mule deer usually have larger racks than whitetails and they are easier to hunt. The major drawbacks to a mule-deer hunt for most of us are the expenses involved in traveling to western areas and paying for guided hunts. Other factors to consider include the type of hunting you enjoy and the kind of country in which you want to hunt.

If you enjoy stillhunting or stalking it's best to forget whitetails. These two methods are far more effective with mule deer. If you like to hunt on your own from a stand, then going after whitetails should be your choice. Mule deer should get your vote if you enjoy the terrain in the West and if you would prefer to hunt from a camp.

How Much to Spend?

I live near a small town in northern Michigan and can walk out my back door to go after whitetails. Last fall I nailed a buck only a half-mile from where I'm writing these lines. Later on during the fall I hunted mule deer with an outfitter in the Colorado Rockies. That trip cost me close to $1500. The meat of my Michigan whitetail cost me practically nothing. The mule-deer meat was expensive, somewhere around $15 per pound. That example serves to illustrate how the differences in costs of deer hunting can go.

There are other variables. The deer hunter who already owns a camping outfit can camp much more cheaply than the man who has to rent one. The man who rents a fold-out trailer and camps can make a hunt in a given area for less money than the man who bases in a motel and eats in restaurants. Four men sharing the costs of a trip can get by for less money than two men who make the same trip. A week's hunt with an outfitter cost less than a ten-day hunt. The list of variables could be almost endless. Cost of transportation alone can be a big item. If you and one or more partners share the costs of driving to a distant hunting area the cost per man would be much less than if you used air transportation.

If you live in the East it will cost you a lot more money to hunt mule deer than whitetails. Vice versa for most hunters who live in the West. What we have discussed in this chapter should give you the basic information you need to decide what kind of a hunt you want to make. The answers to letters you write to game departments, outfitters or guides, tourist associations, and state travel agencies will give you solid clues to how much various trips will cost. Then it's up to you to plan one that will fit your wallet.

Your Physical Condition

As an outdoor writer I talk to lots of deer hunters who make trips away from home. A few years ago I began to get the distinct impression that many of the most successful gunners are those that prepare themselves physically for the type of hunting they're going to do long before they make the trip. They set up training programs that may include dieting, jogging, playing tennis, or any number of regular exercises. These men figure that if they invest a lot of money in a hunting trip they want to be able to get the utmost enjoyment out of it. That theory certainly makes sense to me, and I follow it.

The other important point is that some types of deer hunting are much easier physically than others. Stillhunting, for instance, demands less physical exertion than climbing mountains. If you choose to hunt in mountainous terrain it's a lot easier to reach the back country by horseback than by backpacking. You should consider all such details if you're concerned about your physical condition.

Information Sources

I've also pointed out the basics of how to get information on license costs, season dates, permit applications, and so forth. I've talked about how to go through official channels, but I want to emphasize that there's another route that's more available today than ever before. It will save you some time in planning away-from-home hunts.

In the old days most deer hunters operated relatively close to home. In these modern times more and more gunners are making trips to distant states and provinces in attempts to bag their deer. A guy who has made a trip to the area you want to hunt is a valuable source of information. If you want to hunt deer in Wyoming the chances are there is somebody in your neighborhood who has been there, knows the ropes, and has the answers to many of the questions you're likely to ask.

If you can get in touch with the right man you'll save yourself a lot of trouble in planning a hunt. A good bet is to ask questions in sporting-goods stores. Many gunners who hunt away from home buy gear from their local dealers, and they like to mention that they're going to such-and-such a state to get their buck. Most hunters like to talk about their experiences, especially with strangers. Sporting-goods dealers are often able to suggest the names of great contacts.

And don't pass up chance meetings at such places as service clubs, golf clubs, and sportsman's clubs. If you let it be known that you're looking for information on out-of-state deer hunts you'll be surprised at the contacts you'll make.

Meat Care

Years ago it was common practice to hang deer from tree limbs in a cool area until the hunt was finished. Then the carcasses were tied to car tops or lashed to trailers for the drive home. This procedure involved no cost at all until the hunter arrived home. Then he had his local butcher cut up the meat. This expense was little noticed, for it was paid from the regular family budget.

Today it's obvious that you can't take a whole deer carcass home with you if you're traveling by commercial aircraft. Another important factor is the relatively new government control of meat-cutting plants. Regulations covering the cutting of noninspected meat are far stricter today than they were years ago. Today's butcher who wants to cut up game meat has to have certain facilities and has to follow specific regulations in order to be licensed to handle game.

Many of the smaller operators—those who used to handle game a few years ago—no longer will accept the meat. These men figured that it would cost more money to follow government regulations than they would take in by processing wild animals. In many areas of the East and Midwest it's now impossible to find a butcher who will process, cut up, and freeze game. So, in many cases, nonresident hunters have found it mandatory to have their meat taken care of in the area they hunt. It's no problem to find game processors in prime hunting regions.

It seems to me this is a far better deal than hauling a carcass home. For one thing, the sooner you process game the less chance you run of meat spoilage. Also, you eliminate a lot of problems when you get home. Last year, for example, I picked up my three cardboard boxes of frozen venison in the baggage area of our airport shortly after my plane landed. I loaded them into my station wagon and drove home. It took me only minutes to unpack my meat and stash it in my freezer. I've been doing the same thing for several years. It's far better than hoping unprocessed meat won't spoil on the way home, worrying about getting it into a cold-storage locker, worrying about finding a butcher to cut it up, and worrying about when he'll find time to do it.

Processing meat in the hunting country is my idea of the proper way to handle it regardless of whether my trip is made by plane or car. If I'm driving and it will take me two or three days to get home, I'll have the frozen meat packed with dry ice to keep it from thawing. And don't worry if it does thaw a bit. The old belief that frozen meat which has partially thawed out should not be refrozen has little basis in fact. It can be refrozen once with no damage at all. It should not be refrozen twice. This principle does not apply to fish and other more perishable foods. Once defrosted they should be eaten; refreezing can spoil them.

In the better deer areas of the West many game processors do a great volume of business. I've seen groups of hunters arrive at processing plants in pickup trucks loaded with game carcasses. I've seen cold-storage rooms crowded with deer hanging from meat hooks. I mention this to point out that it's not wise to expect a processor to be able to handle your animal on short notice.

If you're working with a guide or outfitter, chances are he'll have a system worked out with a processor for handling his clients' meat. But don't depend on it. Ask your man at the beginning of the hunt if he can handle your meat processing connections for you. If he can't, or if you're on your own, you should do some planning to avoid delay in heading for home. A mix-up here, in terms of a day or two delay, is another example of how unexpected expenses can dent your wallet.

I've found it best to make contact with a game processor before beginning my hunt in a new area. Find out if he will handle your meat, his hours of operation, and his phone number. When I down a deer I prefer to get it skinned out and hung in cold storage as soon as possible. So when I come in after a successful day I phone the processor and ask if I can bring the carcass right in. If this isn't convenient for him I'll make arrangements to have my animal at his place of business at the agreed-upon time. Businessmen appreciate this kind of consideration, and they'll go out of their way to take care of your needs.

If I'm hunting with companions we follow the same procedure. One man in the group may get his deer the first day of the hunt, another man the last day. If the first animal has been processed early, a lot of last-minute details are avoided at the end of the hunt.

If I fly to my hunting area I ask my meat processor to pack my meat so that each box weighs a bit less than 50 pounds. Such boxes are often accepted by airlines as excess baggage at no extra cost. I discovered that by accident one time in Colorado. The processor who had put up my meat was temporarily out of his larger-size boxes, so all of my venison went into smaller boxes. I checked them in at the airport, asked for charges, and was advised there was no cost for parcels weighing under 50 pounds. The technique won't always work, but in that case I flew a big mule-deer buck 1,500 miles without paying a dime for air freight.

Your boxes of frozen meat should be marked plainly. One time my frozen air freight meat was mostly thawed when I picked it up at the baggage counter of my home airport. It had been placed by a heater. If I'd labeled the boxes "frozen meat—do not store near heat," that problem wouldn't have developed. Another time one of my boxes of meat was half-thawed because I hadn't taken the time to mark the top side of the box, "this end up." The significance is that when dry ice is put in a box it's always put in the top because cold air flows downward, not up. In effect, the dry ice in the upside-down box wasn't accomplishing its purpose. It's no problem at all to mark boxes with a black marker.

Keep in mind, though, that many airlines won't accept boxes of frozen meat that contain dry ice. During recent years I've switched to using the new lightweight insulated portable coolers. They'll keep meat from thawing for up to forty-eight hours. That's usually plenty of time for hunters using air transportation to get home from hunting country. If you drive, dry ice is no problem.

Don't Lament the Old Days

All deer hunters have heard stories of the good old days when deer hunting was of such fabulous quality that it can never again be duplicated. Some of the stories were true, some enormous fabrications. The records of state game departments, old newspaper clippings, and the memories of old-timers can give clues about what deer hunters actually experienced during the past 150 years.

The stories that big bucks were far more common in the old days when there was less hunting pressure are both true and false. Some dramatic facts show why they can be false.

Mule deer have a reputation for not being very smart, plus being easier to hunt than whitetails. It might seem logical that the really big trophy muleys were all shot off years ago. So when was the world-record typical mule deer killed? Doug Burris Jr. of San Antonio, Texas, won the honors with a massive buck he took in Colorado's San Juan National Forest in 1972. Further, nearly all of the top twenty typical mule deer listed in the Boone and Crockett Club record book have been taken since 1960.

Here's another shocker. M. J. Johnson killed a typical whitetail buck in Peoria County, Illinois, in 1965. At that time it was the second-best typical whitetail ever recorded. When somebody tells you that it's too tough to bag a trophy today you might emphasize that Johnson downed his magnificent deer with bow and arrow. Johnson's second-ranked whitetail was replaced in 1971 with a buck taken near Moberly, Missouri, by Larry W. Gibson. Note that both of these outstanding whitetails were taken in heavily hunted farm country. Don't believe the stories that the big bucks were all shot off many years ago. The clincher may be the fact that the current world-record, nontypical whitetail came from St. Louis County, Missouri. It was found dead of natural causes in 1981. It has 19 points on the right antler and 25 points on the left. The rack scored a whopping 333-⅞ points, more than 50 points better than the previous record.

It's true, of course, that the deer herds of yesteryear produced more big bucks than today's herds because the average buck lived long enough to grow a big rack. But even that statement has to be qualified by making it refer to the earlier years of sport hunting. Before then—during market-hunting times—deer were slaughtered to the point of extinction in many areas. During the years of hunting for markets few male deer lived long enough to grow racks of any size. I note these highlights to point out that plenty of big bucks still exist in our deer country.

The trophy bucks of years ago received more attention because fewer people hunted deer. Hunters often camped in groups for the entire season, as opposed to today's custom of hunting for only a few days at a time. When the old-time hunters came back from camp they often brought in six to a dozen bucks which they would hang from front-yard trees to keep the meat cool. Such eye-opening sights are rare today because the modern deer hunter usually has his venison butchered and quick-frozen before or soon after he returns from his hunt.

But the sights of those bucks strung from camp meat poles or tree limbs have been the sources of stories of unlimited deer, and such tales originated with nonhunters who didn't have the best knowledge of what they were talking about. One of my favorite stories concerns a similar situation.

When I was a small boy, one of my older distant relatives told me that many years before I was born our local area in the northwestern part of Michigan's Lower Peninsula swarmed with whitetail deer. He told me that in the early 1900s he knew men who went out in the fall and shot all the deer they wanted just outside of town. He named some of the men, and for many years I remembered those names as if they were legend.

I learned years later that my local area actually had harbored very few deer in the early 1900s. Those men my relative named, didn't find easy hunting at all. They were seasonal farmers and teamsters who in winter used their horses to haul logs for a timber company. During the fall, how-ever, they had plenty of time to hunt deer. A day or two before each deer season opened they loaded their wagons with camping gear and aimed their horses toward distant boondocks. They camped and hunted strictly for the serious business of supplying their families with meat for the long winter ahead.

With their horses these men were able to get back into the remote swamps that held a few deer, and because they hunted for weeks they were able to do quite well. When they returned home they unloaded their largest bucks from their wagons, hung them from a tree limb, and let admiring townsfolk take photos. As the years passed, those photos were handed down through generations of family members until, when I first saw them as a boy, the stories were well-established that deer were all over the place in the good old days.

Meat-pole photos like this one give many people the mistaken idea that deer were generally more plentiful in the old days. But these North Dakota deer were taken before hunting limits had been established. If hunting laws were suspended today, such photos would be common again.

I have another Michigan story that stretched the truth even more. When I first started hunting deer back in the early 1940s I always regretted not having a way of hunting in the state's Upper Peninsula (U.P.). In those days that's where the big bucks were. The Mackinac Bridge that now links the two peninsulas wasn't even a dream then: you had to get your car across the few miles of water on one of several small ferry ships. So great was the appeal of Upper Michigan deer hunting, and so limited the carrying capacities of the small ferries, that lines of cars stretched for miles back of the loading docks during the few days preceding deer season.

233

Many of the old-timers I talked with when I was a boy told me stories of the great hunting in the Upper Peninsula. I about cried when one old man said, "The good hunting is fading in the U.P. Too many hunters now and the habitat is diminishing. I've nailed my share of good bucks, but the hunting is getting tougher every year. When Upper Michigan was inhabited by Indians there were big bucks all over the place. I've heard stories of how the Indians killed deer with arrows as easily as we killed them with rifles."

At the time I believed the old man but now I know better. The truth is that before the coming of the white man there were almost no deer in Michigan's north country. Records of explorers and fur traders mention a few moose and caribou, but none of the early journals made mention of deer. The reason is obvious to anyone who has studied the habitat and habits of whitetails.

Deer are browsing animals. During the Indian era there was no browse because all the timber was mature. Deer also will eat in grain fields and truck gardens, but there was little agriculture before the white man arrived. The equation is simple: no habitat, no deer. Northern Michigan didn't show deer until after the lumbering companies began cutting the pine forests. In cutover areas the slashes fed fires that left the land denuded, but in perfect shape to begin producing second-growth browse.

Hardwood sprouts and cedar began growing and the area became attractive to deer. The late George Shiras III, a leading authority on the early history of Michigan deer, recorded that the animals migrated into the U.P. from southern Wisconsin by the thousands as top habitat became available. By the early 1800s about 80,000 deer were killed annually on lands in the U.P. where 50 years earlier no deer were found.

As more and more of the timber was logged, some of the cutover land was sold to early settlers. As land clearing developed so did the deer herds, until the arrival of the market hunters who considered 200 deer per man per season only average hunting. Such slaughter drastically reduced the previously exploding numbers of deer. In sharp contrast to the previous beneficial slash fires, huge forest fires followed the rape of the pine stands by lumber companies. The fires consumed the new browse required by deer. The effects of market hunting and ravaging fires did in the whitetails. By 1920 Michigan's U.P. had few deer left. Farsighted citizens then demanded legislation to prevent complete extermination of the remaining whitetails.

A buck law was passed and forest fire control began to be serious business. With the absence of raging fires, browse growth exploded all over the U.P., and control of the deer harvest by hunting laws gave the whitetails a new lease on life. Their numbers boomed. By the 1940s deer hunting in Michigan's north country reached its peak. Since then it has been declining because the browse that produced the enormous herds has now itself become mature forest. Michigan's Department of Natural Resources is engaged in a ten-year program to bring back the habitat and rebuild the whitetail herds. The program's goal is to increase the annual current state-wide harvest from 90,000 whitetails to 200,000.

How Deer Herds Developed

The history of building deer herds is a fascinating story because deer, in al-most their present forms, existed in prehistoric times and lived among other forms of life that have long since become extinct. Deer have survived be-cause they are able to adapt to change so long as they have suitable habi-tat. Another factor, their ability to prosper in proximity to man, means that deer herds can be built in conjunction with modern land-use plans that would threaten such species as wild sheep, buffalo, and wolves.

An interesting example of how deer and concentrated human activity can go together is found in Delaware, a small state surrounded by the east-ern megalopolis.

"Our deer herd thrives despite increasing pressures from urbanization," H. Lloyd Alexander, Jr., the state's Supervisor of Wildlife, told me some years ago. "The only deer-management problem we face is one of under-harvest. As areas become closed to hunting because of urbanization, deer populations build to considerable levels. Deer management in Delaware has always included either-sex hunting. We feel that either-sex hunting is the only way to control our herd, and that it is essential to modern manage-ment."

The key to all of today's healthy deer herds is modern management by knowledgeable deer biologists. Consider the situation in Kansas, where both whitetails and mule deer once were common. With the plowing of native grasslands, extensive grazing of livestock, and the lack of adequate legislation protecting deer, the population declined until both species were considered extinct between 1904 and 1933.

The following years saw a limited number of introductions of deer by private individuals and by the Fish and Game Commission. Undoubtedly some deer migrated into Kansas because of stocking and redistribution programs in neighboring states. With a complete ban on hunting, the herd grew slowly until 1956 when there were an estimated 3,000 deer in the state. Then the population increased at the rate of about 30 percent per year till 1964, with deer being found in every county. The rapidly explod-ing population began to cause local crop damage problems and the high-way kill was becoming a major headache.

An effort had to be made at some kind of control and the only logical approach was a hunting season. In 1965 an archery season was authorized for October 1 to November 15, and a firearms season from December 11 through December 15. All hunting would be on a permit basis. Archery permits were mailed to all applicants, but gun permits were limited to 4,575. After the planning was over and the permits were issued, game offi-cials and hunters alike wondered what would happen to deer that had never been hunted.

The result was that the deer herd continued to increase even though many of the animals ended up in hunters' freezers. As the years passed the hunting continued to improve. In 1983 Kansas hunters took 13,359 deer while posting a success rate of 58%. That's startling when you recall that as late as 1956 the state had only 3,000 deer.

And the boom continues. The 4,575 gun permits offered in Kansas in 1965 expanded to 20,616 in 1983. The herd is in excellent shape and continues to produce bumper crops of fawns. The Kansas story shows what can be done by deer managers, and why your future as a deer hunter looks far better than the future of other big-game hunters.

Another success story comes from Missouri. Both the deer harvest and the number of hunters in that state have doubled in the past decade. Still, deer biologists feel that at least part of the state, the timbered Ozarks, could double the deer herd that was present in 1974. In that section hunters take less than two deer per square mile of forest. Biologists believe there is potential for perhaps twenty-five deer per square mile in the Ozarks where now there might be five to ten. In 1973, for the first time in Missouri's modern deer-hunting history, the northern part of the state topped the Ozarks in harvest. How do biologists feel about that? For one thing, they acknowledge that northern Missouri has progressed farther than anyone would have believed possible when the first deer were stocked there. Statewide, in 1975, Missouri deer hunters took 38,149 deer through the first two days of the state's 9-day season, nearly 5,000 more than the highest previous total for an entire season. In 1983 close to 300,000 hunters harvested 57,691 deer, an all-time record kill that beat the 1982 harvest of 56,041 whitetails. Missouri deer hunting, like that in some other states, gets better every year.

Unlike northern Michigan, Kentucky was loaded with deer during the era of early settlers. Daniel Boone never had trouble living off the land, and much of the meat he ate was venison. Years later, Audubon often mentioned the vast numbers of deer he saw in Kentucky.

However, for reasons only partly known, Kentucky's deer dwindled rapidly from the early 1900s to shortly after World War II. By that time the total whitetail herd numbered only a few thousand animals. Open seasons had by then been outlawed. But though most of the state contained no deer at all, Mammoth Cave National Park had so many of the animals they were considered a nuisance.

Kentucky's modern deer-management program got off the ground when hundreds of deer were live-trapped in the Park and relocated in groups of about fifty in scattered areas around the state. Biologists hoped the nucleus herds would adapt to the new territories and multiply. The deer did just that, and the program was so successful that Kentucky went from a non-deer to a deer-hunting state in little more than a decade. The state's first modern deer season was held in 1956. In 1961, 11,650 hunters killed 2,710 deer. By 1973 the number of deer hunters had increased to 40,000, the herd had multiplied to 60,000, and the harvest had jumped to 6,500. In 1984 there were so many deer in Kentucky's Bernheim Forest Refuge that a special herd-reduction hunt was held in early winter to relieve a serious over-population problem.

Deer-management programs have been great successes in many states, but what has happened in Texas is almost enough to boggle the mind. From the early 1900s through the late 1920s there were few deer left in Texas. The future for deer hunters looked dismal. Today, the Texas herd numbers 3,400,000 whitetails and 150,000 mule deer, far and away the largest of any state in the nation. The deer bag limit is four deer per season only two of which have to be whitetail bucks. Texas has so many deer it's begging for hunters. How could such an astounding circumstance take place in just a few decades? I got most of the details from research carried on by Eugene A. Walker of the Texas Game and Fish Commission.

Years ago, as the human population in the state increased, the great and famous cattle empire was founded. Cattle production reached its peak between 1880 and 1890, with the result that many of the major cattle ranges in the state were overgrazed. Sheep and goats were brought in to utilize the scant forage that remained.

With the introduction of sheep and goats came a need for predator control, and ranchers turned to traps and hounds in efforts to reduce losses to livestock. But the hounds much preferred to run deer than the wolves, coyotes, bobcats, and cougars at which control efforts were aimed. To prevent this, deer were shot on sight. Thus, wide areas in the state were virtually depleted of deer.

By the 1920s the deer population in Texas had reached a very low level. But by this time a few conservation-minded landowners and sportsmen initiated efforts to preserve existing deer and provide means for increasing their numbers. Legislation was enacted to afford greater protection to deer in certain portions of the state, while in others the processes of elimination of the deer continued.

With the increased protection of brood stock, and disappearance of the big livestock empires, deer began a comeback. By the late 1930s they had reached saturation in one or two isolated parts of the state.

The Texas Game and Fish Commission initiated its first attempt to trap and transplant wild deer in the mid-1930s in Mason County. Trapping techniques later were improved, and since the program's inception more than 20,000 deer have been moved from areas of overabundance to suitable locations all over the state. The success of this transplanting program is indicated by the large number of deer now present in areas of the state where they were virtually absent in 1938.

The Federal Aid to States in Wildlife Restoration Act, the so-called Pittman-Robertson Act, was enacted by the National Congress in 1937. Under the provisions of this act a 10 percent excise tax was levied on sporting arms and ammunition. These monies were gathered in Washington, D.C., and reallocated to qualifying states. Texas was one of the first states to become eligible to receive these funds and immediately undertook the vast job of wildlife management work.

The state hired its first trained wildlife biologist and studies were immediately initiated to determine the distribution of native game species. Research work on life histories of game animals and birds was begun. Since the whitetail deer is the most important big-game animal in the state, this species has received much of the federally assisted research effort.

The first recommendation by a biologist to harvest anterless deer along with bucks was made in 1941, but it was twelve years later, in 1953, that the first legal antlerless deer were killed by hunters in this state.

Wildlife biologists soon recognized that deer management closely parallels livestock management and that deer numbers must be controlled just as are livestock in order to prevent range depletion and subsequent extensive die-offs. A rancher who owns a thousand acres of ranch land may conceivably be able to run 100 head of cattle on such an area. At the same time, a given number of deer will be able to prosper on the same land with the cattle. Such a rancher knows that he must remove the annual increase of both sexes in his cattle herd in order to prevent overstocking. The same reasoning applies to the deer on the same area. Once the carrying capacity has been reached for either livestock or deer, the annual increase must be removed in order to protect the rancher's investment in livestock and the sportsmen's and landowner's investment in the deer.

By 1961 deer had increased in Texas enough to cause overpopulation in a large number of counties. At that time there were approximately 125 counties in the state in which the harvest of surplus antlerless deer could be allowed if the need became evident. The program for antlerless-deer harvest was carried out in 48 counties in 1961. Deer had reached extremely high numbers in 24 of these 48 counties and provisions were made for the taking of a third or bonus deer in these counties.

There still are too many deer in Texas even though the state's annual harvest is nearly 350,000. Are you welcome to hunt in Texas? I put the question to Richard A. McCune, Information and Education Director of the Texas Parks and Wildlife Department.

"We welcome all the deer hunters we can get because our harvest should be much higher in many areas," he told me. "But the problem of hunter access to the deer supply gives cause for real concern. Most of Texas is private property, and that makes it difficult for the average gunner to find a place to hunt. The harvest could be greater if we find ways to increase landowner-sportsman cooperation. That's one of our modern problems of efficient deer management. Ways and means must be found to permit the taking of 25 to 30 percent of the total deer population in normal years to insure a healthy herd."

Some Problem States

At this point you should understand very well why I titled this chapter "Don't Lament the Old Days." I've painted a pretty bright picture for modern hunters so far, but not all states have the deer-management programs, the lands, or the abilities to follow the examples I've mentioned. This chapter wouldn't present a true picture if I didn't discuss the problems that exist in other states.

As this book goes to press, one has to wonder about what's going on in California. Though the state's game officials say California harbors over 1,200,000 deer (second highest figure in the nation) many of its hunters don't believe the claim.

California game officials say that early state records show deer were plentiful in the valleys and foothills during pioneer days. After the gold rush ran its course deer populations declined rapidly. The use of meat and hides by settlers was unrestricted. Free grazing on public lands caused a livestock buildup that resulted in severe overgrazing by domesticated animals.

The cycle changed when deer hunting laws were enacted and more browse became available through the ever-increasing clearing of mature stands of virgin timber. By 1940 California's deer herds numbered more than one million animals. But, by 1950, the trend reversed again because of urban development created by the demands of the state's 23 million people. In addition, second-growth timber was maturing and crowding out much of the browse required by deer.

Some California game officials privately admit that the state probably doesn't harbor as many deer as it did in the 1940s. Yet the official estimate of the number of deer in the state given by the Department of Game and Fish is 1,200,000 animals. If the herd is obviously decreasing in numbers how could it total 300,000 more deer in 1974 than in 1940?

However, the situation may be turning for the better. The evidence comes from Ray Arnett, who was Director of the California Department of Fish and Game in 1974. He made some enlightening statements at the National Rifle Association annual meeting in March of that year.

"Deer populations throughout the West are decreasing and their habitat condition is worsening," Arnett said. "The decline has been particularly evident along the western slope of the Sierra-Nevada Mountains. Deteriorating range conditions and poor fawn survival are considered to be the major reasons for the decline. In addition to loss of habitat, deterioration of habitat must also be considered.

"Poorer hunting opportunity is directly translatable into hunter dissatisfaction. For the first time in memory we are getting indications of hunter disenchantment with our programs and hunting opportunities in California. The number of complaints is now significant. We are doing something about it.

"We have manipulated some 5,500 acres of deer range in California," Arnett went on. "Our controlled burning results have been encouraging. Deer use of treated areas has increased and even doubled in some areas. Our goal is to manipulate some 25,000 acres of key range. We are developing a deer-management plan to rebuild deer populations and to improve hunting opportunity to maintain and enhance habitat, and to educate the public on deer-management principles."

Other problem areas exist in portions of the prairie states, the Great Lakes states, and the East. The North Dakota story is a good example of what's going on in prairie country.

Game and Fish Department records in that state go back to 1881. The first year a hunting license was required was 1897. A bag limit of five deer per person also became law that year. In 1909 the daily and seasonal bag limit was reduced to two. By this time the once-great deer herds were already being shot off. In 1913 the deer season was closed, and it remained closed through 1920. How's that for the good old days?

Enough deer were present in the state in 1921 and 1922 to allow hunting (1 buck bag limit), but without a deer-management program the animals were shot off in a hurry. The season was closed again from 1923 through 1930. From 1931 through 1939 a deer season was held every other year. From then to 1953 there were closed seasons during six years. Permit hunting for both mule deer and whitetails was initiated in 1959. Deer management has taken hold well enough in North Dakota to permit hunting during each year since 1954.

The problem on the prairie is that deer habitat is limited, so, therefore, must be the number of deer. During soil-bank years the numbers of deer increased because habitat increased. When the program was dropped, deer became fewer. Coupled with this situation is another problem: the ever-increasing number of deer hunters. In 1945 there were only about 15,500 deer hunters in North Dakota. By 1971 that number had exploded to more than 53,000, and by 1983 it was up to 60,000. When you consider that the deer-hunter success ratio on the prairie consistently runs about 60 percent, it's easy to realize that biologists are doing a good job of deer management. But, unless ways are devised to expand habitat, deer hunting on the prairies probably will remain the domain of a relatively few special-permit holders.

Lack of habitat is the problem in the Great Lakes states, too. But unlike the prairie states where deer licenses are limited, Michigan, Wisconsin, and Minnesota sell unlimited licenses to both residents and nonresidents. During recent years, in Michigan and Wisconsin, deer license sales numbered over 600,000 in each state.

The history of deer hunting in the three states closely parallels the situation in Minnesota, so I'll mention some facts from the old records of that state.

Whitetails were all over southern Minnesota when the white man came, but the human population rapidly exploded. In 1850 the state held only a little more than 6,000 people. By 1860 that figure jumped to 172,000, and it boomed to 440,000 by 1870. The entire population was categorized as rural and was concentrated in the southern and western areas. Coupled with that were unrestricted use of game for food, market hunting, and loss of deer habitat due to the clearing of land.

Still, there were so many deer that their numbers held up well. It wasn't until 1895 that a bag limit of five deer was established. In 1899 a hunting license was required for the first time. It cost 25 cents. By 1900 the southern Minnesota deer numbers greatly increased due to timber-cutting operations and the resultant growth of much browse. The situation in the north developed along the same lines I mentioned earlier in this chapter while discussing the early boom of deer populations in Michigan's Upper peninsula.

Great changes in Minnesota's deer-management ideas occurred between 1900 and 1936. The bag limit was reduced to one deer in 1915. Market hunting had been stopped, and many restrictions were applied to sport-hunting methods. In 1923 a law was passed allowing deer hunting in only even-numbered years; it remained in force through 1941.

What happened between 1951 and 1963, compared with the 1964–1971 period, is a dramatic example of what can happen to deer in the snow states. The first period showed only one severe winter. Deer populations boomed and carried over into the beginning of the second period when a series of hard winters hit the state. The whitetail harvest neared 100,000 for 10 years in a row, and it hit an all-time high of 127,000 in 1965. Following that, the hunter take showed a marked reduction, dropping to 45,000 animals in 1970. In 1971 the season was closed. There is no better example proving that when deep snow covers the browse required by whitetails, many of the animals simply starve to death.

Minnesota's solution to rebuilding its whitetail herd to over 800,000 by 1983 is the only solution biologists say will work in the heavily forested states: creation of new deer habitat by intensive range management. The tools are increased logging (which is coming naturally because of paper shortages), controlled burning and bulldozing with enormous dozers equipped with cutting blades. Such operations open the mature forest canopy of trees and enable new browse to begin growing. If the job is done properly, just two back-to-back fawn crops with good survival would provide enough animals to double the hunting-season herd in a managed area. That's how prolific deer can be on ideal range, and that's why the future of deer hunting in states now having habitat problems could be far superior to what it is today.

The situation in New Jersey is typical of eastern states with high human populations.

In the early 1900s deer herds as we know them today were nonexistent in New Jersey. The deer population consisted of a few family groups of whitetails scattered through the pine oak woodlands of South Jersey.

During the period 1900 to 1915 an effort was made by the then Board of Fish and Game Commissioners to increase deer populations statewide by the strict enforcement of regulations pertaining to deer, together with the reintroduction of deer in various sections of the state. Deer were purchased from Pennsylvania and Michigan, as well as from private deer preserves in New Jersey, and released in suitable habitat.

The fact that habitat conditions at that time were highly favorable and could support a much greater deer herd, plus the effects of an expanded law enforcement effort resulted in a rapidly increasing deer population which probably reached the carrying capacity of the deer range as early as 1935 in certain areas of the state (the central pines area of Ocean and Burlington counties).

The state's first modern season was authorized in 1909. The first state-wide harvest of antlerless as well as antlered deer since 1915 took place in 1961. Still, the herd continued to grow. Today, practically all deer habitat in New Jersey is presently supporting a deer herd either at or in excess of its carrying capacity. In 1983 hunters took over 10,000 whitetails from a state-wide herd of an estimated 125,000, and that's about as good as Jersey deer hunting can get.

So the problem in the East and some other areas is more a problem of people management than deer management. If, in the future, people value wildlife more than they do today, deer hunting may get better. It will get worse if the increasing human population continues making more and more demands on the habitat. It should be noted that diminishing and deteriorating deer habitat is a nationwide problem, even though it's most serious in the East and Far West.

Though I've concentrated on telling how much of the future of better deer hunting keys on habitat problems, we may also produce more deer with improved technical knowledge in such fields as disease control. One of the greatest examples of the possibilities has been the successful screwworm control program in southern states. Developed by agriculture interests, this breakthrough made the livestock industry more profitable and at the same time made possible the dynamic deer restoration program across the South. Today, many of the southeastern states have some of the largest deer herds in the United States. Nationwide, regardless of our problems, we now have more deer than when the Pilgrims landed.

By 1885, according to the National Shooting Sports foundation, there were only some 350,000 whitetail deer south of Canada. Today there are at least 12,000,000 in the lower 48 states. That's reason enough not to lament the old days.

Your Odds on
Bagging a Buck

During the past several years I've encountered some interesting examples of what's happening to deer hunting. Last fall I couldn't get it out of my mind that some of the best hunting techniques of years ago have become far less successful. It also seemed apparent that some of the better hunting states of decades past aren't so hot today.

During the winter I wondered how I could determine if my ideas were valid. I decided the answer was in getting opinions from hunting experts and game officials.

I developed a three-page questionnaire with questions pertaining to the how-to of today's deer hunting and where the best action is found. I mailed the questionnaires to game officials and deer-hunting veterans in each of our forty-eight contiguous states and our neighboring provinces of Canada.

Before I get into the answers to my questionnaire I should mention some experiences that prompted development of the project.

My son Jack turned fourteen in 1972. That's the legal age for deer hunting in Michigan, my home state. I had a tough time deciding where I should take him for his first deer hunt. One day during the summer I discussed the problem with Warren Holmes, a veteran of more than four decades of chasing whitetails. Warren owns a cabin and 300 acres of remote woodlands along the headwaters of the Pere Marquette River 50 miles from my home.

"I'll put you and the boy on a stand," he told me. "I've got some good spots, you'll see plenty of deer."

I didn't particularly like the idea of putting Jack on a stand. Teenagers don't have the patience to sit still long, and that's a must when taking a stand. I assumed the relatively remote area would be lightly hunted, so I told Warren it might be better if we did some stillhunting.

He laughed as if I'd told a joke.

"Look," he told me, "this area will be crawling with hunters. The deer become spooked as soon as the hunting army moves into the woods. There's little chance of getting a shot while stillhunting. The trick is to take advantage of other hunters moving deer through the area. If you sit long enough in a good spot Jack will get his chance. The old-time stalkers and still-hunters couldn't kill a buck in this area today."

Jack did get his chance. The first deer we saw was a six-pointer that was spooked past us by other hunters. He didn't offer a very good shot. The boy missed him.

Later that day another member of our four-man hunting group killed a fine buck from a stand. Warren got his opportunity the next morning. I won't forget what he said when we looked at the venison hanging from the buck pole near his cabin.

"The average hunter-success ratio in this area is about 10 percent because there are more hunters each year. Three of the four of us have had good shots at bucks in only 1½ days. That should tell you something about the value of hunting from stands in heavily hunted country."

Fifteen years ago I took a mule-deer hunt in Wyoming. We worked the thickets along creek beds and draws in the bottom of valleys near a ranch. We jumped plenty of deer. I killed a fine three-pointer (western count) the first day of the hunt.

Two years ago I hunted similar terrain in Montana. The rancher who was hosting me said that between 50 and 150 deer could be seen in the huge field behind his house on moonlit nights. I expected to hunt near that field the next morning. I was surprised to learn that easy hunting was out. We would have to climb far up into the foothills long before dawn. Why?

"Mule deer aren't as dumb as they used to be," my host explained. "Lots of hunters come out West now. The deer are reacting to the pressure. They'll leave that field before dawn and climb the mountain to bed down. We've got to be up there to intercept them when they move up the canyon trails. We don't get much shooting in the valleys anymore."

That statement emphasizes another trend of modern deer hunting.

Twenty years ago when I'd ask a local hunter where he got his buck he'd invariably mention some area close to home. In recent years a good share of my townsmen have come up with an answer something like this: "I don't hunt deer in Michigan anymore. Now I head for the western states where game is plentiful."

During a recent Colorado deer hunt I began discovering that the popular opinion, "The West is where the deer are," might not be all that correct.

One of the hunters in my group was Ken Callaway, the outdoor-movie producer from Houston, Texas, I mentioned earlier. He surprised me when he said, "We've got so many deer in Texas our bag limit is four per season in the area I hunt. The only reason I came to Colorado is because I've never hunted mule deer."

A few months ago I talked to another hunter who brought up the subject of deer hunting in Florida, a state not many gunners would recognize as good deer country. "Tell you what," the man told me. "Deer hunter success ratios in Florida average 30 percent. We've got about 650,000 deer in our state."

Those are the types of experiences that made me ponder some questions. Could it really be that Florida has more deer and a higher hunter success ratio than some of the more well-known deer states? Is it true that hunting from stands produces more deer in heavily hunted country than any other system? Further, what are the best systems to use in various parts of the United States?

Such questions led to others. I wondered what states have the largest deer herds and the highest hunter-success ratios. Do game departments in the best states encourage nonresident hunters? Where can a nonresident get information on any given state's deer hunting?

I reasoned that if I had the answers to such questions I'd have a pretty good picture of what modern deer hunting is really all about. What follows is the information gleaned from my project.

Let's start with the question of which states harbor the most deer. The answer may surprise you. Texas leads the list with a herd of 3,400,000 whitetails and 150,000 mule deer. Next in line, and far below Texas, is Mississippi with 1,500,000. Then comes Alabama and California with 1,-200,000 each. Thirty-two states boast herds in excess of 100,000 and—another shocker—ten of those states are in the Southeast. It's interesting to note that some of the western states, well-known for their great deer hunting, don't harbor the largest herds. Colorado, for instance, ranks 14th on the list.

Does the above information suggest that the states harboring the largest herds are *not* necessarily the best states to hunt? You bet it does, with the exception of Texas which reflects a special situation which I'll discuss later. The hunter success ratio in California is only 10 percent. Some eastern states have gun-hunter success ratios of less than 10 percent, and that's another shocker when you consider that the *bowhunter* success ratio in 13 states is 10 percent or better.

A few years ago the Midwest states of Michigan and Minnesota offered some of the best deer hunting in the nation. Not anymore. In 1984 Michigan hunters scored an 11 percent success ratio and Minnesota hunters showed slightly over 30 percent. Those figures don't reflect great hunting.

Hunters in the deer-rich southeastern states don't do too well either, except where hunting with dogs is permitted. Florida is the top example. Game officials in that state told me that 70 percent of their deer harvest goes to hunters with dogs.

The ten top states, from a deer-hunters'-success standpoint, are all west of the Mississippi River. With the exception of Oregon they're all in the prairie and intermountain area. Most of the best states allow nonresident deer hunting by quota only. This last fact points out two important aspects.

One, deer are easier to hunt in the prairie and intermountain states. Two, game officials in those states are well aware of the value of their deer herds and they're not going to permit over-harvest by unlimited numbers of hunters. In fact, the picture isn't too bright for nonresidents.

"Our nonresident deer license quota has been declining in recent years," said George Kaminski of the Wyoming Game and Fish Department. "The drops are results of declining mule-deer populations in some areas. Deer permits are awarded to nonresidents by lottery. In the best hunting regions, especially in big-buck country, there is intense competition for deer tags. Nonresidents pay $105 for a tag, but their success ratio is about 80 percent."

Saskatchewan nonresidents have been restricted to hunting in specified zones. South Dakota's Harvey H. Pietz, Executive Assistant of the state's Division of Game and Fish, told me, "Out-of-stater permits are already very limited in our prairie zone." It's interesting to note that in recent years the limited number of deer permits in South Dakota's Black Hills has not affected hunting opportunity at all. Through 1982 the permit quota for the hills had never been filled, and in 1983 it was dropped in favor of unlimited permit numbers. The situation in the eastern part of the state is directly opposite. There no nonresident permits are issued, and resident permits are very limited. In Kansas nonresidents are not allowed to hunt deer.

In most of the best deer-hunting states the demand for hunting opportunity already exceeds the supply. That's a very important point to remember if you plan to hunt in one of the top hunter-success ratio states.

The key to getting a license is to plan a year ahead. Write the game department in the state you wish to hunt and ask for details on how to apply for a nonresident deer license, then get your application in as early as it will be accepted. Consider this: Many Wyoming nonresident deer licenses are sold out in spring, months before hunting seasons begin.

The picture in Texas is so different from other states that it warrants special mention. If you can work out some "ifs" your odds of bagging a buck in Texas zoom to about 80 percent. Parts of the state have so many deer it's no problem for a good hunter to score, *if* he can find a place to hunt. Most of the good deer country is privately owned. Many of the ranchers book deer hunters on a fee basis, many others lease deer-hunting rights. If you can make contacts—best bets are chambers of commerce in the south-Texas brush country from San Antonio to Del Rio to Brownsville, and in Llano and Mason counties—you'll have great hunting and you won't have to worry about getting a license.

"We welcome all the deer hunters we can get," Richard A. McCune, of the Texas Parks and Wildlife Department, told me. "Our harvest should be much higher for proper management of overpopulated herds in many areas. Licenses are unlimited and good for taking up to four deer in many parts of the state."

The only more astonishing bag limit than that is the one offered in Alabama. Buy a deer license in that state and you can shoot one deer each day of the entire season. The catch is that Alabama's deer aren't very easy to hunt, and only 17 percent of the state's deer hunters go home with venison. That statistic brings us to the question of why relatively few hunters score in the deer-rich southeastern states. I put the question to some experts.

Jack Crockford, former Director of the Georgia Game and Fish Division, had this to say: "Many property owners in the south won't allow hunting except by family and friends. That means a lot of good deer country is underhunted. Also, our terrain is difficult to hunt. The swamps and woods are thick, the advantages are with the deer."

Charlie Elliott, former Southern Field Editor of *Outdoor Life* magazine, brought up another important point. "There are more novices in the woods today," he began. "Most people have more money and more leisure time. Some guys figure they'll go out and shoot a deer with little idea of how to go about it. The expert will get a deer in the South because he knows how to hunt our spooky whitetails. It takes a lot more skill to score here than out West where the novice has a better chance."

The section of my questionnaire dealing with best deer-hunting techniques brought other surprising replies. The answers blow some large holes in many of the popular theories on how to hunt deer.

I asked the experts to rate the harvest in their states in terms of percentage of total kill taken through use of the following techniques: stillhunting, hunting from stands, stalking, driving (including gang drives), calling (including horn rattling), hunting with dogs, snow tracking and hunting from horseback. Note that I did not ask how most deer hunters hunt, but rather which method the successful hunters used.

Though I suspected that hunting from stands in heavily hunted whitetail areas of the East and Midwest would rate high, I was astonished at some of the final figures. In Missouri, for instance, Dean Murphy, Assistant Chief of the state's Game Division, reported that 95 percent of the Missouri deer harvest was taken by hunters working from stands. I thought Murphy's figure was an error, so I asked him to verify it.

"I stand by the 95 percent," he replied. "Many unsuccessful hunters use various techniques, but the vast majority of our deer are taken by hunters on stands. Our aerial surveys show that most hunters sit quietly on stands till about 8:00 A.M., then start stillhunting, walking along roads and moving to cars. The fellow who goes on a stand before dawn and stays there when other hunters begin moving around is the fellow who takes a deer. Most of the deer are moved by impatient hunters."

Results of my survey show that all game officials in the East and Midwest states except Maine and Iowa rate hunting from stands as responsible for over half of their deer harvests. In the same states the driving technique ranked second with about 25 percent, except in Iowa where it scored 70 percent. When it's realized that most deer taken on drives are downed by standers ahead of the drivers you realize how important it is to know how to select a stand and how to hunt from it.

Statistics supplied by William C. Mincher of Maine's Department of Inland Fisheries and Game show that 60 percent of that state's whitetail harvest is taken by stillhunters. Standers ranked second at 30 percent. Because of the heavy influence of Maine, stillhunting in the Northeast accounts for 25 percent of the deer harvest. By contrast, stillhunting rates only 11 percent on similar terrain in north-central states. Stalking in all of the northern whitetail states is mostly a waste of time, accounting for only about 8 percent of the harvest.

Stands get the nod in southeastern states too, by a whopping 65 percent except in areas where hunting with dogs is legal. Stillhunting and stalking account for about 10 percent of the harvest. Driving rates about the same at 11.8 percent.

All of these figures point out that the average gunner going after whitetails east of the Mississippi River had best forget about stillhunting, snow-tracking, and stalking techniques and concentrate on learning how to hunt from a stand. If you can't put up with sitting still your next best bet is to organize a drive, especially in the snow-belt states.

The picture changes west of the Mississippi, especially in mule-deer country where the terrain is more open. In prairie areas your odds on nailing a buck are about even, regardless of the major hunting technique in which you specialize. Here's how my composite figures came out: stillhunting, 20 percent; stands, 26.5 percent; stalking, 29.8 percent; driving, 20 percent; snow-tracking and horseback hunting combined, 4.7 percent.

This is as good a place as any to mention that the techniques of snow-tracking and horseback hunting, very popular years ago, don't account for many of the deer killed today. The highest ratings I got for both systems came from the intermountain states at 5.8 percent and 7.4 percent, respectively.

Basically, deer calling is a waste of time, except for horn rattling, which can work under given precise conditions. I covered all the details of this unique technique in Chapter 9.

Stillhunting rates as the best technique in the intermountain states where it accounts for 42 percent of the deer harvest. The next best system is stalking at 27.4 percent. In this area only 10.3 percent of the deer are taken from stands. Driving rates about the same. So if you hunt the top deer states in the West it's best to learn how to stillhunt and stalk.

Some of the most surprising statistics showing up on my questionnaire were the high success ratios for archers in Midwest and intermountain states. I followed up my survey with some questions. Here's a typical answer:

"I think the archer success in mountain states is high because of the many opportunities bowmen have to shoot at deer," said Gary T. Myers, Big Game Supervisor for Colorado's Division of Wildlife. "Once while I was bowhunting on the Uncompahgre Plateau I saw thirty-six bucks in one day. A fellow from New York hunted near my camp and he couldn't believe the number of deer he saw. In the West a man has a chance to see lots of deer, and he usually has a chance to stalk them."

The archery take also rates high in such midwestern states as Iowa, South Dakota, Kansas, and Nebraska where wooded terrain is often found in small patches. It's relatively easy to scout these small-cover areas, determine deer travel routes, and ambush the animals from stands. Archer success ratios are low in the heavily forested states east of the Mississippi for the opposite reason: It's simply too difficult to pinpoint deer and get close to them. It's interesting to reflect that years ago just about all deer hunters felt that trying to kill a deer with an arrow was simply too difficult anywhere. Today, hundreds of thousands of successful archers know better.

States and Provinces With Over 100,000 Deer

Texas	3,400,000	Arkansas	400,000
Mississippi	1,500,000	New York	400,000
Alabama	1,200,000	Wyoming	400,000
California	1,200,000	S. Carolina	350,000
Michigan	875,000	Tennessee	325,000
Minnesota	800,000	N. Carolina	300,000
Oregon	750,000	Idaho	300,000
Wisconsin	750,000	S. Dakota	300,000
Pennsylvania	750,000	W. Virginia	300,000
Georgia	750,000	New Mexico	278,000
Florida	650,000	Arizona	250,000
Washington	510,000	Maine	200,000
Colorado	500,000	Saskatchewan	200,000
Utah	500,000	Nevada	135,000
Virginia	420,000	Vermont	135,000
Louisiana	420,000		

Percentages of Hunter Success in States and Provinces

This chart shows percentages of hunter success in states and provinces. Note that the top ten areas are all west of the Mississippi River. The Texas figure may be misleading since the best hunting is often done on private property. For license-holders who find good places to hunt in Texas, the success rate is about 80 percent. Figures were not available for New York and Oklahoma.

Montana	70	Virginia	25
Nebraska	66	West Virginia	25
North Dakota	65	Arizona	23
Nevada	63	Alabama	22
Wyoming	60	Ohio	22
Texas	60	Maryland	20
South Dakota	55	New Mexico	20
Saskatchewan	54	Maine	20
Colorado	50	Pennsylvania	20

Utah	50	Missouri	19
Manitoba	50	Kentucky	19
Kansas	50	New Brunswick	18
Mississippi	50	Delaware	18
Louisiana	50	Michigan	12
Nova Scotia	38	Indiana	15
British Columbia	37	Georgia	13
Oregon	35	Arkansas	12
North Carolina	33	Tennessee	11
Iowa	30	Quebec	11
Florida	30	California	10
Minnesota	30	New Hampshire	8
Illinois	29	Vermont	8
Wisconsin	29	New Jersey	8
South Carolina	25	Rhode Island	8
Washington	25	Connecticut	8
Idaho	25		

What Hunting Methods Work Best in Different Sections

Drives		Stalking	
NORTHEAST	18.2%	NORTHEAST	8%
SOUTHEAST	11.8%	SOUTHEAST	6.9%
N. CENTRAL	28.8%	N. CENTRAL	7.5%
S. CENTRAL	10%	S. CENTRAL	10.2%
PRAIRIE	20%	PRAIRIE	28.8%
INTER-MT.	9.8%	INTER-MT.	27.4%
FAR WEST	32.4%	FAR WEST	26%

Stillhunting		Stands	
NORTHEAST	25%	NORTHEAST	44.1%
SOUTHEAST	5.5%	SOUTHEAST	65%
N. CENTRAL	11%	N. CENTRAL	53.5%
S. CENTRAL	30%	S. CENTRAL	49%
PRAIRIE	20%	PRAIRIE	26.5%
INTER-MT.	42%	INTER-MT.	10.3%
FAR WEST	22%	FAR WEST	16%

Your Future as a Deer Hunter

If your experiences are anything like mine, you're seeing more and more of your hunting opportunities going down the drain. Will the future get worse?

I live in a small town in the northwestern section of Michigan's Lower Peninsula. This part of the state is considered to be top deer-hunting country. Let me tell you what has happened to some of that country.

When I was a teenager I hunted whitetails along river flats outside of town. Those flats are now dumping grounds for a chemical company. Another area that contained acres of wild blueberry bushes always harbored deer. Today the blueberries have been replaced by ranch homes.

I shot my first three whitetails in a section of wildland along the shore of one of our nearby inland lakes. If I fired my rifle in those woodlands today I'd be asked to leave in a hurry. The area is now all private and is dotted with expensive summer homes, posted, and patrolled by a caretaker.

Nationwide it's obvious that game habitat has diminished. The last annual Environmental Quality Index released by the National Wildlife Federation reports that more than one million acres of wildlife habitat are lost each year. If you're a long-time hunter you know of many places where you used to hunt that are now out of bounds. Even if they weren't out of bounds the deer may be gone. And there are some important reasons other than the boom in subdivisions, increased agriculture, and growing human populations.

Ray Lyons, a past president of the Colorado Guides and Outfitters Association and a knowledgeable conservationist, points out one reason why deer are becoming fewer in some areas. "In the West we have lands that are overgrazed and waters that show poor fishing," he told me. "If the fish-and-game boys want to rejuvenate a mountain lake they can poison it out, restock it, and produce great fishing in a year or so. But if they want to rejuvenate overgrazed land it will take ten to fifteen years to bring the range back to where it's suitable habitat for deer. It's far easier to produce good fishing than it is to produce good hunting."

An even more discouraging subject came to light during a discussion I had with a game official in a midwestern state who asked me not to identify him or his state. "I don't want our deer hunters to become alarmed yet," he told me, "but we're going to be facing a new situation if the number of deer hunters continues to increase. Our herd is getting close to being overshot. If the trend continues we'll have to eliminate nonresident hunting and we'll have to license residents on a lottery basis. That will come as a shocker because this state has offered unlimited numbers of deer licenses for many years."

Let's look at the situation in some other states.

In 1970 there were 32,300 deer permits authorized in Nebraska. For the 1983 season that number dropped to 31,048. In 1970 more than 1,000 permits went unused because no hunters requested them. When it came time for nonresidents to apply in 1983, only three of the sixteen management units remained unfilled and permits were issued to very few nonresidents.

To get more details on what is happening to the state's deer-hunting picture I asked Jon Farrar of the Information Division of the Nebraska Game and Parks Commission to put some questions to Karl Menzel, the commission's big-game specialist. Here are the questions and Menzel's answers:

The number of permits authorized has been holding steady for three years now. Do you think that lowering the number of permits will mean better hunting and bigger bucks taken in the future?

"It could, but the primary reason for the jump in hunter success during any season is ideal weather conditions. Good hunting weather always means a larger harvest. However, as for the fewer permits, bigger bucks theory, I don't have much doubt that it will work. It's one of the signs of the times."

Is the day of the nonresident deer hunter in Nebraska gone?

"Last year we had four or five units with permits left over after the resident application. I guess we had fewer than 400 nonresident deer hunters last year. This year there were only three units with any permits available when the nonresident application period opened: Sandhills, Platte, and Upper Platte. A few years ago applications used to string in slowly over several months, but in recent years most of them have come in the first few days after they can be accepted. I would say that nonresident hunting for deer in Nebraska is out unless we offer more permits. Even if we did return to the peak number we have a greater resident demand now. We simply have more hunters applying in some units than we can satisfy fairly without going to regulations that limit the number of permits."

Do you think the time is coming when there may be a 2-year waiting period between eligible years in some of the high-demand units?

"I wouldn't expect it to get to the point where a hunter will be excluded for more than one year, unless it would be in one or two very specific areas."

What does the deer hunter have to look forward to 10 years from now?

"I look for it to be hard to find a place to hunt, hard to get a permit, and in some places, lower deer numbers because of loss of habitat due to increased demand for agricultural products, and other factors.

"Most of the land in all units but the Pine Ridge is privately owned. Generally, permission to hunt deer is harder to come by than permission to hunt upland or small game. Today's landowners regard deer on their land a little more personally than they do pheasants or squirrels. The difficulty in finding a place to hunt, coupled with a greater demand for fewer permits, makes getting into the field almost as difficult as finding a deer. The day of sending in for a permit a couple of weeks before the season, driving out to your unit, and uncasing the rifle is gone from Nebraska."

Sounds bad, doesn't it? Here's more bleak news from another prairie state.

"Several problems have been plaguing North Dakota's whitetail herd," a game official told me. "Of most importance, the number of deer hunters has been increasing each year. A record 58,434 deer licenses sold in 1973; the 1983 figure was over 60,000. As the numbers of hunters have increased their success ratios have decreased. This means that more hunters are going without a deer each year.

"Another problem is rooted in the fact that as more hunters are forced to hunt bucks only there are fewer bucks to go around. A recent winter survey showed the ratio of bucks per every 100 does was only 13. The 12-year average has been 36 bucks for every 100 does. There are fewer adult bucks in the whitetail population.

"Also adding to the problem every year has been the loss of wintering areas and general deer habitat because of increasing agricultural programs, strip mining, oil development, and overgrazing of pastures."

In the Far West the situation isn't a lot different, particularly in California. Consider the following letter I received from Ray Arnett, formerly Director of that state's Department of Fish and Game:

"California is particularly concerned with the future of the deer hunter. The deer in California is our most important species as far as the hunter is concerned, and we are faced with some real problems in losses of deer habitat, decline in deer herds, and reduced hunter success. Our Department has been looking into this problem to determine what can be done to reverse the downward trend in deer numbers.

"Our history shows that deer numbers in California were very low at the turn of the century. After about 1910 the population began building, stimulated by such occurrences as clearing for homestead, forest fires, logging, and other events that opened mature forests and created conditions which supported good deer forage.

"This buildup continued until the 1950s and 1960s. Since then a combination of known factors—increased fire control, drought, reservoir and highway construction, increased highway traffic, mountain subdivisions, natural succession—have combined to reduce the quantity and quality of deer habitat as well as deer numbers. Declines have taken place in herds subject to all levels of hunting.

"In spite of increasing numbers of deer hunters the hunter success stayed about the same up to 1960 because of the increase in deer numbers. However, in the last 20 years there has been a significant drop in hunter success. Although the number of deer hunters in California has been relatively stable during the last ten to twelve years we have had problems of heavy hunting pressure in certain populated areas, and serious thought is being given to the possible need to regulate the number of hunters on a unit or area basis.

"As for the future of deer herds in California, we just do not believe that it will be possible to bring deer numbers back to what they were in the late 1940s and 1950s. However, we are hopeful that through working with the large land-management agencies, particularly the U.S. Forest Service, and through better land-use planning, where full consideration is given to the needs of deer, we can halt this decline in deer populations and improve deer numbers, deer-herd condition and hunter success."

Earlier, I pointed out that deer census data tells us we have more deer in the United States today than we had when the Pilgrims landed. Well then, how does that information tie in with the gloomy picture I've painted so far in this chapter?

The point is that we do have more deer in total because some deer-management plans have been extremely successful. Management plans in some states have not been successful, but should they become successful we'll have more deer than we have today. The overall problem is that the army of hunters is increasing more rapidly than the deer herds. Overshadowing everything else is the increasing problem of finding a place to hunt as habitat decreases and parcels of posted land increase.

So what's going to happen? Let's take another look at Missouri, a state whose deer herds and harvests have boomed in recent years.

Because all species of wildlife are affected by weather conditions, land use, community growth, and pressure from sportsmen, game biologists are generally reluctant to forecast future wildlife trends. But when asked to make a long-range prediction on the future of deer hunting in Missouri, Norb Giessman, deer biologist for the Conservation Department proved optimistic.

"Knowing there is going to be a continual increase of the human population over the next twenty-five years, and that there is going to be a decrease in forest cover, I still believe the outlook for the deer hunter is excellent," Giessman said. "Our native whitetail is a hardy animal.

"I'd guess that twenty-five years from now we are going to be managing people more than we're managing deer. We'll have stricter quotas enabling us to put the gun pressure where we want it. Hunters will still be able to hunt, but the number of hunters in certain areas will be controlled. We had about 300,000 deer hunters in 1984, but we still had a record harvest. We're tickled pink at the way the season went because the antlerless deer bag was almost precisely what we planned for. That's what I mean by managing people.

"However, some way, we have to control the poaching problem. This isn't just a Department problem. It's a problem that has to be partially handled in local courts. There has to be a change in public opinion on the local level to make poaching an unpopular activity. The law-abiding hunter has to get more involved and make his feelings known. After all, for every deer poached the legal hunter has one less potential target. There's nothing romantic about deer poaching. These guys are the counterpart of metropolitan thieves; they contribute nothing and take what they can. In the future the average deer hunter won't stand for this nonsense."

From all of the foregoing it seems apparent that herd-management headaches and people-management headaches are definitely the trends of the future. If such problems are solved we'll have good deer hunting in most areas, and exceptional deer hunting in others.

Hunting regulations are more complex today than they were twenty-five years ago, but it seems definite that they'll get more complicated as the years go by. The more hunting pressure there is the more complex the regulations have to become. The reason is basic: the major way to avoid overharvest is to control gun pressure. Make up your mind that you're going to have to put up with more forms to fill out, more regulations to read, and more laws by which to abide.

I queried many game biologists and deer managers for their thoughts about more restrictive regulations while I was preparing the material for this chapter. Here is a representative reply from James J. McDonough, game Biologist for the Massachusetts Division of Fisheries and Game:

"By issuing a regulated number of permits per county it will be possible to control the number of deer harvested and enable manipulation of the deer population within a county for the benefit of all hunters," began McDonough.

"I do not enjoy regulating and restricting deer hunting, but to allow an unlimited and uncontrolled number of deer hunters into limited deer range is to invite disaster to the sport. I believe it is the duty of the Division of Fisheries and Game to impose rules and regulations.

"I believe that one of the limiting factors of future deer populations will be water and/or access to water. Watersheds and reservoirs may be potential deer-hunting areas in Massachusetts. In such limited areas, it will be necessary to limit the number of deer hunters."

But McDonough, like most other deer biologists, is optimistic about the future of deer hunting, even in the East where human populations are high.

"Looking back over forty-two years of deer hunting, I cannot say, other than natural plant succession, there have been any drastic changes in the deer producing-counties, with a few exceptions. The changes that I note were slow and required some readjustment. For instance, in the mid-1950s the Massachusetts Turnpike was built through the heart of some of our best deer range. The harvest dropped for a couple of years, but we will never know whether the declining harvest was due to the influence of the Turnpike or poor deer management such as unregulated harvest of deer of either sex. Plymouth County used to produce good deer harvests; today we have more deer reported killed by cars than by legal harvest. Sure there are more people, homes, shopping centers, dogs, and roads today, but the backbone of our deer range is still intact.

"Cape Cod (Barnstable County) with its summer traffic and people is still producing a healthy harvest of antlered males each year and should continue. I expect the deer harvest on Nantucket and Martha's Vineyard islands to level off. Both islands should produce a sustained harvest for at least the next twenty years, if a limited number of hunters are allowed to harvest the deer on a controlled basis.

"The backbone of the Massachusetts deer herd is located in Berkshire, Franklin, Hampshire, Hampden and north Worcester counties. I feel that at the present rate of amoebic urban sprawl in Massachusetts, deer hunters can continue to enjoy deer hunting in these counties. However, it may be necessary to limit or control the number of hunters."

In short, deer biologists all over the country told me that deer can be managed for population growth to a much higher degree than most other species of wildlife. Game managers, given an adequate degree of hunter control, can insure that deer hunting will be with us far into the future.

The key part of that last paragraph is *"deer can be managed for population growth."* Mismanagement can have a devastating effect.

To cite one example of mismanagement, in 1906 President Theodore Roosevelt, who also was one of the country's top hunters and foremost pioneer conservationists, set aside the beautiful Kaibab Plateau area on the rim of Grand Canyon in the northwest corner of Arizona as the Kaibab National Game Refuge.

In 1906 it was excusable that people—from those in the White House on down—should be unaware that the simple and obvious mathematics of cows in a pasture applied with equal relentlessness to deer. In less than twenty years deer the Kaibab would create one of the worst game disasters this country has ever seen.

Between 1906 and 1910 some 600 mountain lions plus hundreds of smaller predators were done away with in the Kaibab. And during those years the refuge was kept closed to hunting, as game refuges were supposed to be. When warning signs of an impending disaster became clear, no one heeded them.

By 1910 the deer herd had climbed to about 4,000. Fourteen years later it numbered 100,000, and the food supply was gone. In the next two winters 60,000 Kaibab deer died of starvation.

Today the range is still far from what it was when the whole disastrous chain of events began in 1906, and there is little likelihood that it will ever make a complete comeback. Over the years thousands of tons of the Kaibab's best topsoil have been washed down the Colorado River and added to the mud and silt at Lake Mead and has shown up as far away as the Gulf of California.

Something could have prevented the whole tragic mess: hunting—legal, regulated hunting. It's the primary tool in the management of all wildlife populations. If hunters had been allowed to hold the Kaibab deer herd in balance with its available food supply, as they should have, that herd would still be prospering today.

Such disasters no longer occur where modern game managers can maintain healthy deer herds, but we still haven't been able to control habitat destruction in other ways. Want to know how to destroy deer habitat at taxpayers' expense? The question sounds ridiculous, but consider this:

This juniper shows the effects of overbrowsing in the Kaibab National Forest on the North Rim of the Grand Canyon, during the 1920s. The results included mass starvation, severe plant damage, and extensive erosion.

A few years ago, 363 acres of private land in Modoc County, California, were sprayed at government expense, achieving a 100 percent kill of the brush, and subsequently of the deer habitat. About the same time, in Nevada, taxpayers' money was used on a brush-removal project on land administered by the Bureau of Land Management. In another instance 1,150 acres in northeast California, which happened to be prime winter deer range, were treated with a low-volatile solution of 2,4-D herbicide at a cost of $6.50 per acre. The taxpayers paid for that habitat-destruction project, too.

These are examples of one of the ways that deer habitat can be destroyed needlessly. The "public-be-damned" attitude still does rear its ugly head with enough regularity that citizen surveillance is highly advised. It's good news that ordinary citizens, as well as deer hunters, are becoming more opposed to such habitat destruction. Our voices are being heard with more and more authority, and that's a definite trend of the future.

It also looks as though we may be licking some of the image problems the hunter has with the 93 percent of the public who do not hunt. Consider the following statements made by Cotton Gordon, President of the International Professional Hunters Association, during his speech to the National Rifle Association Annual Convention a few years ago.

"I would like to express my very optimistic views of the future of hunting in this country. I am quite certain that this sort of an attitude comes as a shock to many of you and will be contrary to what you have been hearing, reading and seeing in this last decade . . .

"For years now we have heard that the young people in this country seriously oppose hunting. In a recent survey of college students across this country of ours, Dr. Dale Shaw of Colorado State University found that only a small minority did actually oppose hunting, but that a great majority opposed the hunter—not hunting but the hunter. They seriously object to the slob who shoots water tanks, signs, livestock, and who leaves his litter from plains to mountaintop. So, here again, we hear of the hunter image. . . .

"The slob image, if not taken seriously and if not soon corrected, will be the image that every hunter in this country bears. You and I can correct it by not tolerating the illegal or unethical practices that we see in the hunting field. We can correct it by calling them slobs and not hunters, and most certainly never referring to them as sportsmen. We can correct it by reporting all such incidents to law-enforcement people and by testifying when they go to trial. We can correct it by seeing that our individual state have strong laws that will keep these slobs out of the woods by not issuing licenses to those habitual offenders that jeopardize our sport. We must make the public understand that there is a vast difference between the sportsman who loves and respects this sport of hunting and the slob with a gun in his hand."

The slob-hunter problem has been and will continue to be a tough one to solve, but its significance probably will never be as great as the subject of legally shooting does and fawns. Deer managers now rightfully insist that doe hunting is here to stay. All serious hunters should be aware of the facts. Although I just mentioned the Kaibab National Game Refuge disaster, similar overpopulation disasters have occurred elsewhere. Typical was Pennsylvania in the 1920s when 500,000 deer died in a single winter.

New Jersey's more recent and famous Great Swamp National Wildlife Refuge controversy is a modern example. Starvation, disease and slow death of deer became rampant while anti-hunting groups fought in the courts to delay the controlled hunting necessary to reduce the size of the overpopulated whitetail herd.

The situation in New Zealand would be almost comical if it wasn't so serious. That country's deer, without sufficient natural predation and with too low a human population to provide effective hunting harvests, became national pests. The government was forced to offer bounties on deer to reduce their numbers.

These examples emphasize a biological fact that all professional deer managers live by: When habitat is ideal, a deer herd will increase its numbers at a surprisingly rapid rate; but the day of reckoning always comes when the total population exceeds the number that can be supported satisfactorily by available habitat. If the excess deer aren't harvested by controlled hunting, Mother Nature will begin a ruthless thinning of the herd. The cold, hard truth is that disease or starvation may eliminate as much as 85 percent of a herd in a single year.

Back in the early 1900s buck-only laws were an emergency measure to help deer herds recover from the senseless slaughtering of all wild game which was commonplace in the eastern half of the U.S. during the late 1880s. The herds began to recover about the same time the lumber barons finished cutting off the virgin-pine forests. New undergrowth that sprouted up everywhere in the North and East provided ideal browse for deer. By the 1920s deer numbers were never higher in many states.

In Pennsylvania the herds had multiplied right out of their habitat. Farmers complained of crop damage. The state instituted antlerless hunting to help get the herds back in balance with their habitat. But most of the state's deer hunters refused to accept the new idea. They dramatically pointed out their belief that buck-only laws had brought the herd back to where it was. Some hunters paraded through streets with signs saying, "Don't Shoot a Doe." Many purchased the special doe permits and tore them up so they couldn't be used. Then came the disastrous deer die-off I just mentioned.

Since then many Pennsylvania hunters have supported the principles of good deer management. The fact that the Keystone State has one of the largest deer herds in the U.S. is impressive in itself, but comparable harvest statistics are even more enlightening. In 1960 Pennsylvania deer hunters harvested a total of 68,663 whitetails. Of that total 29,887 were antlerless deer. In 1983 the total take was about 175,000, of which over 70,000 were antlerless.

The figures from Michigan are even more impressive. Since 1951 Michigan hunters have taken 1,500,000 antlerless deer, yet the 1982 buck kill was the third highest in the history of the state.

Such management-success figures weren't available years ago when the anti-doe hunters began screaming that the killing of antlerless deer was barbaric, a senseless slaughter, and a sure route to the ruin of deer herds. The feeling that the killing of a doe deer was murder ran rampant even among veteran hunters who never thought twice about shooting female rabbits, ducks, geese, squirrels, grouse and other wild game. There simply were no facts available which would prove that antlerless hunting is an absolute biological necessity in areas where there are more deer than the habitat can support.

Today we have those facts. Why do some deer hunters absolutely refuse to accept biological facts?

I decided to find the answers. I developed a three-page questionnaire asking scores of questions about modern deer management. I sent the questionnaires to deer managers and biologists in the 19 states which I figured had the most at stake in antlerless-hunting programs. I got replies from all 19 states, a 100 percent return. The completed questionnaires and accompanying letters were loaded with pertinent facts that every deer hunter should be aware of.

One of the questions I asked had to do with why sentiment among hunters still runs high against the harvest of antlerless deer. Here are some of the answers I received.

"Many people who don't accept deer-management principles don't accept many other concepts advocated by government agencies. They don't have the technical background to understand mathematical principles and conclusions. They won't accept the methodology or the answers simply because the government says so. It's not a game-management phenomenon but a sociological situation. The willingness of Americans to ignore expert advice is well documented." David A. Arnold, Supervisor Forest Wildlife Section, Michigan DNR.

"Most hunters are urban born with little if any knowledge of the relationship between animals and range. They can envision a strictly defined and enclosed habitat in a very small area, but they cannot transpose the same concepts to the much larger range that deer roam." Richard N. Denny, Big-Game Manager, Colorado Division of Wildlife.

"Hunters most often see deer during hunting seasons when they are in good physical shape. Even severely overbrowsed range can produce fat deer in fall when natural food supplies are most abundant. Later, when diminished food supplies put deer into trouble there are no hunters around to observe the effects. Most hunters have no conception of the reproductive performance of deer on overbrowsed range." Richard W. Whittington, Regional Game Supervisor, Georgia DNR.

"One of the problems in selling deer management is the absolute need to present statistical data to support facts. Many people are turned off by statistics because they don't understand them. They're prone to ignore facts they can't comprehend." Frank Haberland, Supervisor Big-Game Management, Wisconsin DNR.

"Deer range seems to be unlimited to most hunters. They think most plants are deer feed, but many are not. Most hunters have no real appreciation of the actual state of habitat. They don't have the training to know the difference between good and poor range." Victor Simpson, Associate Wildlife Manager, California Department of Fish and Game.

Some of the biologists I talked with brought up the fact that the average fisherman is much more likely to accept the principles of modern fisheries management than the deer hunter is to accept principles of game management. For example, most anglers have no quarrel with the principle that any given body of water will support only a given number of pounds of fish per surface acre. Yet many deer hunters won't agree with the principle that if a given piece of land is able to support only 100 deer that's all it will support and all others will die.

Why is this? Chester F. Banasiak, Big Game Project Leader for Maine's Department of Inland Fisheries and Wildlife, summed it up well.

"The finite limits of fish habitat is much more readily apparent than the limits of habitat for deer," Banasiak began. "The borders of a lake or stream are obvious, the borders of deer habitat appear endless. Problems with stunted fish can be readily demonstrated and compared with well understood limits of habitat. Stunted fawns don't survive. Where size differences among deer can be demonstrated, the hunter is prone to attribute it to hereditary factors rather than the carrying capacity of land which he doesn't conceive."

Several of the biologists gave me case studies which were technical enough to confuse almost anyone lacking a background in game-management principles. Most of this stuff relates to what happens to deer when they overpopulate their range, but a very important part of it concerns quality deer hunting. Many hunters are unaware of the fact that doe shooting can be the only route to more and bigger bucks on properly managed deer range. Here's a boiled-down version of this proven principle.

Let's say that a given piece of range is able to support 100 deer. Assume this range has a buck/doe ratio of one buck to four does. This means we have 20 bucks and 80 does. Let's say further that the hunter success ratio is 10 percent and that hunters are limited to bucks only. It follows that 10 deer will be killed, and those 10 will represent 50 percent of the bucks. Since the range can support only 100 deer, we'll have only 10 fawns that will survive to bring the population back to 100 deer. It's likely that half the fawns will be males, half females. In short, over a period of years, the buck supply will keep diminishing while the doe supply will keep increasing.

If we allowed some of those does to be harvested we would gradually allow more male fawns to survive which would increase the number of bucks in the herd. In the long run more bucks would survive to grow trophy antlers. Further, over a period of years, the herd of 100 deer would approach a sex ratio of closer to one-to-one. Say that we attained a herd showing 40 bucks and 60 does. With such management success we would be doing the deer, the hunter and the general public the greatest service. Such achievement can never be accomplished without harvesting some antlerless deer.

The "catch" in all this, of course, is that it's based on the proposition that the given piece of range is able to support *only* 100 deer. On range that is underutilized we must stay with buck-only laws until deer herds have reached optimum numbers. Herds in some of the western states are in severe trouble because of overharvest and loss of habitat. In Utah, for example, the deer kill dropped from 130,945 in 1960 to a bit over 65,000 bucks in 1983. The Utah hunter-success ratio dropped from 87 percent to 40 percent during the same years.

The overharvest situation has also reared its ugly head in Arizona, California, Colorado, Idaho, Nevada, Oregon and Washington. Doe shooting is certainly not the current answer in these states, but the opposite picture holds true throughout most of the eastern half of the United States. Consider the following comments I received during my survey.

"Alabama's deer herd has increased from an estimated 14,000 animals in 1940 to 1,200,000 in 1983," said Frank P. Hanley, Chief I&E Section, Alabama Department of Conservation and Natural Resources. "This is an increase of more than 7,000 percent. To put it another way, for each deer in our state 43 years ago we now have more than 75. Our bag limit is one deer per day during the entire two-month season, yet many of our hunters will not take a doe. Due to public pressure and local politics, we do not have an antlerless season on a statewide basis. Doe shooting is legal only in selected counties where the public will support an antlerless season. This will probably prove to be a very unfortunate lack of foresight."

"We had about 40,000 deer in Mississippi over 40 years ago, now we have about 1,500,000," said Robert N. Griffin, wildlife coordinator for Mississippi's Game & Fish Commission. "Our bag limit on deer is one buck per day, five per season. We are having losses from natural mortality. These losses of deer are compounded through overpopulation, and they emphasize the fact that you cannot stockpile deer."

"Public opinion caused our bucks-only seasons during recent years," said George M. Purvis, Chief I&E Division, Arkansas Game and Fish Commission. "Our deer management is no longer in the restoration phase; our range is adequately stocked with a statewide herd of about 400,000 whitetails. Our biologists say we could have a longer season and kill more does with no damage to the herd, but our hunters generally won't support this idea."

Similar comments from officials in other states emphasize again the necessity for doe shooting when deer numbers reach the carrying capacity of the range. Let's look at the situation in New Hampshire, a state where range has been limited for many years.

"We had about 40,000 deer in New Hampshire 25 years ago and we have about the same number today," game biologist Joe Wiley told me. "During all those years our harvest has averaged about 54 percent bucks because we've always allowed some antlerless hunting. It is quite likely that we are maintaining our deer population at a level below its maximum potential, but this is preferable to exceeding the carrying capacity because we have healthy deer. To me, the best argument for shooting antlerless deer is the health of the deer themselves. We know from experience that you can safely remove 30 percent of a total herd and have the same number of deer the following year if the herd is in balance with its range."

So the facts modern biologists now have point out over and over again that doe hunting is a deer-management tool which must be used when cropping of deer is necessary to remove surplus animals. Here are some more comments from professional game managers which should help you put the overall picture into more perspective.

"Failure to harvest does in fully stocked range can only result in disastrous mortality at some later date. The more does protected from harvest at present will only increase losses next year or the year later. When that happens, the doe protectors will have only themselves to blame." Wayne R. Porath, Wildlife Research Biologist, Missouri Department of Conservation.

"States having high numbers of deer but relatively low hunter-success ratios usually are faced with a large number of hunters. As the number of hunters increases, the percentage of successful hunters decreases. This holds true even in areas where herds are at maximum carrying capacity. If either-sex hunting is not allowed the end result will be even *lower* hunter-success ratios due to damaged habitat and the loss of deer to diseases and starvation. Many hunters won't agree with this proven principle because they fail to understand the process of energy flow between plant and animal communities. In order for plant and animal communities to function in harmony there must be a proper balance of both." Tom D. Monschein, Wildlife Biologist, North Carolina Wildlife Resources Commission.

"A given piece of land will support a certain amount of biomass. Consequently, it will support a larger number of small deer than big deer. The population level desired for maintenance of quality deer is considerably lower than that of a herd managed for maximum numbers. Both types of management *require* the harvest of antlerless deer." Charles K. Winkler, Program Director Big Game, Texas Parks and Wildlife Department.

"A lot of our anti-doe hunters claim we allow antlerless hunting only to take in more license money. I like to counter it with another money argument. The basic deer herd is our capital asset, like money in a bank. The interest it produces is in the form of the annual deer harvest. We would be very poor managers if we had to dip into our capital assets to maintain an annual return. Eventually we would wipe out the basic herd and be out of business. A deer manager's existence depends on maintaining a good deer population. When that is gone he is out of a job." Frank Haberland, Supervisor, Big Game Management, Wisconsin Department of Natural Resources.

"When antlerless hunting is justified because of overpopulation, starvation, etc., the hunter has already been cheated because the deer manager is several years late. Antlerless hunting should begin while the herd population is below carrying capacity. The carrying capacity of a given range is a delicate line which can be determined only through elaborate measurements. To exceed this line is disastrous. To come close, but never reach it, is perfect." Richard W. Whittington, Regional Supervisor, Game, Georgia Department of Natural Resources.

All the foregoing material in this book should lead you to some conclusions about your future as a deer hunter. In summary, game managers in some states are producing more deer than was ever thought possible. In states where herds have declined, managers are finding ways to bring them back. In the future we may have more deer than ever before, but there will be more hunters who want to share in the harvest. This means there will be more regulations and controls on hunting. One more change we can expect is an increase in the cost of hunting. Though modest license and permit fee increases will be a sign of the times and will produce more deer, it's likely that you'll be shelling out more money in the future if you want the best hunting. The handwriting is already on the wall. Ray Lyons, the Colorado big-game outfitter I mentioned earlier, expressed it this way:

"You take a rancher out here who has fifty head of deer on his place," he began. "If he could get rid of those deer he'd have food for maybe ten more head of cattle. Those deer are costing him money, so he's reluctant to let hunters go after them for free. More and more ranchers and landowners are realizing that they have money invested in the game they produce. We'll never get rid of deteriorating hunter-landowner relationships till gunners realize it's only fair to pay for good hunting. When the day comes that a landowner makes money on the deer he produces he'll produce more deer and he'll be happy to have hunters. Like it or not, the providing of hunting as a profit objective is a trend of the future."

A hidden blessing in lease or fee hunting is the positive control of the slob hunter who has largely contributed to the hunter's image among non-hunters. A landowner who sells hunting rights knows the names and addresses of his hunters, and they know he knows them. Such hunters don't cut fences or shoot at signs and livestock. They behave themselves.

In my surveys of the trends of deer hunting one of my questions was this:
Do you feel that the modern trend is toward less "free" hunting on public lands? In other words do you feel that more hunters are finding better hunting through:
A. Deer clubs where members buy or lease land and manage it exclusively for their private hunting?
B. Leased lands where ranchers or landowners lease their hunting rights to groups or outfitters?
C. Hunting fees charged by ranchers or landowners who now recognize their deer herds as cash crops?

It was surprising to learn that over one-third of the game officials in the lower forty-eight states said that, as yet, there is no trend toward any of these systems.

Deer clubs have come on strong in areas where fairly large tracts of private property—usually worthless for most other purposes—have been purchased by groups of deer hunters. Top states in this category include Alabama, Arkansas, California, Delaware, Georgia, Michigan, Minnesota, New Jersey, North Carolina, Virginia, West Virginia, and Wisconsin.

The advantage of belonging to a deer club can be tremendous, though expensive. Only club members are allowed to hunt, which means a drastic cut in competition. Also, hunting is far better because most club properties are managed by members to produce the best hunting. One example should serve to illustrate:

In my local area I do some of my deer hunting on public lands where the average annual deer hunter success ratio is 10 to 15 percent. My cousin is a member of a deer club whose property borders some of the country I hunt. Last fall forty-six members of the club hunted during the opening weekend of deer season, and they harvested twenty-seven bucks. That's nearly a 60 percent success ratio, and it was achieved in only two days of hunting.

Members of the club use their dues to produce this great hunting. They cut timber to produce browse, they plant crops which are left unharvested to serve as food for deer, and they hire a caretaker to protect their property from poachers.

A cheaper way for deer-hunting groups to purchase good hunting is to lease a block of land for exclusive hunting rights. Under this system no deer-management practices are involved. The theory is simply to lease land that is already good deer country. The owner maintains all rights to his property except the hunting rights which are controlled by the leasing group. The system is coming to the forefront in Colorado, California, Delaware, Montana, Nebraska, New Jersey, New Mexico, Virginia, Wyoming, and Wisconsin. In Texas practically all deer hunting is controlled through leasing.

I've already mentioned that straight-fee hunting is a sign of the times. This system involves no more than the landowner charging a nominal fee for the right to hunt on his property. Numbers of hunters are usually unlimited. You just pay your fee and take your chance. Only sixteen state game departments told me that fee hunting will probably never gain a foothold in their states. In all the rest of the states it's likely to come on stronger as the years roll by.

APPENDIX 1:

From Field Dressing to Freezer

On the surface, dressing out a deer sounds like a difficult and messy job. It really isn't if you go at it correctly. Veteran deer hunters wipe the last blood off their knives about 15 minutes after they walk up to their downed buck.

The first step is to drag the carcass to sloping ground and place it on its back with the head uphill. This is because the carcass will drain best from its rear end after it's cut open. Then follow these steps in order:

1) Cut a circle around the anal vent with your knife point going about one inch deep. Pull the vent out an inch or so and tie it off with a piece of cord. A boot lace will suffice if you don't have a cord. (It's best to keep a short piece of cord in one of your pockets for this specific purpose.) The vent is tied off to prevent droppings from coming into contact with the meat.

2) Begin the abdominal incision at the V formed by the breast bones of the rib cage. Your purpose is to open the animal without puncturing any of the intestines, so this cut is critical. Make the cut with the blade edge up. Guide the blade between two fingers of the left hand which should hold the skin up and away from the gut pouch. Slit the skin and belly membrane down the belly and around both sides of the genitals to the crotch. Some veterans don't bother cutting around the genitals, they just slash them off and make a straight cut from breastbone to crotch. Many guides do this. I've never had any reason to feel that slicing off the genitals has any effect on the taste of the meat, but it seems to me to be a little neater to cut around them.

But don't waste your time cutting the glands from a deer's legs. Years

2.

1.

3.

4.

ago it was believed these glands would taint the meat if not removed. It's now known that this isn't true. Deer have glands not only on their legs but between their toes and at the corners of their eyes. All of these glands become inactive after death.

3) Tilt the carcass sideways, then reach inside and pull the abdominal contents out far enough so you can cut away the diaphragm, which is a wall of thin muscle tissue separating the chest area and the belly.

4) Reach into the chest area with your free hand, grasp the windpipe as far toward the head as possible, and cut it free.

5) Roll the carcass on its side and pull out all the innards. The rectum and its contents will come through the anal cut with gentle tugging. Be careful. The bladder lies within the pelvis and you don't want to cut or break it.

6) Separate the heart and liver from the pile; cut them free; wipe them clean; and lay them on a rock, a log, or the grass to drain. After they have drained, put them into a plastic bag carried for the purpose. These parts of the deer should be eaten fresh.

7) Check for bloodshot muscle or shattered bone and cut these parts away from the carcass because they spoil quickly and will taint the meat.

8) If your deer was gut-shot and water or snow is available, wash it out carefully. The best bet is to tip the deer on its belly to drain puddles of blood.

9) Prop open the belly cavity with a stout stick to hasten the cooling.

10) What you do next depends on your situation. If you have partners it's best to drag the deer out to camp or vehicle and hang it as soon as possible. Animal heat is what spoils game. A deer will spoil as quickly in cold weather as in warm weather if the carcass isn't lifted off the ground and hung as soon as possible so air circulation can cool the meat. If you can't get help till the next day, get the carcass off the ground by hanging it, dragging it over brush, or working poles under it.

Some lone hunters skin and quarter their deer immediately. Then they hang the quarters, go back to camp or vehicle, and return later with a packboard. It is far easier to make two trips with a packboard than to drag a deer out in one.

Most hunters have help available to get their deer out of the woods soon after the kill. It's at this point that two basic mistakes are made, and they're both hangovers from the old days. Years ago it was custom to hang a deer by its head and to leave the skin on during the aging process. A quick look into any slaughter house will show you that modern meat handlers know better.

Hanging a deer by its head tends to allow whatever blood remains in the carcass to drain into the hindquarters, which contains some of the best cuts. Conversely, a deer hung by its hind legs will allow the remaining blood to drain into the neck and head, which contain little edible meat. Commercial meat cutters also skin their carcasses immediately after killing because skin holds in the animal heat that taints the meat. My primary objective after getting my deer field-dressed is to get it skinned as soon as possible. My second objective is to have the carcass aged four days to a week in 35° to 45° temperature before the meat is cut up and frozen. This isn't always possible if I'm hunting away from home, but aged meat is always more tender than non-aged meat.

In my opinion, venison chops and steaks are far more tasty than venison roasts. I tell the guy who butchers my deer to get every last steak and chop out of the carcass, cut them one inch thick and forget about the roasts. The remaining scraps of meat go into deerburger. The old custom was to have pork mixed into deerburger. I don't do this because pork needs thorough cooking. I like my deerburgers and meatloafs on the medium-rare side.

Good quality freezer paper is ideal for wrapping deer meat for freezing. Wrap similar cuts in packages large enough to provide a meal for you and your family. In my case I have one son left at home, so I wrap enough meat in one package to feed three people. I mark all my packages with identifying words such as: "Venison—round steak." This enables me to get the type of meat I want for any particular meal. I don't date my packages; my family loves venison so much that it doesn't last long around my house.

Many deer hunters don't bother saving their animals' hides for clothing or crafts, but if you want to utilize your deer's hide, the first step is to coat the flesh side with salt. The following day remove this coating and the accumulated moisture, then re-salt. Fold it with the salted side in and take it to a taxidermist for tanning.

APPENDIX 2

I certify that I have measured the above trophy on _____ 19____
at (address) _____ City _____ State _____
and that these measurements and data are, to the best of my knowledge and belief, made in accordance
with the instructions given.

Witness: _____ Signature: _____

OFFICIAL MEASURER [ ][ ][ ][ ]

INSTRUCTIONS FOR MEASURING MULE AND BLACKTAIL DEER

All measurements must be made with a ¼-inch flexible steel tape to the nearest one-eighth of an inch.
Wherever it is necessary to change direction of measurement, mark a control point and swing tape at
this point. Enter fractional figures in eighths, without reduction. Official measurements cannot
be taken for at least sixty days after the animal was killed.

A. Number of Points on Each Antler. To be counted a point, a projection must be at least one inch
long and its length must exceed the width of its base. All points are measured from tip of point to
nearest edge of beam as illustrated. Beam tip is counted as a point but not measured as a point.

B. Tip to Tip Spread is measured between tips of main beams.

C. Greatest Spread is measured between perpendiculars at a right angle to the center line of the
skull at widest part whether across main beams or points.

D. Inside Spread of Main Beams is measured at a right angle to the center line of the skull at widest point between main beams. Enter this measurement again in Spread Credit column if it is less
than or equal to the length of longer antler; if longer, enter longer antler length for Spread Credit.

E. Total Lengths of all Abnormal Points. Abnormal points are those nontypical in location such as
points originating from a point (exception: G-3 originates from G-2 in perfectly normal fashion) or
from sides or bottom of main beam or any points beyond the normal pattern of five (including beam
tip) per antler. Measure each abnormal point in usual manner and enter in appropriate blanks.

F. Length of Main Beam is measured from lowest outside edge of burr over outer curve to the tip of
the main beam. The point of beginning is that point on the burr where the center line along the
outer curve of the beam intersects the burr, then following generally the line of the illustration.

G-1-2-3-4. Length of Normal Points. Normal points are the brow and the upper and lower forks as
shown in the illustration. They are measured from nearest edge of beam over outer curve to tip.
Lay the tape along the outer curve of the beam so that the top edge of the tape coincides with the
top edge of the beam on both sides of the point to determine baseline for point measurement. Record
point lengths in appropriate blanks.

H-1-2-3-4. Circumferences are taken as detailed for each measurement. If brow point is missing,
take H-1 and H-2 at smallest place between burr and G-2. If G-3 is missing, take H-3 halfway between
the base and tip of second point. If G-4 is missing, take H-4 halfway between the second point and
tip of main beam.   * * * * * * * * * * * *

FAIR CHASE STATEMENT FOR ALL HUNTER-TAKEN TROPHIES

To make use of the following methods shall be deemed as UNFAIR CHASE and unsportsmanlike, and any
trophy obtained by use of such means is disqualified from entry for Awards.

  I.   Spotting or herding game from the air, followed by landing in its vicinity
       for pursuit;
 II.   Herding or pursuing game with motor-powered vehicles;
III.   Use of electronic communications for attracting, locating or observing
       game, or guiding the hunter to such game;
 IV.   Hunting game confined by artificial barriers, including escape-proof fencing;
       or hunting game transplanted solely for the purpose of commercial shooting.
       ****

I certify that the trophy scored on this chart was not taken in UNFAIR CHASE as defined above by the
Boone and Crockett Club. I further certify that it was taken in full compliance with local game laws
of the state, province, or territory.

Date_____ Signature of Hunter _____
(Have signature notarized by a Notary Public)

Records of North American Big Game	BOONE AND CROCKETT CLUB	205 South Patrick Street Alexandria, Virginia 22314

Minimum Score:
  mule   195
  blacktail   130

TYPICAL
MULE AND BLACKTAIL DEER

Kind of Deer _____

DETAIL OF POINT
MEASUREMENT

Abnormal Points	
Right	Left
Total to E	

SEE OTHER SIDE FOR INSTRUCTIONS			Column 1	Column 2	Column 3	Column 4
A. Number of points on Each Antler	R.	L.	Spread Credit	Right Antler	Left Antler	Difference
B. Tip to Tip Spread						
C. Greatest Spread						
D. Inside Spread of Main Beams	Credit may equal but not exceed length of longer antler					
IF Spread exceeds longer antler, enter difference						
E. Total of Lengths of Abnormal Points						
F. Length of Main Beam						
G-1. Length of First Point, if present						
G-2. Length of Second Point						
G-3. Length of Third Point, if present						
G-4. Length of Fourth Point, if present						
H-1. Circumference at Smallest Place Between Burr and First Point						
H-2. Circumference at Smallest Place Between First and Second Points						
H-3. Circumference at Smallest Place Between Main Beam and Third Point						
H-4. Circumference at Smallest Place Between Second and Fourth Points						
TOTALS						

ADD	Column 1		Exact locality where killed
	Column 2		Date killed By whom killed
	Column 3		Present owner
	TOTAL		Address
SUBTRACT Column 4			Guide's Name and Address
FINAL SCORE			Remarks: (Mention any abnormalities or unique qualities)

I certify that I have measured the above trophy on _____ 19_____
at (address) _____ City _____ State_____
and that these measurements and data are, to the best of my knowledge and belief, made in accordance
with the instructions given.

Witness: _____ Signature: _____
                                                          OFFICIAL MEASURER | | | | |

INSTRUCTIONS FOR MEASURING NON-TYPICAL WHITETAIL AND COUES' DEER

All measurements must be made with a ¼-inch flexible steel tape to the nearest one-eighth of an inch.
Wherever it is necessary to change direction of measurement, mark a control point and swing tape at
this point. Enter fractional figures in eighths, without reduction. Official measurements cannot
be taken for at least sixty days after the animal was killed.

A. Number of Points on Each Antler. To be counted a point, a projection must be at least one inch
long and its length must exceed the width of its base. All points are measured from tip of point to
nearest edge of beam as illustrated. Beam tip is counted as a point but not measured as a point.

B. Tip to Tip Spread is measured between tips of main beams.

C. Greatest Spread is measured between perpendiculars at a right angle to the center line of the
skull at widest part whether across main beams or points.

D. Inside Spread of Main Beams is measured at a right angle to the center line of the skull at widest point between main beams. Enter this measurement again in Spread Credit column if it is less
than or equal to the length of longer antler; if longer, enter longer antler length for Spread Credit.

E. Total of Lengths of all Abnormal Points. Abnormal points are those nontypical in location (points
originating from points or from sides or bottom of main beam) or extra points beyond the normal pattern
of up to eight normal points, including beam tip, per antler. Measure in usual manner and enter in
appropriate blanks.

F. Length of Main Beam is measured from lowest outside edge of burr over outer curve to the most distant point of what is, or appears to be, the main beam. The point of beginning is that point on the
burr where the center line along the outer curve of the beam intersects the burr, then following generally the line of the illustration.

G-1-2-3-4-5-6-7. Length of Normal Points. Normal points project from the top of the main beam.
They are measured from nearest edge of main beam over outer curve to tip. Lay the tape along the
outer curve of the beam so that the top edge of the tape coincides with the beam on both sides of
the point to determine baseline for point measurement. Record point lengths in appropriate blanks.

H-1-2-3-4. Circumferences are taken as detailed for each measurement. If brow point is missing,
take H-1 and H-2 at smallest place between burr and G-2. If G-4 is missing, take H-4 halfway between
G-3 and tip of main beam.

* * * * * * * * * * * *
FAIR CHASE STATEMENT FOR ALL HUNTER-TAKEN TROPHIES
To make use of the following methods shall be deemed as UNFAIR CHASE and unsportsmanlike, and any
trophy obtained by use of such means is disqualified from entry for Awards.
  I.   Spotting or herding game from the air, followed by landing in its vicinity
       for pursuit;
  II. Herding or pursuing game with motor-powered vehicles;
  III. Use of electronic communications for attracting, locating or observing
       game, or guiding the hunter to such game;
  IV. Hunting game confined by artificial barriers, including escape-proof fencing;
       or hunting game transplanted solely for the purpose of commercial shooting.
       ****
I certify that the trophy scored on this chart was not taken in UNFAIR CHASE as defined above by the
Boone and Crockett Club. I further certify that it was taken in full compliance with local game laws
of the state, province, or territory.
Date_____Signature of Hunter_____
(Have signature notarized by a Notary Public)

OFFICIAL SCORING SYSTEM FOR NORTH AMERICAN BIG GAME TROPHIES

Records of North American
Big Game

BOONE AND CROCKETT CLUB

205 South Patrick Street
Alexandria, Virginia 22314

Minimum Score:
  whitetail 195
  Coues'   120

NON-TYPICAL
WHITETAIL AND COUES' DEER

Kind of Deer_____

DETAIL OF POINT MEASUREMENT

Abnormal Points	
Right	Left
Total to E	

SEE OTHER SIDE FOR INSTRUCTIONS	R.	L.	Column 1 Spread Credit	Column 2 Right Antler	Column 3 Left Antler	Column 4 Difference
A. Number of Points on Each Antler						
B. Tip to Tip Spread						
C. Greatest Spread						
D. Inside Spread of Main Beams — Credit may equal but not exceed length of longer antler						
IF Spread exceeds longer antler, enter difference.						
E. Total of Lengths of Abnormal Points						
F. Length of Main Beam						
G-1. Length of First Point, if present						
G-2. Length of Second Point						
G-3. Length of Third Point						
G-4. Length of Fourth Point, if present						
G-5. Length of Fifth Point, if present						
G-6. Length of Sixth Point, if present						
G-7. Length of Seventh Point, if present						
H-1. Circumference at Smallest Place Between Burr and First Point						
H-2. Circumference at Smallest Place Between First and Second Points						
H-3. Circumference at Smallest Place Between Second and Third Points						
H-4. Circumference at Smallest Place Between Third and Fourth Points						
TOTALS						

ADD	Column 1		Exact locality where killed
	Column 2		Date killed By whom killed
	Column 3		Present owner
	Total		Address
SUBTRACT	Column 4		
	Result		Guide's Name and Address
Add line E Total			Remarks: (Mention any abnormalities or unique qualities)
FINAL SCORE			

273

I certify that I have measured the above trophy on _____ 19_____
at (address) _____ City _____ State_____
and that these measurements and data are, to the best of my knowledge and belief, made in accordance
with the instructions given.

Witness: _____ Signature: _____

OFFICIAL MEASURER ☐☐☐☐ .

INSTRUCTIONS FOR MEASURING NON-TYPICAL MULE DEER

All measurements must be made with a ¼-inch flexible steel tape to the nearest one-eighth of an inch.
Wherever it is necessary to change direction of measurement, mark a control point and swing tape at
this point. Enter fractional figures in eighths, without reduction. Official measurements cannot
be taken for at least sixty days after the animal was killed.

A. Number of Points on Each Antler. To be counted a point, a projection must be at least one inch
long and its length must exceed the width of its base. All points are measured from tip of point to
nearest edge of beam as illustrated. Beam tip is counted as a point but not measured as a point.

B. Tip to Tip Spread is measured between tips of main beams.

C. Greatest Spread is measured between perpendiculars at a right angle to the center line of the
skull at widest part whether across main beams or points.

D. Inside Spread of Main Beams is measured at a right angle to the center line of the skull at widest point between main beams. Enter this measurement again in Spread Credit column if it is less
than or equal to the length of longer antler; if longer, enter longer antler length for Spread Credit.

E. Total of Lengths of all Abnormal Points. Abnormal points are those nontypical in location or
points beyond the normal pattern of five (including beam tip) per antler. Mark the points that are
normal, as defined below. All other points are considered abnormal and are entered in appropriate
blanks, after measurement in usual manner.

F. Length of Main Beam is measured from lowest outside edge of burr over outer curve to the tip of
the main beam. The point of beginning is that point on the burr where the center line along the outer
curve of the beam intersects the burr, then following generally the line of the illustration.

G-1-2-3-4. Length of Normal Points. Normal points are the brow and the upper and lower forks, as
shown in the illustration. They are measured from nearest edge of beam over outer curve to tip. Lay
the tape along the outer curve of the beam so that the top edge of the tape coincides with the top
edge of the beam on both sides of the point to determine baseline for point measurement. Record
point lengths in appropriate blanks.

H-1-2-3-4. Circumferences are taken as detailed for each measurement. If brow point is missing,
take H-1 and H-2 at smallest place between burr and G-2. If G-3 is missing, take H-3 halfway between
the base and tip of second point. If G-4 is missing, take H-4 halfway between the second point and
tip of main beam. * * * * * * * * * * * *

FAIR CHASE STATEMENT FOR ALL HUNTER-TAKEN TROPHIES

To make use of the following methods shall be deemed as UNFAIR CHASE and unsportsmanlike and any
trophy obtained by use of such means is disqualified from entry for Awards.
  I. Spotting or herding game from the air, followed by landing in its vicinity
     for pursuit;
 II. Herding or pursuing game with motor-powered vehicles;
III. Use of electronic communications for attracting, locating or observing
     game, or guiding the hunter to such game;
 IV. Hunting game confined by artificial barriers, including escape-proof fencing;
     or hunting game transplanted solely for the purpose of commercial shooting.
     ****
I certify that the trophy scored on this chart was not taken in UNFAIR CHASE as defined above by the
Boone and Crockett Club. I further certify that it was taken in full compliance with local game laws
of the state, province, or territory.

Date_____ Signature of Hunter_____
(Have signature notarized by a Notary Public)

Records of North American
Big Game

BOONE AND CROCKETT CLUB

205 South Patrick Street
Alexandria, Virginia 22314

Minimum Score: 240

NON-TYPICAL MULE DEER

DETAIL OF POINT MEASUREMENT

Abnormal Points	
Right	Left
Total to E	

SEE OTHER SIDE FOR INSTRUCTIONS		R.	L.	Column 1 Spread Credit	Column 2 Right Antler	Column 3 Left Antler	Column 4 Difference
A.	Number of Points on Each Antler						
B.	Tip to Tip Spread						
C.	Greatest Spread						
D.	Inside Spread of Main Beams — Credit may equal but not exceed length of longer antler						
	IF Spread exceeds longer antler, enter difference						
E.	Total of Lengths of Abnormal Points						
F.	Length of Main Beams						
G-1.	Length of First Point, if present						
G-2.	Length of Second Point						
G-3.	Length of Third Point, if present						
G-4.	Length of Fourth Point, if present						
H-1.	Circumference at Smallest Place Between Burr and First Point						
H-2.	Circumference at Smallest Place Between First and Second Points						
H-3.	Circumference at Smallest Place Between Main Beam and Third Point						
H-4.	Circumference at Smallest Place Between Second and Fourth Points						
	TOTALS						

ADD	Column 1		Exact locality where killed
	Column 2		Date killed By whom killed
	Column 3		Present Owner
	TOTAL		Address
SUBTRACT	Column 4		Guide's Name and Address
	Result		
Add Line E Total			Remarks: (Mention any abnormalities or unique qualities)
FINAL SCORE			

275

I certify that I have measured the above trophy on _____ 19_____
at (address) _____
                                        City   State
and that these measurements and data are, to the best of my knowledge and belief, made in accordance
with the instructions given.

Witness: _____ Signature: _____
                                                      OFFICIAL MEASURER

INSTRUCTIONS FOR MEASURING WHITETAIL AND COUES' DEER

All measurements must be made with a ¼-inch flexible steel tape to the nearest one-eighth of an inch. Wherever it is necessary to change direction of measurement, mark a control point and swing tape at this point. Enter fractional figures in eighths, without reduction. Official measurements cannot be taken for at least sixty days after the animal was killed.

A. Number of Points on Each Antler. To be counted a point, a projection must be at least one inch long and its length must exceed the width of its base. All points are measured from tip of point to nearest edge of beam as illustrated. Beam tip is counted as a point but not measured as a point.

B. Tip to Tip Spread is measured between tips of main beams.

C. Greatest Spread is measured between perpendiculars at a right angle to the center line of the skull at widest part whether across main beams or points.

D. Inside Spread of Main Beams is measured at a right angle to the center line of the skull at widest point between main beams. Enter this measurement again in Spread Credit column if it is less than or equal to the length of longer antler; if longer, enter longer antler length for Spread Credit.

E. Total of lengths of all Abnormal Points. Abnormal points are those nontypical in location (points originating from points or from sides or bottom of main beam) or extra points beyond the normal pattern of up to eight normal points, including beam tip, per antler. Measure in usual manner and enter in appropriate blanks.

F. Length of Main Beam is measured from lowest outside edge of burr over outer curve to the most distant point of what is, or appears to be, the main beam. The point of beginning is that point on the burr where the center line along the outer curve of the beam intersects the burr, then following generally the line of the illustration.

G-1-2-3-4-5-6-7. Length of Normal Points. Normal points project from the top of the main beam. They are measured from nearest edge of main beam over outer curve to tip. Lay the tape along the outer curve of the beam so that the top edge of the tape coincides with the top edge of the beam on both sides of the point to determine baseline for point measurements. Record point lengths in appropriate blanks.

H-1-2-3-4. Circumferences are taken as detailed for each measurement. If brow point is missing, take H-1 and H-2 at smallest place between burr and G-2. If G-4 is missing, take H-4 halfway between G-3 and tip of main beam.

* * * * * * * * * * *

FAIR CHASE STATEMENT FOR ALL HUNTER-TAKEN TROPHIES

To make use of the following methods shall be deemed as UNFAIR CHASE and unsportsmanlike, and any trophy obtained by use of such means is disqualified from entry for Awards.
   I. Spotting or herding game from the air, followed by landing in its vicinity for pursuit;
  II. Herding or pursuing game with motor-powered vehicles;
 III. Use of electronic communications for attracting, locating or observing game, or guiding the hunter to such game;
 IV. Hunting game confined by artificial barriers, including escape-proof fencing; or hunting game transplanted solely for the purpose of commercial shooting.
****

I certify that the trophy scored on this chart was not taken in UNFAIR CHASE as defined above by the Boone and Crockett Club. I further certify that it was taken in full compliance with local game laws of the state, province, or territory.

Date_____Signature of Hunter_____
(Have signature notarized by a Notary Public)

Records of North American
Big Game

BOONE AND CROCKETT CLUB

205 South Patrick Street
Alexandria, Virginia 22314

Minimum Score:
  whitetail 170
  Coues'   110

TYPICAL
WHITETAIL AND COUES' DEER

Kind of Deer_____

DETAIL OF POINT
MEASUREMENT

Abnormal Points	
Right	Left

Total to E

SEE OTHER SIDE FOR INSTRUCTIONS	R.	L.	Column 1 Spread Credit	Column 2 Right Antler	Column 3 Left Antler	Column 4 Difference
A. Number of Points on Each Antler						
B. Tip to Tip Spread						
C. Greatest Spread						
D. Inside Spread of Main Beams — Credit may equal but not exceed length of longer antler						
IF Spread exceeds longer antler, enter difference.						
E. Total of Lengths of all Abnormal Points						
F. Length of Main Beam						
G-1. Length of First Point, if present						
G-2. Length of Second Point						
G-3. Length of Third Point						
G-4. Length of Fourth Point, if present						
G-5. Length of Fifth Point, if present						
G-6. Length of Sixth Point, if present						
G-7. Length of Seventh Point, if present						
H-1. Circumference at Smallest Place Between Burr and First Point						
H-2. Circumference at Smallest Place Between First and Second Points						
H-3. Circumference at Smallest Place Between Second and Third Points						
H-4. Circumference at Smallest Place between Third and Fourth Points (see back if G-4 is missing)						
TOTALS						

ADD	Column 1		Exact locality where killed
	Column 2		Date killed By whom killed
	Column 3		Present owner
	Total		Address
SUBTRACT Column 4			Guide's Name and Address
FINAL SCORE			Remarks: (Mention any abnormalities or unique qualities)

Index